**SHORTLIST**

# Sydney

WHAT'S NEW | WHAT'S ON | WHAT'S BEST

www.timeout.com/sydney

# Contents

**Published by Time Out Guides Ltd**
Universal House
251 Tottenham Court Road
London W1T 7AB
Tel: + 44 (0)20 7813 3000
Fax: + 44 (0)20 7813 6001
Email: guides@timeout.com
www.timeout.com

**Managing Director** Peter Fiennes
**Financial Director** Gareth Garner
**Editorial Director** Ruth Jarvis
**Deputy Series Editor** Dominic Earle
**Editorial Manager** Holly Pick
**Assistant Management Accountant** Ija Krasnikova

Time Out Guides is a wholly owned subsidiary of Time Out Group Ltd.

© Time Out Group Ltd
**Chairman** Tony Elliott
**Financial Director** Richard Waterlow
**Group General Manager/Director** Nichola Coulthard
**Time Out Magazine Ltd MD** Richard Waterlow
**Time Out Communications Ltd MD** David Pepper
**Time Out International Ltd MD** Cathy Runciman
**Production Director** Mark Lamond
**Group IT Director** Simon Chappell
**Head of Marketing** Catherine Demajo

Time Out and the Time Out logo are trademarks of Time Out Group Ltd.

**This edition first published in Great Britain in 2008 by Ebury Publishing**
A Random House Group Company
Company information can be found on www.randomhouse.co.uk
Random House UK Limited Reg. No. 954009
10 9 8 7 6 5 4 3 2 1

Distributed in the US by Publishers Group West
Distributed in Canada by Publishers Group Canada

For further distribution details, see www.timeout.com

ISBN: 978-1-84670-104-7

A CIP catalogue record for this book is available from the British Library.

Printed and bound by Firmengruppe APPL, aprinta druck, Wemding, Germany.

The Random House Group Limited supports The Forest Stewardship Council (FSC), the
leading international forest certification organisation. All our titles that are printed on
Greenpeace approved FSC certified paper carry the FSC logo. Our paper procurement
policy can be found at www.rbooks.co.uk/environment.

Time Out carbon-offsets all its flights with Trees for Cities (www.treesforcities.org).

# Sydney Shortlist

The **Time Out Sydney Shortlist** is one of a new series of guides that draws on Time Out's background as a magazine publisher to keep you current with everything that's going on in town. As well as featuring Sydney's key sights and the best of its eating, drinking and leisure options, it picks out the most exciting venues to have recently opened and gives a full calendar of annual events. It also includes features on the important news, trends and openings, all compiled by locally based editors and writers. Whether you're visiting for the first time in your life or the first time this year, you'll find the *Time Out Sydney Shortlist* contains all you need to know, in a portable and easy-to-use format.

The guide divides central and neighbouring Sydney into ten areas, containing listings for Sights & Museums, Eating & Drinking, Shopping, Nightlife and Arts & Leisure, and maps pinpointing their locations. At the front of the book are chapters rounding up these scenes city-wide, and giving a shortlist of our overall picks. We also include itineraries for days out, plus essentials such as travel information and hotels.

Our listings give phone numbers as dialled within Sydney. From abroad, use your country's exit code followed by 61 (the country code for Australia) and the number given.

We have noted price categories by using one to four dollar signs ($-$$$$), representing budget, moderate, expensive and luxury.

Major credit cards are accepted unless otherwise stated. We also indicate when a venue is NEW .

All our listings are double-checked, but places do sometimes close or change their hours or prices, so it's a good idea to call a venue before visiting. While every effort has been made to ensure accuracy, the publishers cannot accept responsibility for any errors that this guide may contain.

Venues are marked on the maps using symbols numbered according to their order within the chapter and colour-coded as follows:

❶ Sights & Museums
❶ Eating & Drinking
❶ Shopping
❶ Nightlife
❶ Arts & Leisure

| Map key | |
|---|---|
| **Area name** ............. PADDINGTON | |
| **Major sight or landmark** ...... | |
| **Park** ................... | |
| **Hospital/university** ............. | |
| **CityRail station** ............. | |
| **Monorail station** ............. ○ | |
| **LightRail station** ............. □ | |
| **Steps** ................... | |

# Time Out Sydney Shortlist

**EDITORIAL**
**Editor** Katie Ekberg
**Deputy Editor** Emily Kerrigan
**Proofreader** Tamsin Shelton

**DESIGN**
**Art Director** Scott Moore
**Art Editor** Pinelope Kourmouzoglou
**Senior Designer** Henry Elphick
**Graphic Designers** Gemma Doyle,
  Kei Ishimaru
**Advertising Designer** Jodi Sher
**Picture Editor** Jael Marschner
**Deputy Picture Editor** Katie Morris
**Picture Researcher** Gemma Walters
**Picture Desk Assistant** Marzena Zoladz

**ADVERTISING**
**Commercial Director** Mark Phillips
**International Advertising Manager**
  Kasimir Berger

**International Sales Executive**
  Charlie Sokol
**Advertising Assistant** Kate Staddon
**Advertising Sales (Sydney)** Ad Pack
  Australia (colin.m@adpacau.com)

**MARKETING**
**Marketing Manager** Yvonne Poon
**Senior Publishing Brand Manager**
  Luthfa Begum
**Sales & Marketing Director,**
  **North America** Lisa Levinson
**Marketing Designers** Anthony Huggins,
  Nicola Wilson

**PRODUCTION**
**Production Manager** Brendan McKeown
**Production Controller** Damian Bennett
**Production Co-ordinator** Julie Pallot

**CONTRIBUTORS**
This guide was researched and written by Juliet Rieden, Katie Ekberg, Sarah Belle Murphy, Carrie Hutchinson, Pip Harry, Eoghan Lewis and contributors to *Time Out Sydney*.

**PHOTOGRAPHY**
Photography by Michelle Grant; except page 35 AFP/Getty Images; page 36 Reuters/Corbis; page 37 Mim Stirling AGNSW; page 38 Getty Images; page 44 Sydney Seaplanes; pages 50, 51, 92, 98, 166 Daniel Boud; page 67 Museum of Contemporary Art Sydney; page 100 Heloise Bergman; page 158 James Pipino, TNSW; page 170 Apartment One.

The following images were provided by the featured establishment/artist: page 10, 89, 120, 174, 177, 178, 179.

Cover photograph: Sydney Harbour Bridge. Credit: Steve Vidler/AISA

**MAPS**
JS Graphics (john@jsgraphics.co.uk).

## About Time Out

Founded in 1968, Time Out has expanded from humble London beginnings into the leading resource for those wanting to know what's happening in the world's greatest cities. As well as our influential what's-on weeklies in London, New York and Chicago, we publish more than a dozen other listings magazines in cities as varied as Beijing and Mumbai. The magazines established Time Out's trademark style: sharp writing, informed reviewing and bang up-to-date inside knowledge of every scene.

Time Out made the natural leap into travel guides in the 1980s with the City Guide series, which now extends to over 50 destinations around the world. Written and researched by expert local writers and generously illustrated with original photography, the full-size guides cover a larger area than our Shortlist guides and include many more venue reviews, along with additional background features and a full set of maps.

Throughout this rapid growth, the company has remained proudly independent, still owned by Tony Elliott four decades after he started Time Out London as a single fold-out sheet of A5 paper. This independence extends to the editorial content of all our publications, this Shortlist included. No establishment has been featured because it has advertised, and no payment has influenced any of our reviews. And, for our critics, there's definitely no such thing as a free lunch: all restaurants and bars are visited and reviewed anonymously, and Time Out always picks up the bill.
For more about the company, see www.timeout.com.

# Don't Miss

# timeout.com

Over 50 of the world's greatest
cities reviewed in one site.

Sydney Harbour BridgeClimb p63

# Sights & Museums

There's really only one place to begin a tour of Sydney – and that's at the national landmark, the Sydney Opera House (p63), which was placed on the World Heritage list and deemed an international treasure by UNESCO last year. With its sweeping white sails, the Jørn Utzon-designed structure sits like a glittering jewel amid the busker-clogged harbourside precinct on the east side of Circular Quay. But don't just admire it from outside – it's well worth going inside for a tour. A costly revamp is finally attending to the long-ignored issue of access – the interior foyer steps are pretty punishing so a new set of escalators and a lift will aim to help elderly and disabled visitors.

## Spot the icons

From the Opera House steps you get a fine view of the Sydney Harbour Bridge (p63), known as the Coathanger. Day and night you'll spot a procession of grey ants scrambling 134 metres (440 feet) to the top via the BridgeClimb. Clip into a safety harness, slip on a jumpsuit and it's just a matter of taking a deep breath, and one step at a time. There is also the slightly tamer Pylon Lookout, which is home to a Harbour Bridge exhibition and accessible via the stairs on Cumberland Street.

To the left of the bridge, on the west side of the Quay, lies the renowned Museum of Contemporary Art (p59). Entry is free, thanks to an initiative by its inspirational director Elizabeth Macgregor (see also box p67) and the museum showcases an impressive range of contemporary Australian and international art.

Adjacent to Circular Quay, also on the west side, is the Rocks, once home to Sydney's convicts and dockworkers, and the site of Australia's first European settlement in 1788. It can be overrun with backpackers warming the barstools of its rollicking pubs, but don't let that put you off exploring its secret alleyways and cobblestone streets.

## Colonial past

The Rocks Discovery Museum on Kendall Lane (p60) is stuffed with artefacts and gives a great overview of the area's interesting and sometimes seamy history. Or take a Rocks Walking Tour (23 Playfair Street, the Rocks, 9247 6678, www.rockswalking tours.com.au) and dive head first into the historic streets, churches and pubs, with a knowledgeable

guide. Susannah Place Museum (p61), located in a 19th-century terrace of four houses, is a unique way to gain an insight into the lives of the working classes who lived in what were then Sydney's slums and are now home to some of its slickest developments. Original wallpaper and floor coverings still exist and modest backyards bear testament to the restrictive lives the hundreds of families who lived in these properties used to lead. You can even buy a trinket from the recreated 1915 corner store, also part of the museum.

The Sydney Observatory (p63), built on the site of one of Sydney's early forts, offers day- and night-time tours. Night tours are guided by an experienced astronomer, must be pre-booked and take about two hours. During the day it's also worth a look at the observatory's beautiful grounds. For a spookier night-time activity, try a ghost tour around the Rocks area with Ghost Tours of the Rocks (9247 7910, www.ghosttours.com.au), which

**Museum of Contemporary Art p59**

start at Cadman's Cottage, one of the nation's oldest houses, now home to Sydney Harbour National Park Information Centre. Tales of murder, hangings and hauntings are guaranteed.

## Open spaces

Head up the hill to the Royal Botanic Gardens (p60), a lush green landscape with incredible flora and fauna fronting the harbour and extending over 30 hectares with stunning views overlooking Woolloomooloo Bay and the harbour. This is where Sydney's office workers let off steam during their lunchbreak and can be seen playing touch rugby or jogging.

Some of the best views of the water and Sydney's chugging green and yellow ferries can be seen from the vantage point of Mrs Macquarie's Chair (p56) in the Domain. Government House (p57) is also inside the Gardens, and can be toured on the hour and half hour (the first tour departs at 10.30am, the last tour at 3pm). Entry is free. It's a magnificent Gothic revival structure, and has been spruced up of late with refurbed state drawing rooms.

From the Gardens, head back up Mrs Macquarie's Road to the Art Gallery of NSW (p57). As well as the big-name touring collections that draw in the crowds, the gallery houses Aboriginal art in the Yiribana gallery. The permanent exhibition has bark paintings and artefacts collected in Arnhem Land in the late 1950s and 1960s, as well as grave posts and more modern pieces depicting fascinating aspects of Aboriginal culture.

A short walk across the Domain are the Hyde Park Barracks (p57). The barracks, located between Macquarie Street and Queens Square, were built by the convict

## SHORTLIST

**Most iconic**
- Sydney Opera House (p63)
- Sydney Harbour Bridge (p63)
- Luna Park (p138)

**Best views**
- Skywalk, Sydney Tower (p64)
- BridgeClimb, Sydney Harbour Bridge (p63)
- Taronga Zoo (p149)
- Scenic World, Blue Mountains (p160)

**Prettiest parks**
- Royal Botanic Gardens (p60)
- Centennial Park (p116)
- Nielsen Park (p146)

**Best free**
- Museum of Contemporary Art (p59)
- Walk across Sydney Harbour Bridge (p63)
- Jazz in the Domain (p34)

**Best Australian art**
- Art Gallery of NSW (p56)
- Brett Whiteley Studio (p100)
- SH Ervin Gallery (p60)
- Museum of Contemporary Art (p59)

**Best for kids**
- Sydney Aquarium (p86)
- Australian Museum (p57)
- Sydney Wildlife World (p87)

**National history**
- Powerhouse Museum (p86)
- Australian National Maritime Museum (p86)
- Rocks Discovery Museum (p60)

**Historic houses**
- Vaucluse House (p146)
- Government House (p57)
- Susannah Place Museum (p61)

**Best law and order**
- Q Station (p142)
- Hyde Park Barracks (p57)

# 7th day free* with Avis

Rent any car with Avis in Sydney for 7 or more consecutive days and receive one day free* of the time and kilometre charges.

Include coupon number **TPPA031** in your reservation.

Offer valid on rentals commenced prior to 31 July 2010.

*Travelling to an unfamiliar city?*
*Add Avis' portable GPS^ to you rental.*

labour force between 1817 and 1819. A visit today is more of a salutary way to learn about the horrifying lives of the prisoners.

The Australian Museum (p57) is in a cavernous sandstone heritage building on College Street across from Hyde Park. Look out for travelling exhibits, including the Wildlife Photographer of the Year, which arrives each summer. Plus there are plenty of dinosaur bones and creepy crawlies.

## Brave new worlds

It's easy to find your way to Australia's tallest structure, the Sydney Tower (p64), also known as Centrepoint, because it is visible from just about every vantage point in the city. On Market Street, in the heart of the CBD, the tower has a viewing platform with binoculars, but its Skywalk is the best way to soak up the jaw-dropping 360-degree views right out to the Blue Mountains 122 kilometres away. The tour takes around two hours and involves walking (slowly and strapped to the edges) around the outside of the turret. Guides encourage walkers to let go of the sides and jump on the perspex glass overhangs for high-altitude photo ops.

Darling Harbour, a ten-minute walk from the CBD, is valiantly trying to shake off its tacky vibe with a clutch of sleek restaurants and bars in King Street Wharf. It's also welcomed a fabulous new attraction, Sydney Wildlife World (p87). Locals scrutinised building of the giant bubble-like structure for months, and were relieved when the doors opened to a classy new venture showcasing the furriest and fiercest native creatures.

Great and small abound with venomous spiders, as well as wallabies hopping around a red

sand desert. Don't miss standing in the middle of the humid tropical butterfly enclosure, arms outstretched, waiting for the winged creatures to land on your nose. Next door is the Sydney Aquarium (p86) with more than 11,500 marine animals including crocs, sharks and rainbow-hued fish. Cut costs by getting a discounted pass for both venues.

The Australian National Maritime Museum (p86) across the Pyrmont Bridge on Murray Street has regular exhibitions, as well as a re-creation of Captain Cook's tall ship, the *Endeavour*.

The Powerhouse Museum (p86) in Ultimo is a must-see. A former working power station, it's now Sydney's grooviest museum with interactive design, history and science experiences. From robot dogs to full-sized steam engines, this place has the lot.

A ferry ride from Darling Harbour to Manly will take you to one of Sydney's newest and most controversial attractions, located in the Sydney Harbour National Park. The former North Head Quarantine Station (a heritage site built in 1828 to house migrants suspected of carrying contagious diseases) has been given a $17.3-million makeover and is now known as Q Station (p142). Locals have opposed the redevelopment throughout its nine-year overhaul, fearing it would be turned into a gaudy theme park. Q Station's owners say they are simply preserving the station's history, keeping the famously macabre and long-running ghost tours operational, as well as adding other experiences. Part of the upgrade includes a theatre, (with actors telling Q Station's often tragic stories), Boilerhouse restaurant in the old steam room used to disinfect luggage, a spa and accommodation.

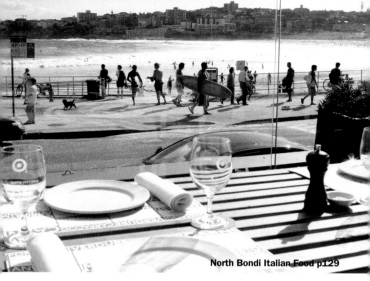

**North Bondi Italian Food p129**

# Eating & Drinking

Sydneysiders are a proud bunch,
no more so than when it comes
to eating out– and with good
reason. World-class chefs, terrific
produce and healthy competition
that keeps prices reasonable and
standards high have together
resulted in a thriving food scene.
And, from top-end restaurants to
local cafés, good food is there for
the tasting, with something to suit
all whims and wallets.

## On the Mod Oz menu

You might have heard of Modern
Australian cuisine, often referred to
as Mod Oz, but what is it exactly?
A precise definition is, in fact, hard
to come by. Australia has been
blessed by waves of migration
throughout its history, each of

which has brought with it the
cuisines of other nations. Italian,
Greek, Chinese and Vietnamese are
some of the more predominant,
both in terms of numbers of
immigrants and the effect they've
had on the city's menus. Add to
that the fact that many Sydney
chefs have travelled extensively in
Europe and had classical French
training, and you begin to see why
it's tricky to pinpoint exactly what
the term Mod Oz stands for. Some
of its leading proponents, however,
are Matt Moran at Aria (p65), Peter
Doyle at est. (p68), Guillaume
Brahimi at Guillaume at Bennelong
(p71) and Luke Mangan at Glass
(p69), all of whom have carved out
their own particular take on Mod
Oz fine dining.

Regardless of whether you're dining at the top end of town or somewhere more modest, the variety of ingredients that you'll find on menus is enormous. Seafood is an obvious highlight, with the fresh catch coming in daily at Pyrmont's Sydney Fish Market (p87). Sitting in the sunshine here while working your way through a plate of freshly shucked oysters washed down with a glass of chilled sémillon is a definitive Sydney dining experience.

As sustainability in all areas of production becomes more of a concern and diners become more interested in where their food comes from, you'll see the provenance of ingredients listed more regularly on menus (be sure to try Bangalow pork, Blackmore wagyu and Rannoch Farm quails if you come across them). Due to the wide variety of climates throughout the country, many fruits and vegetables are 'seasonal' for much of the year. Vegetarians are usually well catered for, with many menus having at least a couple of meat-free options. And if you have food allergies or restrictions, let your waiter know – most kitchens will be only too willing to help.

## A taste of the future

When it comes to eating out, Sydney's only real problem is that there is so much to eat and so little time. Visitors inevitably find themselves at the harbour, but take note: despite the spot's beauty, its restaurants don't always represent good value. Stick to those listed in the guide and, although you might end up with a heftier bill, the views and food will make the expense worthwhile. Above all, be sure to try Sydney's smaller venues where you'll often find young chefs on the road to super-chefdom. Try Daniel

**DON'T MISS**

### SHORTLIST

**Food with a view**
- Aria (p65)
- Forty One (p69)
- Guillaume at Bennelong (p71)
- Icebergs Dining Room (p126)
- Quay (p74)
- Summit (p75)

**In-the-know favourites**
- Billy Kwong (p102)
- Fratelli Paradiso (p95)
- Longrain (p105)
- Sean's Panorama (p129)
- Tetsuya's (p75)

**Best new restaurants**
- Foveaux Restaurant + Bar (p105)
- Glebe Point Diner (p132)
- L'Etoile (p117)
- Universal (p108)

**Best breakfast**
- Book Kitchen (p103)
- Forbes & Burton (p104)
- Jackie's (p117)
- Kafa (p105)

**Best seafood**
- Boathouse on Blackwattle Bay (p132)
- Garfish (p139)
- Rockpool (fish) (p74)
- Sydney Fish Market (p87)

**Clever cocktails**
- Lincoln (p96)
- Madame Fling Flong (p134)
- Rambutan (p106)
- Victoria Room (p108)
- Zeta Bar (p76)

**Posh nosh**
- Assiette (p102)
- Bilson's (p66)
- Marque (p106)

**Best people-watching**
- North Bondi Italian Food (p129)
- Opera Bar (p72)
- Otto (p96)

Puskas's Oscillate Wildly (p133), Darrell Felstead's Foveaux Restaurant + Bar (p105) and Alex Kearns's Glebe Point Diner (p132) for a taste of the hotly tipped culinary stars of tomorrow.

## Aussie café rules

Sydneysiders are serious about their coffee and it's the first thing most cafés will be judged on. For a prime example, head to Single Origin (p107) and order a flat white – an Antipodean coffee consisting of a heart-stopping shot of espresso topped with textured milk.

You can grab a cheap, tasty and quick meal any time of the day at one of hundreds of cafés in the city. Try the hole-in-the-wall Plan B (p74), younger sibling of top French dining room Bécasse (p66), or the popular Badde Manors (37 Glebe Point Road, Glebe, 9660 3797, www.baddemanorscafe.com). The latter's frosty staff seem to have twisted the meaning of the café's name and adopted it as their ethos, but the city only seems to love the place more for it. Be sure to try an all-day café breakfast while you're in town, invented for shift workers but embraced by all, especially those who like to stay out late.

## Ethnic eateries

From spicy Thai and Malaysian to freshly sliced sashimi, Peking duck and delicate Vietnamese dishes, Asian cuisine is ubiquitous across Sydney. It ranges from the cheap and cheerful to the truly decadent, but rarely fails to impress. For authentic Thai, try hip Longrain (p105) or head to the unassuming Spice I Am (p107). The quirky Uchi Lounge (p108) serves a Japanese menu with a twist, while Golden Century (p88) is top of Sydney's list for Chinese seafood.

## Euro vision

Australian chefs who've trained in Europe, international ones who have settled here for the lifestyle – what it all adds up to is some of the best European cuisine you'll find anywhere (even when compared to the country of origin). Sometimes it's given an Australian update with spices from Asia or unusual produce, but for authentic French, head to the charming Tabou (p108), or for cracking Italian in artistic surrounds, visit Lucio's (p117). The city has also recently embraced the trend for small-plate, tapas-style dining. Take a seat at Spanish eateries Alhambra (p143) and Emmilou (p104) and find out what all the fuss is about.

## Table talk

At the weekends, Australians tend to eat whenever they feel like it – it's not unusual to meet a friend for breakfast at 11.30am. Formal establishments have set hours, which means a lunch service from midday to 3pm, and dinner from 6pm to 10pm or 11pm.

Prices for fish and seafood will sometimes be listed on menus as 'market price' so ask for an approximation if you don't want a nasty surprise at the end of the meal. Any extras, such as a weekend or public holiday surcharge, corkage for BYO wines, or service, will also be specified on the menu. One bone of contention with Sydney diners is the price of water. Some restaurants will ask if you want it and then serve up expensive imported varieties. If you prefer tap water, let your waiter know. Tipping is appreciated but not expected. In a café you might leave the change, although if you think the service at a restaurant has been particularly good, a tip of ten per cent is considered reasonable. Bars and pubs have different opening times depending on their licences, but most close somewhere between midnight and 3am.

## Raise a glass

Sydney's drinking scene is almost as diverse as its eating. Restaurants will serve wines from Australia's many grape-growing regions as well as drops from around the world. At most places, you can BYO or 'bring your own' (check when booking). This normally only applies to wine and the restaurant will charge a fee for doing so.

It won't come as a huge surprise to learn that beer is a popular drink in restaurants as well as pubs, since it's often a better match with Asian food than wine. In NSW, beer from a tap comes in two main sizes: a schooner (425ml) and a middy (285ml). Many locals, however,

drink bottled beer. For true Aussie authenticity, order a round of Cooper's Pale Ale.

The great Australian pub is an egalitarian institution. You invariably get a mixed crowd, cheap beers and a TV in the corner showing sport. Confusingly, many pubs in Australia are called hotels, even though the places where you book a room for the night are called the same thing. Sydney did go through a designer pub phase in the late 1990s – read original features gutted, shiny hard surfaces installed, atmosphere lost – but that, thankfully, seems to have come to an end. For local flavour, head to the Australian Hotel (p65), the Gaslight Inn (p105) or the Hotel Hollywood (p105).

## Small bar none

One thing you'll notice about Sydney is the distinct lack of small venues where you can sit with a good glass of wine and chat with friends. It has to do with the state's draconian licensing laws. However, legislation has been passed that should make it much easier, and a whole lot cheaper, to open a small bar. By the time you're reading this, it's possible that the city will already have started reaping the benefits. Until then, most of the places you'll go for a quiet drink are also likely to serve food, even if it's just small sharing plates. There are some larger venues in the city, notably Justin Hemmes's new temple to hedonism, Ivy (p71), where the atmosphere is amped and the crowd is huge, particularly on Friday and Saturday nights. For great wine by the glass, try Vini (p108) or Bentley Restaurant & Bar (p102). And if you're feeling flush or have something to celebrate, head to Hemmesphere (p71) or Zeta Bar (p76).

**Bentley Restaurant & Bar p102**

**Paddington Market p121**

# Shopping

While Sydney's shops cannot rival the world's top shopping cities – Paris, London, New York, Hong Kong – wandering through its vibrant markets, meandering down the boutique-lined, terraced streets or getting lost in the old-school multi-storey malls still offers shoppers variety both in terms of choice and experience. There's also a good pool of local design talent to be tapped – particularly in fashion, homewares and art. Shopping opportunities reach beyond the city's main hub (which is dominated by malls and department stores) to the suburbs, each of which boasts its own individual personality and vibe.

Explore the nation's most esteemed and up-and-coming designer outlets in the picture-perfect eastern suburb of Paddington, where a well-heeled crowd flocks to keep up with the latest looks. Next door in Woollahra, you'll find a clutch of antiques shops and if you head west to Newtown's alternative scene, you'll uncover thrift stores, record shops and quirky fashion emporiums. For crafts try Balmain or the many markets all over the city; for beachwear head to Bondi and Manly.

## Funky threads

This is a city passionate about fashion and its colourfully clad inhabitants are renowned for their polished but laidback sense of style. Starting in the CBD, Sydney has its fair share of indoor shopping havens that are perfect during the heat of winter. The imposing MLC Centre (p78), whose towering hexagonal form pierces the city's skyline, has a fantastic collection of high-end fashion brands, including Gucci and Jimmy Choo. Those on a more realistic budget can find reasonably priced labels in the bountiful floors of department stores Myer (p80) and the elegant David Jones (p77), both housing international and Australian labels.

The most magnificent shopping arenas are those set in Victorian arcades. The Queen Victoria Building (p80) stretches over an entire block with four levels of boutiques, big-name labels, cute cafés and salons, all bathed in natural light thanks to the stained-glass windows. A similar but far more compact version is the Strand Arcade (p80) on Pitt Street, which gives consumers a rare glimpse back in time – the narrow corridor flanked by specialist shops on either side still shows off its beautiful original features from the spiral staircase to the tiled floors.

Local designers' boutiques are bountiful and clustered most densely around the cosmopolitan area of Paddington. Set in the heart of Oxford Street's busy strip is style favourite Sass & Bide (p122). Arguably the country's best-known fashion export, the creative duo now churn out a lot more than just skinny jeans – devoting more time and floor space to their high-end fashion creations from sparkly dresses to chi-chi underwear. Another big name not to be missed is the quirky but infinitely feminine Alannah Hill (p118), whose boudoir-esque flagship store is filled with intricately adorned creations. If it's sharp suits or sassy party attire you're after, Morrissey

**S H O R T L I S T**

**Designer flair**
- Easton Pearson (p119)
- Lisa Ho (p121)
- Kirrily Johnston (p119)
- Parlour X (p122)
- Sass & Bide (p122)
- Scanlan & Theodore (p122)

**Best beach gear**
- Aussie Boys (p109)
- Between the Flags (p76)
- Big Swim (p129)
- Billabong (p77)
- Mambo (p130)
- Zimmermann (p122)

**Best gifts**
- Collect (p109)
- Mimco (p121)
- Opus Designs (p121)

**Best beauty**
- Mecca Cosmetica (p121)
- Napoleon Perdis Make-up Academy (p121)

**Best shoes**
- Gary Castles (p78)
- Midas (p78)
- Nine West (p121)
- Platypus Shoes (p144)

**Best jewellery**
- Dinosaur Designs (p77)
- Family Jewels (p119)

**Best sweet treats**
- Jones the Grocer (p119)
- Just William (p119)
- Max Brenner (p117)
- Sweet Art (p122)

**Best all-in-one shopping**
- David Jones (p77)
- Galeries Victoria (p78)
- Queen Victoria Building (p80)
- Strand Arcade (p80)

**Best undies**
- David Jones (p77)
- Dress Me Darling (p135)
- Myer (p80)

(p121) will have you decked out in no time. Clean lines and sharp tailoring are the trademarks of both his menswear and ladies' fashions.

The vintage scene is thriving in Sydney and no matter where you are in the city, you're never too far away from a treasure trove of pre-loved fashions. Sydneysiders love to mix modern-day pieces with old-school one-offs that they buy on Crown Street at a string of quirky outlets such as the Rockabilly-inspired Route 66 (p110) and the twee boutique Grandma Takes A Trip (263 Crown Street, Surry Hills, 9356 3322, www.grandmatakes atrip.com.au). It all makes interesting browsing, even if you don't intend to buy.

Unsurprisingly, given the city's blissful coastal setting, swimwear is a wardrobe essential and there's no shortage of options when it comes to buying new gear to hit the surf. Some of the world's most famous swimwear brands are Australian-grown and have their own stores; look for Billabong (p77), Rip Curl (p80) and Mambo (p130), all of which can kit you out with a wide selection of cossies, as well as street-inspired fashions to take you from dawn till dusk.

## Market value

Sydney's vibrant markets are a much-loved institution and have long acted as a platform for launching the careers of local talent. The longest-running and most popular is Paddington Market (p121), held in the grounds of the Paddington Uniting Church on Oxford Street every Saturday. The tightly packed lines of stalls sell a plethora of handcrafted goods from soft furnishings and fashion right through to jewellery and plants. The creative trio behind the rainbow-bright Dinosaur Designs

**Alannah Hill p118**

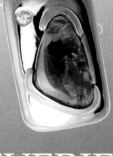

**DON'T MISS**

(p77) began their career in this very spot and they're not the only ones – so it's worth keeping your eyes peeled for potential big names.

Bargain hunters who revel in the opportunity to rumble through tangled piles of vintage clothes or precariously stacked furniture should visit the artsy Surry Hills Market (p110). Unlike the more reserved Paddington version, this is very much a case of empty out the attic and see what flies. Vendors range from OAPs selling 'antique' jewellery to designers not yet established enough to earn a spot at more prestigious markets.

When it comes to choice, however, Glebe Market (p136) wins hands down. The western suburb is known for its alternative traits and the collection of stalls here mirrors its personality with tie-dye tees, organic clothes and even Japanese imported fashions all on colourful display. With the scent of incense in the air, the sound of folk singers on the breeze and wind chimes reverberating around the grassy patch, it's all strangely relaxing despite the buzzing crowds.

## Words and notes

Sydney doesn't just do a good trade in second-hand clothes – the second-hand book scene is bouyant as well. While you can, of course, pick up all the brand new bestsellers at the likes of Borders (p77), tatty old classics, dog-eared travel guides and well thumbed coffee-table books add character not to mention affordability to your literary buys. Glebe Point Road has a handful of enchanting little stores including Sappho Books (p136), which incorporates a beautiful courtyard café into its premises. Come to enjoy home-baked cakes and potent coffee as you flick through the piles of books.

Music fans will have no problem finding a record store to cater to their aural tastes, be they jazz, hip hop or country. Local favourite Red Eye (p80) specialises in the kind of old-school vinyl that's ideal for bedroom DJs, as well as carrying an impressive choice of CDs from a mixed bag of global artists. Fish Records (p135) offers all the top chart tracks while a more eclectic mix of folk can be found at Oxford Street's Folkways Music (p119).

Bear in mind that the majority of weekend markets will have record vendors too, many of whom sell well preserved LPs from decades past. Another fantastic opportunity is the Parramatta Music Fair held regularly throughout the year (www.collectables.zip.com.au).

## Opening hours

Shops open Monday to Friday between 9am and 10am and close between 5.30pm and 6pm, except on Thursdays when most shopping areas stay open until around 9pm. On Saturday most places tend to shut pretty sharpish between 5pm and 6pm. Sunday trading is the norm, with most shops open between 11am and 4pm, or 5pm in the summer – though hours can vary quite a bit.

Sale time is usually at the end of summer and winter, but department stores also hold sales to coincide with public holidays. The big ones to watch out for are David Jones's twice yearly clearance at the end of June and after Christmas, and Myer's Boxing Day sale. Get there early for the best bargains.

In all cases, what you see on the price tag is what you pay; it includes GST (Goods & Services Tax). For details of the goods you can and can't take out of the country when you leave see p185.

Slide p112

# Nightlife

For a city renowned for its fickle tastes and ever-revolving venue hot-spots, Sydneysiders love any excuse to party, so there's no shortage of options for a night on the town. Between Sunday and Tuesday the city tends to be fairly sleepy, but come Wednesday (or 'hump day' as it's known here) there's a giant spike in numbers that balloons as the weekend beckons for the party faithful and night owls alike. The gay community is well served along the infamous strip of Oxford Street with a range of clubs and bars, while straight clubbers tend to stick to predictable venues dotted around the CBD and their uber-cool counterparts in Kings Cross (the latter can get pretty crowded and rowdy after midnight). Bouncers in clubs are more than ready to eject anyone sneezing the wrong way so it pays to choose your late-night spot carefully. Live music remains a stable part of nightlife in Sydney, with a resurgence of local up-and-coming bands and a variety of venues for big-name acts, ranging from small clubs and theatres to massive arenas. Comedy is more of a cottage industry by international standards (Melbourne has the edge on Sydney by a mile), with its centre at the Entertainment Quarter (Bent Street, Driver Avenue, Moore Park, 8117 6700, www.eqmoore park.com.au) and annual comedy festivals held at the Enmore Theatre (p136) – aka the finest rock venue in town.

One general rule of thumb for night-owls: don't try and head home around 3am. It's the much-criticised 'changeover time' for Sydney's less-than-impressive taxi fleet, so plan to leave a good half hour earlier or later unless you fancy a long walk home.

## Clubs

Considering the dance music boom came relatively late to Australia – a good decade after the UK and US – Sydney has more than made up for lost time, even if the venue boom has now eased. There is literally something for everybody and every occasion, with the city offering both long-established and effective dancefloor beats. The Slip Inn (p82) remains the finest straight club in town after the demise of the much-loved Sublime, (since relegated to a 'night' status at Home, p90, every Friday) and fresher-faced attempts at major dance nights – the ArtHouse Hotel (p81) and Cargo Bar (p90) – both attract a younger, more suburban straight crowd.

For cool vibes and underground beats, head to Kings Cross. Lady Lux (p99), in a renovated old terrace, is the place to head first, and home strictly to well-dressed inner-city types with 'tude, while Moulin Rouge (p99) is exactly what it says, albeit with a younger-than-expected crowd. The Bourbon (p95) and Sapphire Suite (p99) tend to attract a mainstream, boozy audience, the latter being an attempt to bling-up the Cross. Nearby, Yu at Soho Bar (p99) is more elegantly wasted and offers an earthier vibe for the late-nighters. And for an alternative scene later in the night, head to Q Bar (p112) along Oxford Street, a mixed club that can resemble scenes from *A Little Shop of Horrors* if the night's right.

**S H O R T L I S T**

**Best for after dark**
- Lady Lux (p99)
- Q Bar (p112)

**Best for gigs**
- Enmore Theatre (p136)
- Hordern Pavilion (p122)
- Oxford Art Factory (p111)

**Best for young blood**
- Hopetoun Hotel (p111)
- Spectrum (p112)
- Yu at Soho Bar (p99)

**Best supper clubs**
- Basement (p82)
- Will & Toby's (p112)

**So Sydney**
- Colombian (p110)
- Stonewall (p112)
- Tilbury (p99)

**Best gay nights**
- Arq Sydney (p110)
- Colombian (p110)
- Midnight Shift (p111)

**Best for bling**
- Sapphire Suite (p99)
- Tank (p82)

**Best Friday night**
- Slip Inn (p82)

**Best for sound**
- Home (p90)
- Tank (p82)

**Best for Sunday sessions**
- Arq Sydney (p110)
- Cargo Bar (p90)
- Stonewall Hotel (p112)

**Best for cabaret**
- Slide (p112)
- Will & Toby's (p112)

**Best for international acts**
- Acer Arena (p159)
- Hordern Pavilion (p122)
- State Theatre (p83)
- Sydney Entertainment Centre (p90)

**DON'T MISS**

# Music

One of the longest traditions of Sydney nightlife has been its live music scene. Overcoming a threat in the late 1990s from the onslaught of pokie (gambling) machines – brought in to replace bands for a quick buck – live music is very much alive and rocking in the Emerald City (with the pokies tucked away out of sight). Many pubs have some sort of live entertainment laid on (check local press for details), with the likes of the Hopetoun Hotel (p111) in Surry Hills and Spectrum (p112) on Oxford Street showcasing up-and-comers every night of the week.

Just down from Spectrum is the latest and greatest live music space that Sydney has seen for years: the Oxford Art Factory (p111). Here, a mix of DJs and dance nights together with ultra-hip bands (Danish outfit the Raveonettes, for instance) make for a modern blend of all things music. Better still, it's one of the very few live venues where two bands can play

simultaneously in adjacent rooms, the main stage offset by the next door mini-stage, in front of which there are chairs and poufs to hang out on and soak up the vibe. The bouncers are typically bone-headed, but the staff are friendly and helpful. Close by, the Supper Club at Will & Toby's (p112), above the Oxford Hotel (p111), increasingly caters to straight band crowds as well as the eastern suburbs cocktail set. Upstairs again, the Polo Bar is a super-stylish cocktail-quaffing scene controlled by a steely door policy – but if you can get past the decor the vibe up here is very Rat Pack.

The inner-west remains the heart and soul of young bands, with the University of Sydney campus neighbouring Glebe, Newtown and Annandale. Among the many venues worth frequenting for a fresh take on who may (or may not) make it: Newtown's Sandringham Hotel (p137), once scene to a residency from Danielle Spencer (aka Mrs Russell Crowe) before she

Cargo Bar p90

became a mum; and, most importantly of all, the legendary Annandale Hotel (17 Parramatta Road, Annandale, 9550 1078, www.annandalehotel.com). Newtown's much-loved the Vanguard (p137) – an inner-west version of the Basement (p82) in Circular Quay tends towards jazz and blues, while art deco favourite the Enmore Theatre (p136) remains an essential part of any muso's pilgrimage. Ignore what anyone else may tell you, this represents the heart and soul of Sydney's music scene. For opulence and big-namers, there's the outstanding State Theatre (p83). Sydney Entertainment Centre (p90) down the road in Darling Harbour is exactly what you'd expect: an aircraft hangar of a place with little atmosphere and plastic seats. Big names out to make money can be found here, out west at the Acer Arena (p159) in Olympic Park and, more intimately, at Fox Studios' Hordern Pavilion (p122), another barn of a place.

## Gay and lesbian

The gay scene is focused on the strip of Oxford Street that runs from Hyde Park's southern tip to the imaginary crossroads marked by Taylor Square and the fringes of Darlinghurst. Pretty much anything goes at the likes of popular hotel and drag club Stonewall (p112) and rave joint Midnight Shift (p111), but it's the Colombian (p110) these days that is the focal point of the scene, with drinkers sitting at the open window checking out the action on the strip. Palms (p111) is a popular dance spot where Kylie is frequently on the sound system, while stalwarts such as the recently revamped Oxford Hotel (p111) and Slide (p112) offer eye-candy for a male

crowd. The latter also serves up some truly innovative girls' nights. Indeed lesbian nights are popping up all over town; check freesheets the *Sydney Star Observer*, *SX* and *Lesbians on the Loose* for venues.

Gay clubbers gravitate to Arq (p110), a notoriously camp space that hosts shows from local heroes such as Marcia Hines and standard dance nights. Nearby, the Taxi Club (p112) is the grotto of we-can't-stop-the-music types.

Beyond the strip, a quintessential eastern suburbs drinking hole – the Tilbury (p99), across Hyde Park, in waterside Woolloomooloo – caters for a mixed crowd (the pub closes at midnight, though), while across town, in the inner-west suburb of Erskineville (down the road from Newtown) lies the infamous dive that is the Imperial Hotel (35 Erskineville Road, Erskineville, 9519 9899,www.theimperialhotel. com.au). Famed for drag shows and immortalised on the big screen in *The Adventures of Priscilla, Queen of the Desert*, the cleaned-up Imperial reopens in 2008 and the gay community waits nervously to see what's been done.

## Comedy

Standup struggles in Sydney although quite why remains a mystery. Venues have come and gone over the years (notably the Comedy Club in Glebe), but comics and promoters remain determined. The Comedy Store at the Entertainment Quarter (p24) is the modern home of Sydney comedy, while the Enmore Theatre (p136) packs 'em in for the Cracker Comedy Festival. On the rare occasions that big-name talents, such as Chris Rock, pitch up, expect to pay three figures and sit it out in one of the Entertainment Centre's (p90) dreadful seats.

**OpenAir Cinema p83**

# Arts & Leisure

Forget the cliché of Melbourne as the self-appointed cultural capital of Australia, the Sydney arts scene has never looked or felt so buoyant. Leading the charge, understandably, is Sydney's iconic Opera House (p63), which has actively broadened its remit in the last decade to showcase its most diverse range of live performances to date.

Now boasting a staggering 1,500 performances a year, Jørn Utzon's new-world arena offers everything from spoken word and assorted instrumental performances to traditional set pieces such as opera, ballet and drama, alongside comedy, rock gigs – even reality TV finales. In addition, the hallowed steps in front of the house play host to outdoor gigs (Björk and local heroes Powderfinger are recent highlights) and often act as the finish line to sporting events. On 28 June 2007, it was also announced on the same steps that the Opera House had been awarded a World Heritage listing.

Added to this tangible cultural buzz is a massive resurgence in all things drama and dance, due in no small part to the work of Cate Blanchett and playwright husband Andrew Upton at the helm of the Sydney Theatre (p83). Elsewhere, the massive arts space CarriageWorks (245 Wilson Street, Eveleigh, 8571 9099, www.carriage works.com.au) is doing much to promote experimental artforms, while the reality TV smash *So You*

*Think You Can Dance* has seen the Sydney Dance Company play an active role both in front of and behind the camera.

Similarly, the Sydney Festival – a fortnight-long arts bash that takes over the city immediately after New Year – has gone from an elitist highbrow affair to an en masse event buzzing with talent from around the world. It kicks off with a series of free-for-all gigs dotted around the CBD (the biggest of which is in the Domain) and is followed each year by its big-screen cousin, the Sydney Film Festival.

All this means that the Harbour City can now proudly boast the cream of the cultural crop all year round. And with year-on-year record attendances for its Festival, Sydneysiders are proving to be just as culturally curious as their Melbourne counterparts.

## Sports & leisure

An inherent part of daily life in Sydney lies in the local obsession with fitness, physical perfection and all things sport. On any given day in the inner city, thousands gleefully jog, walk, work out, swim, and play (or watch) tennis, cricket and rugby league.

For a hearty swimming session, there are outstanding pools in the east, notably Bondi's famed Icebergs ocean pool (p130), and in the north try North Sydney Olympic Pool (p139), with its stunning city skyline and harbour backdrop. The centrally located Andrew (Boy) Charlton Pool (p82) offers fitness classes as well as swimming, and a similarly glistening outlook.

But it's the city's west that is the most spoilt, its Olympic Park with its athletics, tennis, aquatic and sports centres (p159) catering admirably for both spectators and participants. The giant ANZ Stadium (p159), also housed in Olympic Park, plays host to Australia's national rugby team as well as to various other one-off games. Meanwhile, the Sydney Cricket Ground (p123), built in 1848, and the adjacent Football Stadium (built in 1988) next to Moore Park between them host Sydney Swans (AFL) games, international cricket series, World Cup qualifying matches with Australia's Socceroos and several rugby league and union fixtures. Looking after oneself – via spas, massages, steam rooms and body scrubs – is big business in a town as image conscious as Sydney, and there are plenty of options to choose from, including Zen Day Spa (p113) and the famed spa at the Observatory Hotel (p167).

**Belvoir Street Theatre p113**

# Cinema

For a city so embracing of an outdoor lifestyle, it can be surprising to find Sydneysiders enthusiastic about indoor pursuits such as cinema. Mainstream multiplex fare is nonetheless everywhere – the busiest cinema being the city's Hoyts-Greater Union monolith on George Street (p83), and the most civilised being Fox Studio's Entertainment Quarter (p123). Art-house cinema is well served (and well loved) – choose from Dendy Newtown (p137) in the inner-west, the Palace Verona (p123), Palace Academy Twin (p123) and Chauvel (p123) cinemas in Paddington, and the classy Dendy Opera Quays downtown (p82). Given their inherent patriotism, Aussies are strangely less enamoured with local releases, a perennial sticking point in an industry beset with funding issues. Despite this, a number of mini-festivals are laid on to reflect and serve the culturally diverse melting pot of Sydney, with French, Spanish, German, Russian, Korean, Japanese and Mexican films all showcased throughout the year.

During the summer, movies head outdoors with a series of alfresco screenings in idyllic settings. Bondi's OpenAir (p130) and Centennial Park's Moonlight cinemas (p123) are casual, come-as-you-are affairs, while the OpenAir Cinema (p83) at Mrs Macquarie's Chair offers the priceless backdrop of the Bridge and Opera House, super-quality sound and a fully stocked bar and restaurant to boot. The latter is so popular with locals that it sells out in a flash, so get in quick (it's an unforgettable experience). Once you've bought your ticket in advance, nothing short of gale-force winds will engender a refund (ie the films play

**SHORTLIST**

**Best for movies**
- Dendy Opera Quays (p82)
- Chauvel (p123)
- Palace Verona (p123)

**Best outdoor cinemas**
- OpenAir Cinema (p83)
- Bondi OpenAir Cinema (p130)
- Moonlight Cinema (p123)

**Best theatre**
- Sydney Theatre (p83)
- Belvoir Street Theatre (p113)

**Best for musicals**
- Capitol Theatre (p90)
- Lyric Theatre (p91)

**Best pools**
- Bondi Icebergs (p130)
- Ian Thorpe Aquatic Centre (p91)
- North Sydney Olympic Pool (p139)
- Andrew (Boy) Charlton Pool (p82)
- Sydney International Aquatic Centre (p159)

**Best sports space**
- Sydney Cricket Ground (p123)
- Sydney Olympic Park (p159)

**Best for location**
- Ensemble Theatre (p139)
- Sydney Opera House (p63)
- Sydney Theatre (p83)

**Best for talent**
- Cate Blanchett at the Sydney Theatre (p67)
- Geoffrey Rush at the Belvoir Street Theatre (p113)

**Best arts festival**
- Biennale of Sydney (p35)
- Jazz in the Domain (p34)
- Sydney Festival (p34)
- Sydney Film Festival (p35)

**Best spas**
- Observatory Hotel Spa (p167)
- Zen Day Spa (p113)

**DON'T MISS**

# THE SHORTLIST

## WHAT'S NEW | WHAT'S ON | WHAT'S BEST

 **Amsterdam**

 **Barcelona**

 **Berlin**

 **Cyprus**

 **Dubai**

 **Dubrovnik**

 **Edinburgh**

 **Florence**

 **Las Vegas**

 **London**

 **Malta**

 **Manchester**

 **Marrakech**

 **New York**

 **Nice & Cannes**

 **Paris**

 **Prague**

 **Rome**

 **San Francisco**

 **Sydney**

 **Tokyo**

 **Venice**

- **Pocket-sized guides**
- **What's on, month by month**
- **Full colour fold-out maps**

**TIME OUT GUIDES
WRITTEN BY
LOCAL EXPERTS**
timeout.com/shop

**Time Out Guides**

come rain or shine). For kids, the 3D IMAX experience in Darling Harbour (p91) is a must. Both 2- and 3D selections are on the billing, and the films themselves run longer than your typical blockbuster.

## Theatre

Australia's major acting talent may often relocate itself to the US for work purposes – think Hugh Jackman, Nicole Kidman, Toni Colette – but many remain loyal to their thespian roots and are actively involved in theatre. Geoffrey Rush, for instance, has long been a patron and a performer at the well attended and highly regarded Belvoir Street Theatre (p113). The city's Capitol Theatre (p90) and Star City's Lyric Theatre (p91) tend to be reserved for big-scale musicals such as *Billy Elliot: The Musical* and *The Phantom of the Opera*, which tend to have a 12- to 18-month run, if successful. The Sydney Theatre (p67), meanwhile, remains the stalwart venue for the dramatic arts, along with the Sydney Opera House's Drama Theatre (p63). North of the bridge, the likeable Ensemble Theatre in Kirribilli (p139) offers solid professional acts for theatre lovers too tired of traffic to head south into the city.

## Dance

Dance in Sydney may have been newly inspired by reality TV hit *So You Think You Can Dance*, but there's still a bit of catching up to be done in theatres – both by the performances themselves and attendance levels. The shock departure of inspirational choreographer Graeme Murphy from the Sydney Dance Company and the introduction of Cuban Yosvani Ramos to the Australian

Ballet are both shaking up the scene. For truly cutting-edge work, the Bangarra Dance Theatre (9251 5333, www.bangarra.com.au) is the company to watch. This Sydney-based troupe tours all over the world with its unique collaborations of contemporary dance and ancient Aboriginal traditions of physicality, movement and bodily storytelling.

## Classical music

Australia may not be renowned for its classical composers, but there remains a healthy appetite among the well-to-do and the so-inclined for performances at the city's two main classical venues: the Sydney Opera House's hallowed Concert Hall (p63) and its younger cousin, the City Recital Hall (p82). The latter was completed in time for the 2000 Olympics to cater for increased demand and to ease the burden on the former, so that its remit could be broadened. Both venues offer a wide range of classical performance in a stylish, comfortable setting. The Recital Hall has the edge acoustics-wise (hardly surprising, given that it was purpose-built in the last decade) – but both are worth experiencing for their wow factor.

Beyond these semi-elitist affairs lies a programme of mainstream outdoor summer events – both Jazz and Opera in the Domain (p34) draw tens of thousands each year who rock up with picnic hampers and champers to enjoy an evening's entertainment. And beefing up the classical calendar in January 2009 is internationally acclaimed conductor and music director Vladimir Ashkenazy, who will join the Sydney Symphony Orchestra as its principal conductor and artistic advisor, taking over the reins from Gianluigi Gelmetti.

**DON'T MISS**

# Calendar

News Year's Eve fireworks p38

Sydney loves to celebrate the incomparable natural beauty of its open spaces and, consequently, many of its biggest and brightest festivals are held outdoors, be they day or night. Here is a selection of the hottest annual events, all of which underline the diversity of Sydney's cosmopolitan society and its growing interest in cultural pursuits. For further details, visit www.cityofsydney.nsw.gov.au or pick up a copy of *Time Out Sydney*'s weekly magazine.

## January

Early Jan **Flickerfest**
Bondi Pavilion, Bondi Beach
*www.flickerfest.com.au*
Australia's only short-film festival to be officially recognised as an Oscar-qualifying event.

Mid-late Jan **Sydney Festival**
Various venues
*www.sydneyfestival.org.au*

Three weeks of dance, theatre, opera and music. Ticketed events are supplemented by a free outdoor programme which includes Jazz in the Domain.

26 **Australia Day**
Various venues
*www.australiaday.com.au*
Celebration of European settlement in Australia with music and flag-waving.

26 **Ferrython**
Sydney Harbour
*www.sydneyfestival.org.au*
Catamaran ferry race finishing at the Harbour Bridge.

## February

Early Feb **Chinese New Year**
Belmore Park, Darling Harbour & Chinatown
*www.cityofsydney.nsw.gov.au*
Fifteen days of festivities, including a lively parade and dragonboat racing.

Late Feb-early Mar **Mardi Gras**
Various venues
*www.mardigras.org.au*

Huge annual gay and lesbian carnival that sees thousands parade and party.

Late Feb **Tropfest**
The Domain, Sydney
*www.tropfest.com.au*
Free outdoor short-film festival broadcast on giant screens to thousands.

## March

Early Mar-mid May **Archibald, Wynne & Sulman Prizes**
Art Gallery of NSW, Art Gallery Road, The Domain
*www.artgallery.nsw.gov.au*
One of Australia's oldest, finest, most prestigious and most controversial art awards (see also box p37).

## April

Early-mid Apr **Royal Easter Show**
Sydney Showground, Sydney Olympic Park, Homebush Bay
*www.eastershow.com.au*
A Sydney institution with livestock prizes and sheepdog trials.

25 **Anzac Day**
Along George Street
A dawn service at the Martin Place Cenotaph followed at 9am by a march and a 12.30pm service at the Anzac Memorial in Hyde Park.

## May

Mid May **Sydney Writers' Festival**
Various venues
*www.swf.org.au*
Sydney's biggest annual literary event.

## June

Mid June **Darling Harbour Jazz & Blues Festival**
Darling Harbour
*www.darlingharbour.com*
Free jazz on the harbour over the Queen's Birthday long weekend.

3 weeks in June **Sydney Film Festival**
Various venues
*www.sydneyfilmfestival.org*
Indie films and mainstream premieres from around the world.

June-Sept **Biennale of Sydney**
Various venues
*www.bos2008.com*
Major three-month long contemporary art festival showcasing the very best work by world-class Australian and international artists.

**Chinese New Year**

## July

Mid July **World Youth Day**
Around CBD
*www.wyd2008.org*
Sydney comes to a halt for the Pope who attends this Catholic celebration.

## August

Early Aug **City to Surf Fun Run**
Corner of Park & College Streets to Bondi Beach
*www.city2surf.sunherald.com.au*
Upwards of 60,000 runners tackle this 14km (8.7-mile) course.

## September

Mid Sept **Festival of the Winds**
Bondi Beach
*www.waverley.nsw.gov.au*
Australia's largest free kite-flying festival attracts upwards of 50,000 enthusiasts each year.

Mid Sept **Sydney Running Festival**
Various venues
*www.sydneyrunningfestival.org*
Sydney's marathon is made up of four runs – a Bridge Run, fun run, marathon and half-marathon – all of which finish at the Opera House.

## October

Early Oct **Sleaze Ball**
Entertainment Quarter, Driver Avenue, Moore Park
*www.mardigras.org.au*
Spectacular dance party organised as a fundraiser for gay Sydney's main event, Mardi Gras in February.

Early Oct **Manly International Jazz Festival**
Manly
*www.manly.nsw.gov.au/manlyjazz*
Australia's largest and longest running community jazz festival.

3 weeks in Oct **Art & About**
Various venues
*www.cityofsydney.nsw.gov.au/artandabout*
The city's parks, squares and streets become a blank canvas for local artists.

All month **Good Food Month**
Various venues
*http://gfm.smh.com.au.*
Top restaurants offer cut-price menus and there are plenty of outdoor fairs.

**Mardi Gras**

# Canvassing attention

'Heath' by Vincent Fantauzzo

It may be the old man of Aussie art prizes, first awarded in 1921, but there's nothing staid about the Archibald Prize (p35). Controversy swirls around this annual contest and the exhibition of shortlisted portraits is always one of the year's best attended events.

JF Archibald was a journalist and co-founder of Australia's now defunct news magazine the *Bulletin*. He was also a supporter of young artists. In 1900, he commissioned John Longstaff to paint a portrait of poet Henry Lawson for 50 guineas. The story goes that Archibald was so happy with the result that he left money in his will for an annual prize.

What makes the prize so special is the manner in which it has chronicled the social changes of the nation. The first woman to win was Nora Heysen in 1938, with a portrait of the wife of the Consul General for the Netherlands. But her triumph wasn't met with enthusiasm – far from it. Her many critics felt she was betraying the fairer sex by her indulgence in the arts. As painter Max Meldrum, who ironically (or possibly not) won the prize himself the following year, famously crowed, 'If I were a woman, I would certainly prefer raising a healthy family to a career in art.' And while Meldrum's dated sexism is ever trotted out as a humorous sign of the times, the cold facts remain – only seven women have ever won the Archibald in its 87-year history.

The prize requires its subject to be a 'distinguished' man or woman, meaning that the majority of entries depict well known faces. In 2008, a triptych of Heath Ledger (painted just weeks before the actor's tragic death) proved especially poignant. Some of Australia's greatest painters have won the prize, but it still carries the frisson of tapping new talent.

## November

16-2 Dec **Sculpture by the Sea**
Bondi to Tamarama coastal walk
*www.sculpturebythesea.com*
The country's largest free outdoor exhibition of modern sculpture.

Mid Nov **Newtown Festival**
Camperdown Memorial Park, corner of Lennox & Australia Streets, Newtown
*www.newtowncentre.org*
Inner-west free festival boasting music, workshops, food and activities for kids.

Mid Nov **Glebe Street Fair**
Glebe Point Road, from Parramatta Road to Bridge Road, Glebe
*www.glebechamber.com.au*
Sydney's longest-running street fair with food stalls, wine tasting, arts and crafts, clowns and music stages.

## December

6 **Homebake**
The Domain, Mrs Macquarie's Road, Royal Botanic Gardens, CBD
*www.homebake.com.au*
This outdoor music festival features some of Australia's best home grown talent. Tickets sell out well in advance. Bring ID if you want to drink alcohol.

Mid-late Dec **Carols in the Domain**
The Domain, Mrs Macquarie's Road, Royal Botanic Gardens, CBD
*www.carolsinthedomain.com*
Join the 100,000 who fill the Domain for an evening of carols by candlelight. The event is televised live.

25 **Christmas Day on Bondi Beach**
Bondi Beach
Thousands of travellers gather on Bondi for an impromptu party. Since the council introduced an alcohol ban on the beach, this has become more of a family affair, with the backpackers heading instead to the Bondi Pavilion.

26 **Sydney to Hobart Yacht Race**
Sydney Harbour
*www.cyca.com.au*
Hundreds turn out on Boxing Day to watch the spectacular start of this notoriously gruelling yacht race.

31 **New Year's Eve Fireworks**
Sydney Harbour & Darling Harbour
*www.cityofsydney.nsw.gov.au/nye*
Two displays – one at 9pm and then the midnight extravaganza. If you're lucky (or loaded) enough, you'll be watching on a boat; failing that, the best views will cost you an all-day wait, as you'll have to pitch up very early to stake out a front-row position.

**Sculpture by the Sea**

# Itineraries

# Building Sydney

For most of its history, Sydney relied on the sheer beauty of its harbour, easily forgetting the intimate backdrop of urban life, its streets and public spaces. With little architecture other than that derived from the cold-climate styles of London and New York, and a sprawling, low-density urban model inspired by Los Angeles, one might expect Sydney to be somewhat stuffy and derivative. And yet most are surprised by its intimacy and warmth, by the fineness of its urban pattern, so closely connected to topography, that reminds one more of an old European city that has grown incrementally over time than the new-world American variety of planned cities.

Sydney is full of contradictions and this walk zigzags across these contradictions as evidenced by Sydney's architecture. In the course of a leisurely day you will meander west through the formerly industrial precinct, traipse through the central business district, before finishing on the eastern edge with views out across Elizabeth Bay and Potts Point. Included are projects imported and home grown, old and new, all of which reveal Sydney's schizophrenic relationship to this most sublime of landscapes.

Where better to start than the **Sydney Opera House** (p63), Danish architect Jørn Utzon's half-finished 20th-century masterpiece. After a painstaking study of naval maps of the harbour, the 38-year-old architect's inspired, almost naïve, gesture of billowing clouds hovering over an abstract geology won over Finnish American judge Eero Saarinen, who in turn convinced the other judges: 'Gentlemen, here is your opera house!' With its freshness and poetic economy, Utzon's building became the unlikely symbol of a brash young nation.

The platform, concrete vaults and ceramic skin were built almost precisely to his design, but his intentions for the acoustic interiors, he likened to a 'violin within its case', and the glass walls or 'gulls' wings' were relegated to the scrap heap following his forced departure in 1966 at the hands of the irascible Askin Liberal government. In 1973, after a whopping $102 million had been spent on what was supposed to have been a $7 million project, Queen Elizabeth II officially opened the building. The architect's name was not mentioned.

In 1998, Utzon was invited back to the project, due to the acoustic inadequacy of the interior, and the fruit of his collaboration with Sydney architect Richard Johnson is finally becoming evident – have a look at the new colonnade that skirts the western boardwalk. Sydney Architecture Walks (8239 2211, www.sydneyarchitecture.org) offers tours of the building.

On your left as you head back towards Circular Quay you'll see the building nicknamed the Toaster, a highly controversial apartment block that was built following no less than a decade of discussion debating the best use of the land (most Sydneysiders think planners got it badly wrong with a block that resembles a kitchen appliance). Behind the Quay is **Customs House** (p57), designed by James Barnet in 1885, an elegant classical revival building that has

experienced constant makeovers, most recently by Sydney architects Tonkin Zulaikha Greer (1997) and Lacoste and Stevenson (2006). Once the hub of early trading, the building features a six-storey atrium and houses the city library. There is a 1:500 scale model of the city in the foyer – use it to orient yourself before heading out again to explore.

As you exit the building, look at the paving, which interprets the natural history of Circular Quay by expressing the original shoreline in the abstract graphic of a stone-paved plaza. As you walk under the Cahill Expressway towards Circular Quay, it seems hard to believe that this bland two-storey freeway, cutting the city off from its most public space, was once seen as progress. It was built at the end of the 1950s, symbolically replacing Sydney's vast tram network. During the same period the city's 150-foot height limit was lifted. Essentially, it was the period when Sydney chose to ape the style of Los Angeles's sprawling, automobile-fed urban model, resulting today in more than 12,500sq/km of dreary, low-density suburban sprawl.

Turn left along the Quay until you hit George Street, which runs behind the Overseas Passenger Terminal and the **Museum of Contemporary Art** (p59). Turn right up George Street and then take a sharp left on Gloucester Walk. You will immediately see the Sirius Apartments, the tallest structure in the Rocks and a perennial feature both on people's most-loved and most-hated lists of Sydney architecture. One of the last remaining bastions of a genuinely egalitarian Sydney, Sirius recalls the days when exceptional views were the right of almost all, not merely the affluent. Designed by

Tao Gofers in 1979, the building came at the end of a tumultuous period of community opposition to the then government's urban policies. Pickets were positioned around proposed development sites like the Rocks, effectively saving them from demolition. A mix of one- to four-bedroom apartments, aiming to cater to a social mix, as well as those specifically designed for the elderly, Sirius was a clear sign that social housing would remain in the area. Constructed entirely from precast concrete, its orthogonal concrete austerity nods playfully to Utzon's more sensual curves across the harbour.

Head up to Cumberland Street, under the **Sydney Harbour Bridge** (p63) and up to Observatory Hill, the highest natural point in Sydney. From here the city's geological and urban patterns are apparent. Contours and landscape were the early dictators of planning, as well as an unruly populace, which resisted attempts at straightening streets and setting road widths. The sandstone ridges were the walking tracks of the locals and became arterial ridge-roads like King and Oxford Streets. Social differences were articulated in the layout of the settlement from the start; the convicts were placed to the west of Circular Quay, while the officers settled on the gentler eastern slope. Across the harbour, large tracts of land were given to the Navy to fortify the colony from French invasion (Britain and France were at war in 1801) and, as a result, many of these sites remained undeveloped. The Harbour Trust now manages these sites, many of which have been returned to public ownership, including the spectacular Cockatoo Island. For details on visiting the islands, go to www.harbourtrust.gov.au.

Descend into Walsh Bay, a family of five formerly industrial finger wharves, designed by engineer RD Walsh and built between 1910 and 1920. Once the largest timber structure in the world, and the first construction in Australia nominated for World Heritage status, they were made redundant in the 1970s due to the containerisation of shipping and faced demolition through successive governments' neglect. At the end of the 20th century, the site was folded into private ownership. Wander the strip and marvel at these incredibly robust structures constructed entirely of local hardwoods. Hundreds of turpentine trunks support each wharf, pushed deep into the mud with an ironbark structure above. The most interesting structure is wharf 8/9, adapted by architects Bates Smart, and a fine example of what is known as 'adaptive re-use'.

Continue south along Hickson Road until you come to the Lend Lease Headquarters, 30 The Bond, built on the site of Sydney's gas works and the first building in Australia to commit to an ecologically progressive five-star energy rating. It is clever outside and stunning inside, the building hugging the five-storey sandstone cut, creating a lively atrium space with projecting kitchen and meeting pods hovering in the space. There is a public café at the back.

Cut back up to George Street to the stunning **Queen Victoria Building** (p80), designed in a Romanesque style by George McRae in 1898. Famously described by Pierre Cardin as 'the most beautiful shopping centre in the world', it was up for demolition as recently as 1959, before foreign money was injected and the building restored in 1986. Walk the length of its atrium before heading north on George Street to the heroic modernist work Australia Square.

Bauhaus-educated Harry Seidler designed the towering block, widely recognised as seminal to Australian modernist architecture. Australia Square was a collaboration with brilliant Roman engineer Pierre Luigi Nervi and features an Alexander Calder Stabile in the forecourt. Sadly, the LeCorbusier tapestry that hung in the foyer since the 1960s was recently sold. Pop up to the level 48 **Summit** revolving restaurant (p75) for a cocktail with a view.

Continue north along George Street, turning right into Bridge Street. The **Museum of Sydney** (p59), designed by Melbourne outfit Denton Corker Marshall in 1995, sits on the site of Governor Phillip's house and interprets and reveals the ruins inside and out. The sculpture *Edge of Trees* adjacent to the entrance (by artists Janet Lawrence and Fiona Foley) is well worth investigating. Head through the stunning foyers of the two skyscrapers looming behind the museum – also designed by Denton Corker Marshall – and Governor Phillip and Macquarie Towers, also completed in 1995, are both very impressive.

Across the road on the corner of Phillip and Bent Streets sits Italian maestro Renzo Piano's elegant 44-storey commercial and 17-storey residential towers, Aurora Place, completed in 2000. For Piano, these buildings pay homage to Utzon and reflect his ambition to create indigenous buildings, that is, structures that grow out of intelligent response to place. Look carefully at the tower and the way it flares out at the top, thereby creating a public space at the base. You may also notice the winter gardens on the north and south of every floor, conceived as

green, social spaces to be shared by the workers. The greatest poetic and technological achievement of this project is Piano's 'kinetic crystalline skin' – the eastern façade of the Macquarie Street apartments and one of the finest and most transparent structures ever built.

Continue south along Phillip Street to Lord Norman Foster's Deutsche Bank tower. Completed in 2005, this hard-edged corporate structure boasts 140-metre-high (460-foot) atriums that separate the office space from the 16 high-speed glass lifts and allow natural light to penetrate through all sides.

Head up to Macquarie Street towards Hyde Park and you will come across the diminutive HQ of the **Mint** (p59), home of the Historic Houses Trust. Head on and you'll be surprised by the gorgeous renovation recently completed by Sydney architects FJMT; a deft conversation between old and new, realised in the urban courtyard that carefully peels away the layers of the old Mint.

Have a quick look at the adjacent building on the corner of Hyde Park, the **Hyde Park Barracks** (p57). Built in 1819 by Governor Macquarie's convict architect Francis Greenway, the barracks were sympathetically renovated by local heroes Tonkin Zulaikha Greer back in 1992.

Continue around Art Gallery Road to the **Art Gallery of New South Wales** (p56). The Asian extension to the gallery, conceived by local firm Johnson Pilton Walke as a translucent white glass lantern, works in counterpoint with the gallery's main stone building, reflecting the sky and filtering natural light. Kick back here with a cool drink at the café and you can enjoy views out to the north and south heads.

ITINERARIES

**Seaplane from Rose Bay p47**

# Trains, Boats, Planes

You can't get anywhere near to covering all of central Sydney's highlights in one day, but if you have 12 hours, you can tick off most of the main attractions with the help of the various transport options the city has to offer.

Start the day by the harbour (where else?) in the luscious **Royal Botanic Gardens** (p60). Head to the Palm Grove area tucked away inside (it's signposted), where you'll find visitor information, toilets, a café, restaurant and shop. From here, climb aboard the 'trackless train' (tickets cost $10), which takes you around the gardens at a leisurely pace. Stop-offs cater for such highlights as the Tropical Centre, the stunning rose gardens, the equally impressive cacti collection and an alarmingly large

colony of fruit bats ('flying foxes') that hang upside down asleep in the trees near Palm Grove (it's quite an experience, especially when they sleepily stretch out a wing mid-nap). There's also the ultra-rare Wollemi pine, a so-called 'living fossil', to see before your train whisks you through the greenery to the iconic **Sydney Opera House** (p63). Pause for a photo op on the Fleet Steps in front of the famed arts centre before heading to Circular Quay Ferry Terminal (see map inside back cover).

From there, catch the **Milsons Point ferry**, which leaves from either Wharf 4 or Wharf 5 (check the departures board for details). Not just a mode of transport but a means of soaking up some major sights – the imposing **Museum of**

**Contemporary Art** (p59), the historic **Rocks** area with its **Rocks Discovery Museum** (p60) and **Overseas Passenger Terminal** to your left, and, across the harbour, the smiling face of **Luna Park** (p138) funfair and the splendid **North Sydney Olympic Pool** (p139), which itself is nestled up against the base of the **Sydney Harbour Bridge** (p63). Milsons Point is the perfect spot to stretch your legs along the boardwalk, which runs all the way to McMahons Point to the west. Soak in the double delights of the Opera House and the Harbour Bridge, also dubbed the Coathanger in one picture-postcard shot. You can enjoy the rides inside Luna Park, although the much-loved Big Dipper has long since gone to appease noise-obsessed apartment dwellers who demanded its removal after the 2000 Olympics.

Next, pick up on the Darling Harbour ferry from the same wharf at Milsons Point and head back across the harbour, with the Rocks (which demands its own excursion) on your left. You'll be dropped off at the **Sydney Aquarium** (p86), one of the largest of its kind in the world. To the right are a number of cafés and restaurants – sit out on the boardwalk, recharge and have a bite to eat before you head inside.

The aquarium itself contains over 650 species of fish and a number of sharks that swim above you in a coral setting that replicates the Great Barrier Reef. In addition, there are crocs, seals, penguins and platypuses in four key areas representing the different aquatic habitats of Australia: the Southern and Northern rivers, and Southern and Northern oceans.

As you leave the aquarium, take a left and follow the water round along the boardwalk until you reach the connecting drawbridge

that contains Cockle Bay, an enormous area of reclaimed land that houses shops, the giant **IMAX** cinema (p91), **Home** nightclub (p90) and an array of restaurants and bars. Head up the escalators to the Darling Park Metro Monorail station and catch the westbound train, which takes you across the bridge and past the **Australian National Maritime Museum** (p86) on your right. Filled with boats and fascinating maritime history, the museum is well worth a quick look – and it's free. The Monorail then takes a sharp left and passes through stations servicing the Star City casino (which, cynics insist, was the real reason behind the 20-year-old system's inception) and the convention centres that play host to various international exhibits and conferences.

Pass overhead through the tail end of Chinatown and hop off at the next stop, **Paddy's Market**, for a taste of China, as well as warehouse-sale shopping and well known labels in the adjacent Market City shopping centre. Head to any of the nearby Chinese eateries on Sussex Street – the main strip of Chinatown – for a quick, cheerful and cheap lunch stop.

Back on the Monorail, continue on another three stops, past Hyde Park on your right, and alight at City Centre station. For those keen to shop some more, the station is housed within the very slick **Galeries Victoria** (p78) retail complex, opposite the **Queen Victoria Building** (p80), a multi-level shopping mecca inside a massive domed building. The QVB is full of boutique and chain stores, and was originally built to celebrate Queen Victoria's golden jubilee in 1898.

Head back east two blocks to Elizabeth Street, and cross into

ITINERARIES

Hyde Park (named after its London counterpart). Stroll north towards the Archibald Fountain (so-called after the Australia-French alliance of World War I). Continue north down Macquarie Street back towards the Sydney Opera House.

To your right, you'll pass the **Hyde Park Barracks Museum** (p57), the **Mint** (p59), **Sydney Hospital**, **Parliament House** (p59) and the **State Library of New South Wales** (p61), all well worth visiting separately.

As you arrive at the foot of Macquarie Street – it's a five- to- ten-minute walk downhill via an array of imposing 19th-century buildings on your left, and **Government House** (p57) on your right – hang a sharp left on to Alfred Street, then right, back to the Quay, where a sea of cafés, burger bars and newsstands await.

Catch the Watsons Bay ferry – which these days is one of the smaller, Rivercat-style vessels – from Wharf 4 and alight at **Rose Bay**, once home to Australia's first international airport. If you're not shopped out, Rose Bay (like its wealthy neighbour Double Bay, serves up a typical eastern suburbs selection of boutique-style shops offering expensive antiques, interior furnishings and accessories, bookshops, galleries, cafés and restaurants, all with a quaint European feel.

To top off your whistlestop tour, head out and left to the rear of the beach to **OzPaddle** (corner Vickery Avenue and New South Head Road, Rose Bay, 0416 239 543, www.ozpaddle.com.au) for another unique Sydney Harbour experience: kayaking. Australia is a nation of sports and fitness crazies, and Sydneysiders are especially obsessed with watersports. There are a range of other water activities on offer here, but if time is at a premium, a good hour in a kayak on the harbour ($20 for a single, $30 for a double) is a novel way to catch the Sydney vibe. Your 60 minutes

Royal Botanic Gardens p44

**Milsons Point ferry p44**

of paddling go in a flash, so you're unlikely to head out very far, certainly not into the main thoroughfare of the harbour traffic. Bear in mind that OzPaddle shuts up shop at 6pm. Bookings are recommended, although not essential. Don't be intimidated by the buff staff who are outrageously fit and toned – steering oneself on the harbour waters is an exquisite experience, particularly after taking it easy on a ferry all day, and you don't want to miss it.

Once you're back on dry land, head to waterside restaurant **Catalina** (Lyne Park, off New South Head Road, Rose Bay, 9731 0555, www.catalinarosebay.com.au) off to the left near the wharf. Once home in the 1950s to one of Sydney's most stylish nightclubs, it offers breathtaking views of the bay and harbour with exquisite seafood to match (and it's open all afternoon until midnight). Grab a waterfront spot on the deck and watch the yachts come in and out of the bay as you take a load off and sip a well earned aperitif.

A meal at Catalina, enjoyed with superlative Rose Bay views of the Harbour Bridge stretching across the skyline, is *the* way to finish off a full day's sightseeing in style. But if your wallet can stretch to it, there's one last way to cap it all: chartering your own **Sydney Seaplane** (Seaplane Base, Lyne Park, Rose Bay, 9388 1978, www.seaplanes.com.au). The planes take off from the harbour before flying over the city and taking in the eastern suburbs, including **Bondi**. Better still, you can catch a plane up to the northern beaches for a picnic or an overnight stay in chi-chi **Jonah's** boutique hotel (p152) overlooking Whale Beach. With prices for these aerial jaunts starting from $300 per person, it's certainly not cheap – but there's no better way to see the world's most beautiful harbour than looking down on it from your own private plane.

Shelly Beach p51

# Metropolitan Walkabout

Pressed for time on a short visit to Sydney, but still want to fit in some bush-walking and see indigenous rock carvings? If you can spare around four hours, this north shore to the start of the northern beaches walkabout is the perfect diversion – and possibly the world's most scenic walk to be found in a metropolitan area.

Regarded by some of Sydney's (many) early-morning joggers as the ultimate workout before a day at the office, the famed **Spit Bridge to Manly walk** is not for the faint-hearted, whatever the time or day. What makes it worth all the huff and puff? Its sheer natural beauty, tranquillity and its treasure trove of Aboriginal carvings and caves, dotted along the way.

The walk has its devotees and regulars, and you'll pick up some handy tips by taking note of what they wear and what they carry before you set off yourself. Go for walking shoes/sandals or boots and carry a light rucksack containing layers of clothing, plus something waterproof. Pack a swimsuit for the many swimming opportunities en route and take a light picnic or at least some snacks to enjoy in one of the secluded bays along the way. Most importantly, wear sun protection, insect repellant and carry plenty of drinking water.

You can enjoy this unforgettable walk solo, or, if you prefer, join one of the guided walks organised by Manly Council (booking essential, phone 9976 1661).

First you must get yourself to the Spit Bridge, and the best way is to take the 20-minute or so (subject to traffic) journey from Wynyard Station on either a 169 or 190 bus. This scenic journey passes through some of the north shore's most beautiful suburbs including Mosman. The hairpin right-hand bend that drops down to the Spit Bridge itself – that's where you will get off – affords your first spectacular view of the water and the millionaires' mansions that cling to the cliffs above.

It's from here you must start the trek over the Spit Bridge footpath, to take a left fork down under the bridge to Ellery's Point Reserve, the start of the (just shy of) ten-kilometre (six-mile) walk. You can anticipate it taking anything from four to five hours, depending on your fitness and the number of stops you make along the way.

Ellery's Point Reserve is the historical site of the city's very first punts, which connected the Spit to Manly, and would carry pedestrians, horseback riders, early trams and cars. The crossings began in the 1880s, the first hand punt pushing off in 1850 and the government punts setting out in 1888. The following year saw steam punts chugging across and eventually these were replaced by trams, which ran until 1939. The walkway follows the old tram route for 200 metres towards Fisher Bay.

Along the way, spot the fat eastern water dragons that sit territorially on the boulders and sandy paths and many varieties of lizards that dart across your path. Observe the polite nodding and g'daying to fellow walkers – some of whom will be approaching from the other direction and nearing the end of their trek (you can do the walk in reverse, starting in Manly).

Fisher Bay boasts subtropical rainforest vegetation at its head and along the exquisite creek that runs into the bay. Aboriginal footsteps are everywhere and you will come across a semicircular rock shelter right on the path, quite possibly Aboriginal in origin. The Aboriginal Shell Midden site is more of a certainty – this protected archaeological area contains layers of shells, likely to be food scraps left by the Guringai Aborigines who once inhabited the land. Over time, the shells piled high and are now bleached on the surface.

Pass Sandy Bay – a delightful sand flat that is exposed at low tide and across which crabs scuttle and dig – and head for Clontarf Beach, a generous swathe of sand adjoining a grassy picnicking area much loved by locals. Sit down for a bite to eat and you'll likely be joined by a council ranger whose job it is to protect the area.

If you came without a picnic, try Clonny's On The Beach – a well stocked café with a good selection of snacks, including baguettes, chips, seafood, pastries and cold drinks. The coffee is good and strong and it's open seven days a week, from 9am to 4.30pm. Even if you bought your own food, it's still worth a meander down to the beach itself before continuing on your way – the idle waters rock a few boats and it's pleasant for a paddle to cool off. Failing that, hold out until Castle Rock, a popular little harbour beach on the outskirts of the lush Sydney Harbour National Park, accessed via steps from Ogilvy Road, for a full-on swim.

Next up, stop at Grotto Point Lighthouse. It was here that a First Fleet survey party made camp on 28 January 1788. The lighthouse was built in 1911 and guides ships entering Sydney Harbour.

Spit Bridge to Manly walk p48

Whatever you do, don't miss the unmarked right-hand turn to the Aboriginal engravings site. Your landmark is a bench on your left; to the right you will spot a large railway sleeper jutting out that will lead you to the site. There are some heart-stirring engravings here including kangaroos and fish.

Worth stopping for the view are both Crater Cove Look-out – with its sweeping vistas across the harbour and the Heads – and Tania Park, which affords excellent views of Manly. The park is a windy spot, and popular with kite-flyers. Reef Beach marks the spot where Aboriginal men, women and children once dived for shellfish. It's also known as Pirates Camp on account of the campsite set up here in the 1930s.

Next up is Forty Baskets Beach, a splendidly tranquil, fresh and blissfully deserted spot that offers public barbecues and a refreshingly salty sea pool for those ready to take a plunge. It's a good spot to stop for a bite to eat before embarking on the next hearty stretch, which takes in Wellings Reserve, a native flora reserve and open forest of rich Hawkesbury sandstone vegetation, before hitting the North Harbour Reserve, a two-hectare (five-acre) picnic area, very popular with locals at weekends.

Fairlight Beach beckons and the flurry of busy Manly is not far away, signposted by its signature Norfolk Pines which start to appear on the horizon as you continue on.

All along the path here you'll see clusters of intricate spider webs glinting in the sunlight, each with a large female Golden Orb-weaving spider at its centre. The spiders' abdomens are covered in silver hairs, their legs banded in yellow and black. Their webs are some of the strongest in the world but fear not, they're completely harmless.

The Promenade to Manly Wharf, arrival point for ferries out of the city, is popular with young and old, the fit and wheelchair-bound, and still carries a pleasant air of the genteel seaside resort about it.

**Oceanworld** (p143), an aquarium with sharks and seals, sits in its circular glory to the right, and the **Manly Art Gallery & Museum** (p141) – established in 1930 – is next door.

Walk along the Manly Pathway of Olympians, which celebrates those Manly residents who have represented Australia at the Olympics over the past century.

Turn left at the ferry terminal and cross the road to the Corso, a lively stretch of shops, cafés, bars and restaurants, which leads to Manly Beach, connecting the harbour to the ocean.

Manly Beach is always busy and a great place to throw yourself into the surf (swimming between the flags, of course). Lifesavers are on patrol every day and if you've still got the energy after your walk, you can get a surfing lesson from the Manly Surf School (opposite North Steyne Surf Lifesaving Club, be sure to book in advance: Pine Street, Manly, 9977 6977, www.manlysurfschool.com).

Cabbage Tree Bay Coastal Walk from Manly Beach to the delightful **Shelly Beach** is plain sailing – flat and relaxing. Shelly Beach is a must-do – the secluded bay is something of a secret for locals and offers a great café and gentle waters. Le Kiosk (1 Marine Parade, Manly, 9977 4122, www.lekiosk. com.au) is right next to the beach (look out for its smart blue awning) and serves fish dishes such as grilled snapper and an irresistible roast duck dish with watercress and radicchio. It's open daily from noon until 3pm for lunch and from 6.30pm onwards for dinner.

For rewarding views, walk into the Sydney Harbour National Park beyond Shelly Beach. Pass the old sandstone wall (built in the 1880s to separate quarantine land from that owned by the Catholic Church) and the Quarry and head to the Anti-aircraft Battery, a World War II installation that protected Sydney. The views from here are well worth the effort. Breathe in the sea air and marvel at the big blue.

# Sydney by Area

Andrew (Boy) Charlton Pool p82

# CBD, Circular Quay & the Rocks

SYDNEY BY AREA

While Sydney's character and soul may be found in its sprawling suburbs, its heart is seen proudly beating on its sleeve down at **Circular Quay**. This is the shimmering centre of the Sydney that all the tourists come to see – the stunning harbour dotted with ferries and boats, the white sails of the **Sydney Opera House** and the steel struts of the **Sydney Harbour Bridge**. There's a lot to be proud of. It's also the best place to start a tour of Sydney, walking first around the Quay itself and then to the **Museum of Contemporary Art** and the historic area of the **Rocks**. While it all looks lush and pretty today, much of Sydney's murky history

stemmed from these cobbled streets. Venture away from the water into the CBD and you'll soon see the juxtaposition between the colonial and the contemporary.

Over in the **Royal Botanic Gardens** – with its unique flora and fauna and fruitbats swinging from the trees – Sydney's tropical climate becomes apparent. Next door is the **Domain**, quite possibly one of the world's most beautiful public spaces, boasting views out over the water that will take your breath away. The Domain used to be Governor Macquarie's private park, and its tip was the favourite spot of his wife, Elizabeth. A seat has been carved into the rock –

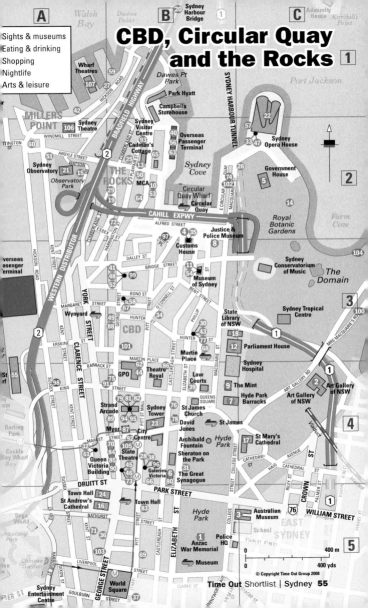

# CBD, Circular Quay and the Rocks

Opera Bar p72

**Mrs Macquarie's Chair** – and the view is still one of Sydney's finest (see also box p79).

When you're tired of sightseeing, there are plenty of cafés, bars and restaurants serving fresh local food where you can sit back and take in those views. If you head to the **Opera Bar** on the east side of the Quay on a balmy summer's evening, you'll get live jazz to boot.

## Sights & museums

### Anzac Memorial

*Hyde Park, between Park & Liverpool Streets, CBD (9267 7668). CityRail Museum.* **Open** 9am-5pm daily. **Admission** free. **Map** p55 B5 ❶
Sydney architect Bruce Dellit was just 31 when he won a 1930 competition to design this beautiful greyish-pink granite memorial to the Australian and New Zealand troops who fell in World War I (and to commemorate above all those who fought in the bloody battle for Gallipoli). Dellit's art deco vision caused a sensation when it opened in 1934. The memorial's striking bas-reliefs are the work of Rayner Hoff, who also made the bronze sculpture in the 'Well of Contemplation' of a Christ-like naked figure held aloft on a shield by three women, and intended to symbolise the sacrifices of war. Some $2.4 million is currently being spent to spruce up the monument in time for its 75th anniversary in 2009. A service of remembrance takes place here at 11am daily and tours can be arranged at the desk in the monument's base, where you'll also find a military museum.

### Art Gallery of New South Wales

*Art Gallery Road, The Domain (9225 1700/www.artgallery.nsw.gov.au). CityRail Martin Place or St James then 10min walk/bus 441.* **Open** 10am-5pm Mon, Tue, Thur-Sun; 10am-9pm Wed. **Admission** free; charges for some exhibitions. **Map** p55 C4 ❷
NSW's main art gallery moved to its present site in 1885. It includes a solid collection of 19th- and 20th-century Australian artists, as well as Aboriginal and Torres Strait Islander art, big names of European art history and international modern artists, plus a fine Asian art collection. One of its most popular exhibitions is the annual Archibald Prize (see box p37).

## Australian Museum

*6 College Street, at William Street, CBD
(9320 6000/www.austmus.gov.au).
CityRail Museum or St James.* **Open**
9.30am-5pm daily. **Admission** $10;
$5 reductions. **Map** p55 C5 ❸
This museum houses the nation's most
important animal, mineral, fossil and
anthropological collections, and prides
itself on its innovative research into the
country's indigenous cultures and
unique environment.

## Customs House

*31 Alfred Street, between Loftus
& Young Streets, Circular Quay (9242
8551/www.cityofsydney.nsw.gov.au/
customshouse). CityRail/ferry Circular
Quay.* **Open** 8am-midnight Mon-Fri;
10am-midnight Sat; 11am-5pm Sun.
**Admission** free. **Map** p55 B2 ❹
Built in 1885, Customs House was one
of government architect James Barnet's
finest works. The building is heritage-
listed, but its use continually changes
– it currently houses a highly stylish
public library, with a decor and fit-out
so slick it makes interior designers
practically drool. A number of local
businesses also make Customs House
their home.

## Government House

*Royal Botanic Gardens, CBD (9931
5222/www.hht.net.au). CityRail Circular
Quay or Martin Place/ferry Circular
Quay.* **Open** Guided tour only; every
30mins 10.30am-3pm Fri-Sun. Garden
10am-4pm daily. **Admission** free.
**Map** p55 C2 ❺
Designed in 1834 by William IV's chief
architect, Edward Blore, the original
plans for Government House (then the
official residence of the NSW governor)
had to be modified to take into account
the local climatic conditions, such as
the sun being in the north rather than
the south. These days, its impeccably
restored State Rooms are the country's
best example of Victorian pomp.

## Great Synagogue

*166 Castlereagh Street, Entry for
services 187A Elizabeth Street, CBD
(9267 2477/www.greatsynagogue
.org.au). CityRail St James or Town
Hall.* **Open** *Services* 5.30pm (winter),
6.15pm (summer) Fri; 8.45am Sat.
*Tours* noon Tue, Thur. **Admission** $5;
$3 reductions. **Map** p55 B4 ❻
Sydney's Jewish history dates back to
convict times – there were around 16
Jews on the First Fleet – and the Great
Synagogue, consecrated in 1878, is
deemed the mother congregation of
Australian Jewry. Thomas Rowe's
building is a lavish confection of
French Gothic with large amounts of
Byzantine thrown in.

## Hyde Park
## Barracks Museum

*Queens Square, corner of Macquarie
Street & Prince Albert Road, CBD
(8239 2311/www.hht.net.au). CityRail
Martin Place or St James.* **Open**
9.30am-5pm daily. **Admission** $10;
$5 reductions. **Map** p55 B4 ❼
Designed by convict architect Francis
Greenway, the Hyde Park barracks
were completed in 1819 with the aim of
housing 600 male convicts, who
remained in government employment
until 1848. Subsequently used first as
an immigration depot and then as an
asylum for women, the barracks were
eventually transformed into a museum.

# 1000 ways to change your life

Makes an ideal gift

On the top level you'll find recreated convict barracks: rough hammocks hang side by side in the dormitories and recorded snippets of conversation surround you.

## Justice & Police Museum

*Corner of Alfred & Phillip Streets, Circular Quay (9252 1144/ www.hht.net.au). CityRail/ferry Circular Quay.* **Open** 10am-5pm Sat, Sun (*Jan* 10am-5pm daily). **Admission** $8; $4 reductions. **Map** p55 B3 ❽

Fittingly, the Justice & Police Museum has been a Water Police Court (1856), Water Police Station (1858) and plain old Police Court (1886). Death masks of some of Australia's more infamous crims are on display, as well as mugshots, assorted deadly weapons and newspaper reports of the city's most sensational wrongdoings.

## Mint

*10 Macquarie Street, between Queens Square & Martin Place, CBD (8239 2288/www.hht.net.au). CityRail Martin Place or St James.* **Open** 9am-5pm Mon-Fri. **Admission** free. **Map** p55 B4 ❾

This attractive building with its bright yellow façade and two-storey, double-colonnaded veranda was built between 1811 and 1816 as the southern wing of the Sydney Hospital. Following the discovery of gold in New South Wales in the 1850s, it became the home of the city's coin-making operations – the first branch of the Royal Mint outside of London – and continued to churn out money until 1926.

## Museum of Contemporary Art

*140 George Street, between Argyle & Albert Streets, Circular Quay (9245 2400/24hr recorded information 9245 2396/www.mca.com.au). CityRail/ ferry Circular Quay.* **Open** 10am-5pm daily. *Tours* 11am, 1pm Mon-Fri; noon, 1.30pm Sat, Sun. **Admission** free. **Map** p55 B2 ❿

The MCA is the only major public gallery in Sydney that has a serious interest in contemporary art. The museum has fared particularly well under the directorship of Elizabeth Ann Macgregor (see also box p67), a feisty and inspirational Scot who has been instrumental in spearheading the museum's renaissance.

## Museum of Sydney

*Corner of Bridge & Phillip Streets, CBD (9251 5988/www.hht.net.au). CityRail/ferry Circular Quay.* **Open** 9.30am-5pm daily. **Admission** $10; $5 reductions. **Map** p55 B3 ⓫

This modern building stands on one of the most historic spots in Sydney, site of the first Government House, built in 1788 by Governor Arthur Phillip and home to the first nine governors of NSW. In 1983, archaeologists unearthed the original footings of the house, which had survived since the building's 1846 demolition and these are now a feature at the museum.

## Parliament House

*6 Macquarie Street, opposite Hunter Street, CBD (9230 2111/tours 9230 3444/www.parliament.nsw.gov.au). CityRail Martin Place or St James.* **Open** 9am-5pm Mon-Fri. *Tours* (groups only) 9.30am, 11am, 12.30pm, 2pm, 3pm, 4pm *non-sitting days*; 1.30pm Tue *sitting days*. Individual tours also available on demand between opening hours. **Admission** free. **Map** p55 B3 ⓬

Known to locals as the Bear Pit, the New South Wales Parliament is said to be the roughest and toughest in the country. Its impressive sandstone building was constructed between 1811 and 1814 as the northern wing of the Rum Hospital, but was taken over in 1829 to house the new colony's key decision-makers. Only the Legislative Assembly (lower house) existed until the 1850s, when the parliament became bicameral. The Legislative Council (upper house) meets in chambers that were originally intended to be used as a church; the cast-iron prefab was being shipped from Glasgow to Victoria when, mid-voyage, it was abruptly diverted to Sydney. The parliament is largely modelled on its mother in London: there's a Speaker and Black Rod, and even the colour scheme follows the British tradition of green for the lower chamber and red for the upper. Legislative sessions are open to the public, with viewing from a public gallery; booking is essential for the tours.

## Rocks Discovery Museum

*The Rocks Centre, Kendall Lane, at Argyle Street, The Rocks (1800 067 676/9251 8804/ www.rocksdiscoverymuseum.com). CityRail/ferry Circular Quay.* **Open** 10am-5pm daily. **Admission** free. **Map** p55 B2 ⑬

Housed in a restored 1850s coach house, this new museum covers the Rocks' history from the time of the indigenous Cadigal people to the 1970s demonstrations that saved many of the area's historic buildings from the clutches of avaricious developers.

## Royal Botanic Gardens

*Mrs Macquarie's Road, CBD (9231 8111/weekends 9231 8125/www.rbg syd.nsw.gov.au). CityRail Circular Quay, Martin Place or St James/ferry Circular Quay.* **Open** *Gardens* 7am-sunset daily. *Visitor Information* 9.30am-4.30pm daily. *Tropical Centre* 10am-4pm daily. *Shop* 9.30am-5pm daily. **Admission** *Gardens* free. *Tropical Centre* $4.40; $2.20 reductions. **Map** p55 C2 ⑭

The beautiful Royal Botanic Gardens, established in 1816, form an elegantly sweeping green curve from the Opera House round to Woolloomooloo Bay. It's a gorgeous spot, full of majestic old trees, well manicured lawns, bird-filled ponds and impeccably maintained ornamental flowerbeds. The Domain surrounds the gardens: back in colonial times the land actually acted as a buffer between the governor's home and the penal colony, but by 1831, roads and paths had been built to allow public access, and it has remained a people's place ever since. The Palm Grove area is a good place to start: there's a shop, a visitor information desk, a decent café, restaurant and clean toilets.

## SH Ervin Gallery

*National Trust Centre, Watson Road, next to the Observatory, The Rocks (9258 0173/ www.nsw.nationaltrust.org.au/ ervin.html). CityRail Circular Quay or Wynyard/ferry Circular Quay.* **Open** 11am-5pm Tue-Sun. Closed mid Dec-mid Jan. **Admission** $6; $4 reductions. **Map** p55 A2 ⑮

A spectacular setting on Observatory Hill and an impressive calendar of exhibitions and themed shows are the main drawcards at this National Trust gallery. It specialises in Australian art (painting, sculpture and works on paper), showcasing both contemporary pieces and historical surveys.

## St Andrew's Cathedral

*Sydney Square, corner of George & Bathurst Streets, CBD (9265 1661/ www.cathedral.sydney.anglican.asn.au). CityRail Town Hall.* **Open** 10am-3pm daily. **Admission** free. **Map** p55 A5 ⑯

This imposing late-Gothic edifice – the oldest cathedral in the country– was conceived with astonishing confidence and foresight by Governor Macquarie when Sydney was still the size of a small village. Macquarie named his cathedral after the patron saint of his native Scotland, laying the first stone in 1819. By 1868, the cathedral had been consecrated. No less than three architects contributed to its design, the most notable being Edmund Blacket, city architect between 1849 and 1854. Special elements link the cathedral to the motherland, including a marble floor from Canterbury Cathedral and two stones that were brought from the Palace of Westminster.

## St Mary's Cathedral

*Corner of College Street & Cathedral Square, CBD (9220 0400/www.stmarys cathedral.org.au). CityRail St James.* **Open** 6.45am-6pm Mon-Fri; 9am-6.30pm Sat; 7am-6.30pm Sun. *Tours* 10.30am Sun. **Admission** free. **Map** p55 C4 ⑰

St Mary's Cathedral is the seat of the Roman Catholic archbishop of Sydney (currently the controversial Cardinal

Justice & Police Museum p59

George Pell) and stands on the site of Australia's first Catholic chapel. William Wilkinson Wardell's design replaced the original cathedral, ruined by fire in 1865. Built from local sandstone, St Mary's is the largest Gothic cathedral in the southern hemisphere – 106m (348ft) long with a 46m (150ft) central tower – dwarfing many of the European models from which it took inspiration. Don't miss the cathedral's crypt, decorated with a beautifully designed terrazzo floor depicting the six days of Creation.

## State Library of New South Wales

*Corner of Macquarie Street & Cahill Expressway, CBD (9273 1414/ www.sl.nsw.gov.au). CityRail Martin Place.* **Open** *Library* 9am-8pm Mon-Thur; 9am-5pm Fri; 10am-5pm Sat, Sun. *Exhibitions* 9am-8pm Mon-Thur; 9am-5pm Fri; 10am-5pm Sat, Sun. *Tours* 11am Tue; 2pm Thur. **Admission** free. **Map** p55 B3 ⑱
The State Library is essentially two libraries in one: the modern General Reference Library (GRL) provides access to five million books, CD-Roms and other media stored over five floors below ground, while the 1910 Mitchell Wing (closed Sun) holds the world's best collection of Australiana, among it James Cook's original journals and the log book belonging to Captain Bligh. The latter wing has fine bronze bas-relief doors depicting Aboriginal peoples and European explorers. The library's Shakespeare Room is a fine example of mock-Tudor style, with a ceiling modelled on Cardinal Wolsey's closet in Hampton Court and stained-glass depicting the 'seven ages of man'.

## Susannah Place Museum

*58-64 Gloucester Street, at Cumberland Place Steps, The Rocks (9241 1893/ www.hht.nsw.gov.au). CityRail/ferry Circular Quay.* **Open** 10am-5pm Sat, Sun (daily in Jan). **Admission** $8; $4 reductions. **Map** p55 B2 ⑲
This museum actually consists of a terrace of houses, built in 1844, and fully restored. With its shop, original brick privies and open laundries it gives an idea of what 19th-century community living was really like.

SYDNEY BY AREA

**Yum Cha lunch 7 days**
**Banquet and a la carte menu**
**Live seafood tanks**
**Private rooms**

Open daily
Lunch 10am to 3pm
Dinner 5.30pm to 11pm

**MARIGOLD**
Level 4 & 5
683 George Street
Haymarket
**Tel: 9281 3388**
www.marigold.com.au

**REGAL**
347 Sussex Street
Sydney
**Tel: 9261 8988**
www.regal.com.au

## Sydney Harbour Bridge & Pylon Lookout

*Accessible via stairs on Cumberland Street (9240 1100/www.pylonlookout. com.au). CityRail/ferry Circular Quay.* **Open** 10am-5pm daily. **Admission** *Pylon Lookout* $9.50; $4-$6.50 reductions. **Map** p55 B1 ⑳

Long before the Opera House was built, Sydney had 'the Coathanger' as its icon. Locals had dreamed for decades of a bridge to link the north and south harbour shores before construction of the 'All-Australian Bridge' began in 1924, by which time Sydney's ferries were struggling to cope with carrying their 40 million passengers a year. The winning design came from English firm Dorman, Long & Co, but used Australian steel, stone, sand and labour. Families within the path of the new bridge and its highways were displaced without compensation, and 800 houses were demolished. A total of 1,400 workers toiled on the structure, which is 134m (440ft) high and 1,149m (3,770ft) long – when it was first built it was the world's largest single-span bridge. It took eight years to complete, and workers, grafting without safety rails, took great risks: 16 of them died. The 1932 opening ceremony was broadcast around the world – and interrupted by a lone horseman, the disaffected Irishman Francis de Groot, who galloped forward and slashed the ribbon with his sword, declaring the bridge open in the name of 'His Majesty the King and all the decent citizens of New South Wales'. De Groot's organisation, the New Guard, resented the fact that a representative of the King hadn't been asked to open the bridge. The police removed him (he was later fined £5), the ribbon was retied, and the ceremony resumed.

Today's refurbished Pylon Lookout is well worth a visit. Climb 200 steps past several exhibits celebrating the history of the bridge and its builders. Stained-glass windows feature a painter, riveter, stonemason, surveyor, concreter and rigger. Memorabilia from the 1930s is also on display; more up-to-date souvenirs are on sale in the shop. The open-air views from the top are magnificent – the more intrepid can take a BridgeClimb tour to the top of the bridge itself, strapped in to a safety harness (see also box p79).

The bridge has been called 'one of the seven wonders of the modern world' – although it's not to everyone's taste. Writer James Michener wrote in the 1950s that it was 'big, utilitarian and the symbol of Australia... But it is very ugly. No Australian will admit this.'

## Sydney Observatory

*Watson Road, Observatory Hill, The Rocks (9921 3485/www.sydney observatory.com.au). CityRail/ferry Circular Quay.* **Open** *Museum* 10am-5pm daily. **Admission** *Museum & gardens* free. *Day tours* $7; $5 reductions. *Night tours* $15; $10-$12 reductions. **Map** p55 A2 ㉑

Built in 1858, the Observatory gained recognition under Henry Chamberlain Russell, who involved Sydney in the International Astrographic Catalogue, the first complete atlas of the sky. The Sydney section alone took 80 years to complete and filled 53 volumes. Increasing air pollution spelled the end for the observatory, and it became a museum in 1982. Interactive displays include a virtual reality tour over the surfaces of Venus and Mars, and there are lessons on how telescopes work. Night tours (booking essential) include a talk, 3-D Space Theatre session and viewing through a 40cm (16in) telescope (see also box p79).

## Sydney Opera House

*Bennelong Point, Circular Quay (box office 9250 7777/information 9250 7111/tours 9250 7250/ www.sydneyoperahouse.com). CityRail/ferry Circular Quay.* **Open** *Tours* every 30mins 9am-5pm daily. **Admission** $32 adult; $23 reductions. **Map** p55 C1-C2 ㉒

Set in a heavenly harbour, its cream wings reminiscent of the sails of the First Fleet, the Sydney Opera House is the city's most famous asset. It took 14 troubled years and $102 million to

build – $95 million more than at first anticipated (the shortfall was met by lotteries). This cultural cathedral has never once been visited by its creator, Danish architect Jørn Utzon, who resigned halfway through the project following a clash with the Minister of Public Works. On its opening night in 1973, an impromptu appearance was made onstage by two small possums.

In its five auditoria the Opera House holds 2,400 opera, concert, theatre, film and dance performances every year, attended by 1.5 million people. The first performer was Paul Robeson who, in 1960, at the invitation of the militant builders' union, sang 'Old Man River' at the construction site. The building recently received World Heritage recognition as an architectural wonder of the world.

In 1999, an apologetic government re-hired Jørn Utzon to develop a set of design principles to be used as a guide for all future changes to the building. Then, in 2001, a series of upgrading projects began under Utzon's guidance with the help of his son and business partner Jan, who visited his father's masterpiece and is overseeing work.

## Sydney Tower

*Centrepoint Podium Level, 100 Market Street, between Castlereagh & Pitt Streets, CBD (9333 9222/ www.sydneytoweroztrek.com.au/www.sk ywalk.com.au). CityRail St James or Town Hall/Monorail City Centre.* **Open** *Tower & OzTrek 9am-10.30pm Mon-Fri, Sun; 9am-11.30pm Sat. Skywalk 9.30am-8.45pm daily.* **Admission** *Tower & OzTrek $24.50; $14.50-$18.50 reductions. Skywalk $64.50; $44.50 reductions.* **Map** *p55 B4* ㉓

Three high-speed lifts take 40 seconds to travel to the golden turret of this well-known city symbol, which boasts two levels of restaurants, a coffee lounge and an observation deck at 250m (820ft) with 360° views. Skywalk, the latest of the city's 'thrill' tours, allows visitors to wander around the outside of the turret (see also box p79).

## Sydney Town Hall

*Corner of George & Druitt Streets, CBD (9265 9189/ concert information 9265 9007/ www.cityofsydney.nsw.gov.au). CityRail Town Hall.* **Open** 8.30am-6pm Mon-Fri. **Admission** free. **Map** p55 A5 ㉔

Built on a graveyard and completed in 1889, the Sydney Town Hall is an impressive High Victorian building, topped by a clock tower with a two-ton bell. It has retained its original function and interiors, including the council chamber and lord mayor's offices.

## Eating & drinking

### Argyle

*12-18 Argyle Street, at Playfair Street, The Rocks (9247 5500/ www.theargyle.biz). CityRail/ferry Circular Quay.* **Open** 10.30am-3am Mon-Sat; 10.30am-midnight Sun. **Bar**. **Map** p55 B2 ㉕

This 1826 wool store, built around a grand sandstone outdoor courtyard, has become the chosen place for smart drinkers on week nights. Seek out the cocktail area with its fab red daybeds.

### Aria

*1 Macquarie Street, at East Circular Quay (9252 2555/www.aria restaurant.com.au). CityRail/ferry Circular Quay.* **Open** noon-2.30pm, 5.30-11pm Mon-Fri; 5-11.30pm Sat; 6-10.30pm Sun. **$$$$**. Licensed. **Mod Oz**. **Map** p55 B2 ㉖

Matt Moran is much more than just another TV celebrity chef – he really can cook. Few restaurants compare to the service at Aria, the wine list is multi-award winning and the stylish room makes for a special evening. The five-spice duck consommé is a highlight, as is slow-roasted pork belly. And then there's the fantastic view of the Opera House.

### Arras

*24 Hickson Road, at Pottinger Street, Walsh Bay (9252 6285). CityRail/ferry Circular Quay then 15min walk.* **Open** noon-2pm, 6-10pm Tue-Sat. **$$$**. Licensed. **English**. **Map** p55 B1 ㉗

Northern English food in Walsh Bay. Expect to find anything from crab bread and butter pudding to jammy dodgers and eggy bread. There are even Union Jack printed chairs complete with authentic rips and tears.

### Attic Bar

*2nd Floor, Art House Hotel, 275 Pitt Street, between Park & Market Streets, CBD (9284 1200/www.thearthouse hotel.com.au). CityRail St James or Town Hall/Monorail Galeries Victoria.* **Open** 5.30pm-late Thur-Sat. **Bar**. **Map** p55 B4 ㉓

Almost hidden atop three levels of suits drinking Becks and domestic fizz, the Attic is an eyrie of good drinking.

### Australian Hotel

*100 Cumberland Street, at Gloucester Street, The Rocks (9247 2229/ www.australianheritagehotel.com). CityRail/ferry Circular Quay.* **Open** 11am-midnight Mon-Sat; 11am-10pm Sun. **Pub**. **Map** p55 B2 ㉙

Locals and tourists flock to this old-school pub just by the Harbour Bridge. There's no view to speak of, but the neighbourhood is very much olde Sydney towne and just a step away from backpacker ground zero. It's a great place to play two-up on Anzac Day and the pizzas are popular. It also offers accommodation.

### Azuma

*Level 1, Chifley Plaza, 2 Chifley Square, corner of Phillip & Hunter Streets, CBD (9222 9960/www.azuma.com.au). CityRail Martin Place.* **Open** noon-2.30pm, 6-10pm Mon-Fri; 6-10pm Sat. **$$$$**. Licensed. **Japanese**. **Map** p55 B3 ㉚

The deluxe skyscraper setting will have you squinting and pretending you're in Roppongi Hills or some other such moneyed Tokyo setting, but the lightness and boldness of this Aussie kitchen's take on traditional Japanese flavours will tell you otherwise. When Azuma-san suggests you try sashimi with a squeeze of lemon rather than the ubiquitous soy, follow his advice and experience raw fish perfection.

## Bambini Trust Restaurant & Café

*185 Elizabeth Street, between Park & Market Streets, CBD (9283 7098/ www.bambinitrust.com.au). CityRail Museum or St James/Monorail City Centre.* **Open** 7am-11pm Mon-Fri; 5.30-11pm Sat. Licensed. **Café**. **Map** p55 B4 ③①

To walk into Bambini for a breakfast meeting is to meet with some serious scrutiny. To have lunch here mid-week, doubly so. Designed with echoes of Milan in its wooden Venetian blinds and dark timber against crisp linen and white tiles, this is the canteen for Sydney's media elite. The coffee is great, the food is OK, but the buzz is the real deal.

## Bécasse

*204 Clarence Street, between Druitt & Market Streets, CBD (9283 3440/ www.becasse.com.au). CityRail Town Hall.* **Open** noon-2.30pm, 6-10pm Mon-Fri; 6-10pm Sat. **$$$$**. Licensed. **French**. **Map** p55 A4 ③②

Justin North is one of the city's brightest young chefs, and with a French-based menu bursting at the seams with delights such as John Dory with scallops or the seriously protein punched rib eye, his restaurant is especially big with the lunchtime business crowd. The stunning room is decked out in muted mushroom, heavy curtains and hula-hoop chandeliers.

## Bennelong Bar

*Sydney Opera House, Bennelong Point, Circular Quay (9241 1999/ www.guillaumeatbennelong.com.au). CityRail/ferry Circular Quay.* **Open** 5.30pm-late Mon-Sat. **Bar**. **Map** p55 C2 ③③

Here's a spot to give designer bars the world over a solid run for their money – although to be fair to the rest of the globe, pitching your bar in one of the sails of the Sydney Opera House does give Bennelong Bar something of an unfair advantage. The soaring ceiling is stunning, the harbour views are superlative, the superb wine list and service make you feel grown-up and

sexy, and the Saarinen chairs are God's gift to lounging. Tapas dishes start at $22 for four: don't miss the very good crab sandwiches – the ultimate in posh bar-snacking and perfect partners to a flute of ice-cold French. The bar is set on the top level of top-notch restaurant Guillaume at Bennelong (p71).

## Bilson's

*Radisson Plaza Hotel, 27 O'Connell Street, at Hunter Street, CBD (8214 0496/www.bilsons.com.au). CityRail Wynyard.* **Open** 6pm-late Tue-Thur, Sat; noon-3pm, 6pm-late Fri. **$$$$**. Licensed. **French**. **Map** p55 B3 ③④

Tony Bilson is something of a legend in these parts, having cooked in Australian kitchens for over 30 years. The unashamedly francophile elder statesman of Sydney dining creates marvels, whether turning his practised hand to grilled fillet of John Dory with artichoke bargoule caviar or a plate of Angus beef. Order the degustation for the full Bilson's experience. The wine list is pretty spectacular.

## Café Sydney

*5th Floor, Customs House, 31 Alfred Street, Circular Quay (9251 8683/ www.cafesydney.com). CityRail/ferry Circular Quay.* **Open** noon-11pm Mon-Fri; 5-11pm Sat; 12-4pm Sun. **$$$**. Licensed. **Mod Oz**. **Map** p55 B2 ③⑤

It's the building and the view that draw people to this place. You soar to the top of Customs House in a glass elevator and step out into a light-filled room with that dreamy view at the end over the harbour. There's a cool cocktail bar by the lift and then it's all about what table you get. The menu is dominated by fresh fish and seafood, which is what the chef does best here – meat dishes can be a little pedestrian given the high prices.

## Chat Thai

NEW *Food Avenue, 500 George Street, CBD (9264 7109/www.chatthai. com.au). CityRail Town Hall/Monorail City Centre.* **Open** 9am-8pm Mon-Wed, Fri-Sun; 9am-9pm Thur. **$**. Licensed. **Thai**. **Map** p55 A5 ③⑥

# Hear them roar

**Elizabeth Macgregor**

Three women: an actor/director, a museum director and a movie costume and production designer. All three living and breathing the Australian arts, and all with one vision – to bring their work to the masses and to do so from Sydney.

And between actor Cate Blanchett – joint artistic director with husband Andrew Upton of the **Sydney Theatre Company** (p83); Elizabeth Macgregor – director of the **Museum of Contemporary Art (MCA)** (p59); and Catherine Martin – production designer on *Australia*, probably the country's biggest movie export of all time; they have enough power and clout to see their vision through.

While Dundee-born Elizabeth Macgregor is a rogue Scot among Aussies, her MCA directorship has already seen big changes during her nine-year helm. A $10-million boost to its coffers in 2008 from the NSW premier was the icing on the cake following a massive growth in visitor numbers due to her inspired removal of the MCA's general admission charge.

Macgregor – who literally used to take art to the masses in Scottish prisons, factories, hospitals and inner-city estates, as curator of the Scottish Arts Council's travelling gallery – was awarded the Centenary Medal for services to the Australian public and contemporary art in 2003.

Oscar-winning Hollywood A-lister Cate Blanchett's own career was fostered at the Sydney Theatre Company where, at the beginning of 2008, she and Upton took up the role of artistic directors and also pledged to introduce green policies by taking the space off the national grid, harnessing solar energy instead to power art. Blanchett has already secured one of the biggest-ever financial donations to an Australian theatrical company from fashion guru Giorgio Armani, who has become the theatre's main patron.

Back in 1988, Baz Luhrmann's fledgling production *Strictly Ballroom* benefited from being taken under the wing of the STC's development programme. Today he and wife Catherine Martin, partners in Bazmark Inq, are pioneers of one of the world's most innovative film and theatre production houses. Martin won two Oscars for set and costume design for *Moulin Rouge* and, with Luhrmann, is dedicated to creating unique works that push the boundaries of film. Their next project, *Australia*, stars Nicole Kidman and Hugh Jackman in an epic World War II story about the bombing of Darwin.

The queues wind halfway down the street and nearly everybody eating in the restaurant is Thai. And with a dining room this stylish and dishes such as redfish mousse fritters and the kitchen's version of chicken rice with bitter melon soup, you can see why.

### Civic Dining

*388 Pitt Street, at Goulburn Street, CBD (8080 7040/www.civichotel. com.au). CityRail Central/LightRail Capitol Square.* **Open** noon-2.30pm Mon-Fri; 6pm-late Tue-Sat. **$$$**. Licensed. **Greek**. Map p55 B5 ⓷
Peter Conistis is one of Sydney's most applauded chefs so the whole city held its breath when his Omega restaurant hit the skids in December 2006. At the Civic, thankfully, he's back on form, creating modern Greek delicacies, only this time catering to a less hoity-toity crowd. The cooking is inspiring and includes Conistis's signature dishes of scallop moussaka and rabbit pie. And all now available to the masses.

### Dome

*ArtHouse Hotel, 275 Pitt Street, CBD (9284 1230/www.thearthouse hotel.com.au). CityRail St James or Town Hall/Monorail Galeries Victoria.* **Open** noon-3pm, 6-10pm daily. **$$**. Licensed. **Mod Oz**. Map p55 B4 ⓸
This classy restaurant inside the ArtHouse Hotel is led by talented head chef Tim Michels, whose take on Mod Oz cuisine is winning him devoted fans. On a Wednesday or Friday, Sydney icon Franca Manfredi serves up the sensational handmade pasta dishes for which she has become justifiably famous.

### Element Bistro

*163 King Street, at Phillip Street, CBD (9231 0013). CityRail Martin Place or St James.* **Open** 11.45am-3pm Mon-Fri; 5.30-10pm Tue-Sat. **$$**. Licensed/BYO. **French**. Map p55 55 B4 ⓹
Chef Matthew Barnett cooks up bistro classics like steak-frites, salade niçoise and calf's liver with onion rings, but it's his Boston Bay mussels with basil sauce that really hit the spot.

### Ember

*Overseas Passenger Terminal, Circular Quay West, The Rocks (8273 1222/ www.wildfiresydney.com). CityRail/ferry Circular Quay.* **Open** noon-1am Mon-Fri; 6pm-2am Sat; 6pm-midnight Sun. **Bar**. Map p55 B2 ⓴
It's all about the manhattans at Ember. Fitting, really, for a bar that adjoins Wildfire, a big, brash restaurant with a strong American accent. Kick back and crunch some popcorn shrimp while you peruse the selection of infused bourbons and the lengthy and distinguished cocktail list.

### Est.

*Level 1, Establishment Hotel, 252 George Street, between Bridge Street & Abercrombie Lane, CBD (9240 3010/www.merivale.com.au). CityRail Circular Quay or Wynyard/ferry Circular Quay.* **Open** noon-2.30pm, 6-10pm Mon-Fri; 6-10pm Sat. **$$$$**. Licensed. **Mod Oz**. Map p55 B3 ㊶
To step out of the lift and into the bright, colonnaded Est. dining room is to enter a bubble of total assurance. Peter Doyle's menu is pretty much

flawlessly presented, always skilfully cooked and hits its mark every time. And what you'll lose in pocket change, you'll gain in pure joy per bite.

## Firefly

*Pier 7, 17 Hickson Road, Walsh Bay (9241 2031/www.fireflybar.net). CityRail/ferry Circular Quay then 10min walk/bus 343, 431, 432, 433, 434.* **Open** Dec-Mar noon-10pm Mon-Sat; 3-10pm Sun. Closed Apr-Nov. **Bar**. **Map** p55 A1

We reckon Firefly's owners must have picked the name on the strength of the spot being so small and shiny. Firefly's indoors-outdoors shtick runs to coffee all day, good cocktails and small, smart, snacky plates of an upmarket order after dark. It's all pretty sublime on a balmy evening.

## Forty One

*Level 42, Chifley Tower, 2 Chifley Square, corner of Phillip & Hunter Streets, CBD (9221 2500/www.forty-one. com.au). CityRail Martin Place.* **Open** 6pm-late Mon; noon-2pm, 6pm-late Tue-Fri; 6pm-late Sat. **$$$$**. Licensed. **Modern European**. Map p55 B3 ❸

While the talk of the views from the urinal in the men's room (it's glass from the waist up, with 41 floors below so quite something) is a constant at Fort One, so too is the quality of chef/owner Dietmar Sawyere's cuisine. Try the sauté of green asparagus and salted walnuts, served with perfectly truffled and creamy polenta.

## GG Espresso

*175 Pitt Street, between Martin Place & King Street, CBD (9221 1644). CityRail Martin Place or Wynyard.* **Open** 6.30am-5.15pm Mon-Fri. Unlicensed. **Café**. Map p55 B4 ❹

The GG in this café's name stands for George Gregan. Seemingly not content with making his mark in the world of rugby union, the former Wallabies' champ has set about making his initials synonymous with good coffee in the inner city. The food on offer is pretty basic, but the shots of espresso pack plenty of oomph.

**Sydney Tower p64**

## Glass

*2nd Floor, Hilton Sydney, 488 George Street, between Park & Market Streets, CBD (9265 6068/www.glass brasserie.com.au). CityRail Town Hall/ Monorail City Centre.* **Open** 6am-3pm, 6pm-late Mon-Fri; 7am-11am, 6pm-late Sat, Sun. **$$$**. Licensed. **French**. Map p55 B4 ❺

Bad news, folks. Glass is one of those hotel dining rooms that seems to have been dreamed up by the damned. The same panel must also have thought that yoking culinary whizz Luke Mangan to a steak-frites-and-soufflés brasserie-by-numbers menu was a good idea. Sadly, the schismatic result does little service to either – but the room is still seriously splashy and some real effort has been made in the wine department.

## Glass Bar

*2nd Floor, Hilton Sydney, 488 George Street, between Park & Market Streets, CBD (9265 6068/www.glassbrasserie. com.au). CityRail Town Hall/Monorail City Centre.* **Open** noon-11pm Mon-Fri; 6-11pm Sat, Sun. **Bar**. Map p55 B4 ❻

**SYDNEY BY AREA**

Shimmering with designer gimmicks such as towering shelves of wine, and with a stunning view of the Queen Victoria Building's architectural curlicues, this cool wine bar is everything a big-city hotel bar should be, offering assured cocktail service, good snacking and an outstanding wine experience for both greenhorns and connoisseurs alike. Upstairs is the very glam Zeta Bar (see p76).

## Guillaume at Bennelong

*Sydney Opera House, Bennelong Point, Circular Quay (9241 1999/ www.guillaumeatbennelong.com.au). CityRail/ferry Circular Quay.* **Open** noon-3pm Thur, Fri; 5.30-11.30pm Mon-Sat. **$$$$**. Licensed. **French**. **Map** p55 C2 ❼
Given the following that Guillaume Brahimi picked up while working with Joël Robuchon in Paris, it's tempting to call his food French (not least of all on account of his note-perfect rendition of the great Robuchon's Paris mash). But there's a lightness that is pure Sydney to his signature dish of tuna infused with basil, for example, or the crab sandwiches that are the mainstays of the bar menu. Wine and service are of a similarly high order, and the Opera House is a nonpareil setting. The Bennelong Bar is a treat too (p66).

## Hemmesphere

*Level 4, Establishment Hotel, 252 George Street, between Bridge Street & Abercrombie Lane, CBD (9240 3040/www.merivale.com). CityRail Wynyard or Circular Quay/ferry Circular Quay.* **Open** 5.30pm-late Mon-Thur; 3pm-late Fri; 6pm-late Sat. **Bar**. **Map** p55 B3 ❽
On the ground floor of the enormous Establishment building, lots of guys and girls in near-identical suits shout orders for pricey beers and stare blankly at the talent. But upstairs is a much rosier picture. Here couples lounge around a high-ceilinged bar, sipping their way through expertly shaken cocktails and discussing the various merits of the deluxe absinthe drinks offered on the hip drinks list.

Celeb-spotting is a bonus; the downside is that it's wise to book in advance. Sushi E, adjoining the lounge, serves fabulous Japanese delicacies.

## Ivy

NEW *320-330 George Street, opposite Wynyard station, CBD (9240 3000/ www.merivale.com.au). CityRail Wynyard.* **Open** 11am-late Mon-Sat. **Bar**. **Map** p55 B3 ❾
At the time of writing, Ivy's pleasure dome is slowly unfolding, with new openings popping up as the building reaches completion. The exterior is still a concrete work in progress and you have to pick your way through rubble to reach the majestic staircase at the back of a corridor off George Street. But at the top of the grand staircase is an oasis of lush, airy, Miami-meets-Dubai chic. With candy-striped yellow and white throughout, Lloyd loom chairs and a mass of scatter cushions and opulent sun umbrellas in the open central courtyard, it feels as if you're in a six-star hotel in the desert. Open air means smokers can puff away and food outlets on the side mean you can choose to graze as well as booze. Upstairs there are more suites and bars, which are policed by door girls.

## La Renaissance Patisserie

*47 Argyle Street, off George Street, The Rocks (9241 4878/www.larenaissance. com.au). CityRail/ferry Circular Quay.* **Open** 8.30am-6pm daily. Unlicensed. **Café**. **Map** p55 B2 ❺⓿
This family business, established in 1974, is highly recommended for its gateaux, which are made daily by a team of pastry chefs and can be savoured in the lovely courtyard. Afterwards, check out the Aboriginal and contemporary art in the Gannon House Gallery just down the street.

## Lord Nelson Brewery Hotel

*Corner of Argyle & Kent Streets, Millers Point (9251 4044/www.lord nelson.com.au). CityRail/ferry Circular Quay.* **Open** 11am-11pm Mon-Sat; noon-10pm Sun. **Pub**. **Map** p55 A2 ❺❶

Real ale fans rejoice – the Lord Nello is one of the best places to explore the joys of Sydney's varying microbrews. The rest of us will be admiring the pub's colonial stonework and tucking into the seriously hearty bar plate – pickled onions, cheese, pickles, doorstop wedge of bread and all. Keep an eye out for the sign announcing the occasional treat that is Nelson's Blood, the pub's signature beer.

### Mad Cow

NEW *330 George Street, CBD (9240 3000/www.merivle.com.au). CityRail Wynyard.* **Open** noon-2pm; 6pm-late Mon-Sat. **$$$$**. Licensed. **Steak**. **Map** p55 B3 🔟

The Mad Cow is serious about its beef – and it makes diners pay for it. Try the rib eye on the bone or the ultra-flavoursome wagyu skirt steak. Sides are small but sensational and the decor is mum's lounge meets 1950s diner.

### MCA Café

*Museum of Contemporary Art, 140 George Street, between Argyle & Alfred Streets, The Rocks (9241 4253/ www.mca.com.au). CityRail/ferry Circular Quay.* **Open** 10am-11.30pm Sat, Sun; noon-3pm daily. Licensed. **Café**. **Map** p55 B2 🔟

Not for the Museum of Contemporary Art the glam stylings of the eateries at the Guggenheim at Bilbao, say, or the flash new MOMA in New York. Instead, the deco design, with its solid marble bar, takes its cues from the building's days housing the Maritime Services Board, rather than from Emin or Warhol. The food is seasonal and light Mod Oz fare. The timber deck at the front of the museum (with both umbrellas and heaters to handle all weathers) makes this one of Circular Quay's best bets for a classy lunch.

### MOS Café

*Museum of Sydney, corner of Phillip and Bridge Streets, CBD (9241 3636/www.moscafe.com.au). CityRail/ ferry Circular Quay.* **Open** 6.30am-9pm Mon-Fri; 8.30am-5pm Sat, Sun. Licensed. **Café**. **Map** p55 B3 🔟

This is a popular spot for breakfast and lunch. The trad porridge with thick slices of poached apricots and peaches is a fave with the money men, drawn by the opportunity to sit in the middle of the city's skyscraper canyons over-looking a nice patch of open space and drink a decent cup of java.

### Nick's Bar & Grill

*King Street Wharf, Darling Harbour (9279 0122/www.nicksseafood.com.au). CityRail Town Hall/ferry Darling Harbour/Monorail Darling Park.* **Open** noon-3pm, 6-10pm Mon-Sat; noon-10pm Sun. **$$$**. Licensed. **Seafood**. **Map** p55 A4 🔟

You can eat brilliantly at Nick's or you can not. The trick is simple: order fish from the extensive selection (don't ever pass up an opportunity to eat red emperor) and get it cooked as simply as possible.

### Ocean Room

*Ground Level, Overseas Passenger Terminal, West Circular Quay (9252 9585/www.oceanroomsydney.com). CityRail/ferry Circular Quay.* **Open** noon-3pm, 6-11pm Mon-Thur; noon-3pm, 6pm-midnight Fri, Sat. **$$$**. Licensed. **Fish**. **Map** p55 B2 🔟

Japanese chef Raita Noda's wilfully out-there Japanese fusion cuisine had a loyal following at Darlinghurst's obscure Rise, but something has been lost in the translation to this tourist-tempting gastro-barn by the water. Noda's work is in there somewhere, along with some superb seafood, but a throw-everything-at-the-wall-and-see-what-sticks approach from the man-agement means you'll be as likely marooned and confused as riding high on waves of inspiration.

### Opera Bar

*Lower Concourse Level, Sydney Opera House, Bennelong Point, Circular Quay (9247 1666/www.operabar.com.au). CityRail/ferry Circular Quay.* **Open** 11.30am-late daily. **Bar**. **Map** p55 C2 🔟

Loved by Sydneysiders and visitors alike, the Opera Bar is one of those multi-purpose venues that actually

La Renaissance Patisserie p71

gets it right. It offers better-than-it-needs-to-be lunch for quayside rubber-neckers; a lovely environment for an afternoon beer; quick, reasonably priced dinners for the pre-theatre crowd; and live music and cocktails most nights for groups on a night out. The views – the Opera House above and the bridge across the water – are particularly pretty at dusk, and this place won't hurt your wallet as much as rival Bennelong Bar (p66).

## Orbit Bar

*Level 47, Australia Square, 264 George Street, between Hunter & Bond Streets, CBD (9247 9777/www.summit restaurant.com.au). CityRail Wynyard.* **Open** 5pm-late Mon-Thur, Sun; noon-late Fri, Sat. **Bar. Map** p55 B3 ❸

Don't adjust your set, and don't worry, your drink hasn't been spiked: it's the bar itself that's spinning. And, 47 floors up, you get a fat eyeful of the city in plush retro-modern surrounds. The drinks are decent, and the bill might not hurt you if you're careful. The building

itself is a city landmark, designed by Harry Seidler.

## Ottoman

**NEW** *Pier 2/13 Hickson Road, Dawes Point (9252 0054). CityRail/ferry Circular Quay.* **Open** noon-3pm, 6-10pm Tue-Fri; 6-10pm Sat. **$$$.** Licensed. **Turkish. Map** p55 B1 ❸

Sister restaurant to Ottoman Cuisine in Canberra, this Sydney joint opened with a few coughs and splutters. Service was slow and faltering and prices seemed high. But the food has always been worth the wait, its Persian spices singing through every dish. The restaurant's setting, on the wharf at Dawes Point, is sublime.

## Palisade Hotel

*Corner of Bettington & Argyle Streets, Millers Point (9251 7225/www.palisade hotel.com). CityRail/ferry Circular Quay.* **Open** noon-3pm, 6-10pm Tue-Fri; 6-10pm Sat. **$$$.** Licensed. **Mod Oz. Map** p55 A2 ❻

A hidden gem, the upstairs dining room in this lovely old pub is certainly worth the fossick. Brian Sudek crafts food that sings with freshness, balance and simplicity. Service can sometimes be as laidback as the atmosphere, but that's not necessarily a bad thing. Be warned however that the bridgeside location doesn't always necessarily translate to views for all.

## Plan B

*204 Clarence Street, CBD (9283 3450). CityRail Town Hall/Monorail Galeries Victoria.* **Open** 8am-4pm Mon-Fri. Unlicensed. **Café**. **Map** p55 A4 ⑥⓪

This cute hole-in-the-wall café next to its big brother (and owner) fine-dining gaff Bécasse (p66) is a great place for a mouth-watering lunch that's a whole lot easier on the wallet than its older sibling. The Plan B wagyu burger is a no-nonsense deal of beef, fresh roasted beetroot, cheddar and tomato. And the coronation chicken sandwich is an excellent second choice if you can't wait for the burger (it takes a couple of minutes as they're made in Bécasse). Try the honeycomb muffin too.

## Prime

*Lower Ground Floor, GPO Sydney, 1 Martin Place, between George & Pitt Streets, CBD (9229 7777/ www.gpo sydney.com). CityRail Martin Place or Wynyard.* **Open** noon-3pm, 6-10pm Mon-Fri; 6-10pm Sat. **$$$**. Licensed. **American**. **Map** p55 B4 ⑥②

The closest Sydney gets to a big, New York-style steakhouse, this designer basement in the old GPO building is all about the blokey business of heavy stone, big-dollar blockbuster reds, and meat – lots of it. The red wine sauces are finger-lickin' great, and the knives are made from German surgical steel.

## Quay

*Upper Level, Overseas Passenger Terminal, Circular Quay West (9251 5600/www.quay.com.au). CityRail/ferry Circular Quay.* **Open** 6-10pm Mon; noon-2.30pm, 6-10pm Tue-Fri; 6-10pm Sat, Sun. **$$$$**. Licensed. **Mod Oz**. **Map** p55 B2 ⑥③

Quay is, quite simply, one of Sydney's greatest dining experiences. Peter Gilmore's food roves the world. Try the mud crab congee or ravioli of slow-cooked rabbit, rare-breed pig belly with green lipped abalone or the eight-hour slow-braised Flinders Island milk-fed lamb – every dish is its own concerto. What's more there's not a bad seat in the house, with beautiful views of the harbour, all round.

## Rockpool (fish)

**NEW** *107 George Street, between Alfred & Argyle Streets, The Rocks (9252 1888/www.rockpool.com). CityRail/ferry Circular Quay.* **Open** noon-2.30pm, 6-11pm Mon-Fri; 6-11pm Sat. **$$$**. Licensed. **Fish**. **Map** p55 B2 ⑥④

For 18 years, Neil Perry's Rockpool was one of Sydney's finest dining establishments. Then in 2007 he did a brave thing and recreated his star venue as a more casual seafood diner. So now, fish is the main focus, even though his culinary creations remain a delicate combination of Asian-inspired Mod Oz. The snapper poached in coconut and garam masala broth is inspirational in its combination of flavours, as are the freshly shucked live scallops with a spicy black bean and chilli dressing.

## Sailors Thai Canteen & Restaurant

*106 George Street, opposite Mill Lane, The Rocks (9251 2466). CityRail/ferry Circular Quay.* **Open** *Canteen* noon-10pm Mon-Sat. *Restaurant* noon-2pm, 6-10pm Mon-Fri; 6-10pm Sat. **$$$**. Licensed. **Thai**. **Map** p55 B2 ⑥⑤

Chef-restaurateur David Thompson now spends most of his time running Nahm, his superb, Michelin-starred Thai dining room in London's Belgravia. Meanwhile back in Sydney, you can eat food every bit as dynamic in Thompson's Rocks eaterie – and at a snip of the London prices. Upstairs at Sailors Thai is a more casual offering, where you can get the usuals of pad thai and som tum, while the downstairs restaurant is a touch more swanky (and expensive). The Thai sweets are particularly special – don't look past the coconut custard.

## Speedbar

*27 Park Street, between Castlereagh & Pitt Streets, CBD (9264 4668). CityRail Town Hall/Monorail Galeries Victoria.* **Open** 7am-6pm Mon-Fri; 8am-2pm Sat. Unlicensed. No credit cards. **Café**. Map p55 B4 66

The focus at Speedbar has always been on coffee, done right, done fast and done consistently well.

## Summit

*Level 47, Australia Square, 264 George Street, CBD (9247 9777/www.summit restaurant.com.au). CityRail Wynyard.* **Open** noon-3pm, 6-10pm Mon-Fri; 6-10pm Sat, Sun. **$$$**. Licensed. **Mod Oz**. Map p55 B3 67

In general, the propect of a revolving restaurant tends to strike gloom in to the hearts of most diners, conjuring up as it does images of tourist traps and gimmicks – but the Summit proved the exception to the rule when it relaunched in early 2007. Chef Michael Moore used to work at Bluebird in London, as well as at a clutch of top-notch eateries in Sydney and all that experience shines through. Moore makes good use of local seafood in his kitchen and there's a definite Asian frisson to dishes such as blue swimmer crab with red chilli salt and coriander. More hearty fare, such as juicy pork with satisfyingly thick crackling, keeps the traditionalists happy too (see also box p79).

## Sushi Tei

*1 Chifley Square, CBD (9232 7288). CityRail Martin Place.* **Open** 11.30am-2.30pm, 5.30-9.30pm Mon-Sat. **$**. Licensed. **Japanese**. Map p55 B3 68

For inexpensive Japanese in the middle of the city, you can't go wrong with relative newbie Sushi Tei, which seemed to mushroom almost overnight across the road from smooth operator and Japanese restaurant-to-the-stars Azuma (p75). Japanese standards such as edamame and gyoza are to a good standard but the menu's standout dish is its sea urchin roe – a real winner especially at these prices.

## Sydney Madang

*371A Pitt Street, CBD (9264 7010). CityRail Museum.* **Open** 11.30am-1am daily. **$**. Licensed. **Korean**. Map p55 B5 69

Korean food is taking over the world – well, Pitt Street, at least. The service at Sydney Madang is outstanding and the kimchi pancake is tasty as hell. The fried dumplings with rice vinegar are a must-order and sides of pickle and tofu will leave you feeling virtuous.

## Tearoom

*Level 3, Queen Victoria Building, 455 George Street, between Market & Druitt Streets, CBD (9283 7279/ www.thetearoom.com.au). CityRail Town Hall/Monorail Galeries Victoria.* **Open** 11am-5pm Mon-Fri, Sun; 10am-3pm Sat. Licensed. **Café**. Map p55 B4 70

It's a little-known fact that this ornate, soaring space, hidden at the top of the QVB shopping complex, does killer coffee in addition to its many premium-leaf teas. Sit with the grannies sipping single-estate Darjeelings and attacking three-tiered platters of pretty cakes and finger sandwiches.

## Tetsuya's

*529 Kent Street, between Bathurst & Liverpool Streets, CBD (9267 2900/www.tetsuyas.com). CityRail Town Hall/Monorail Galeries Victoria.* **Open** 6-10pm Tue-Fri; noon-3pm, 6-10pm Sat. **$$$$**. Licensed. **Mod Oz**. Map p55 A5 71

You must eat here at Tetsuya's – no arguments. Yes, it's a very large amount of money to pay for food. But, given that Tetsuya Wakuda is a culinary Olympian of the order of Alain Ducasse and Thomas Keller, the prices are a bargain of sorts. Don't be put off by the numerous courses in the fixed menu; each is so light and small that you're guaranteed to leave groaning only with pleasure. And don't worry: everyone ends up eating the entire dish of gorgeous butter whipped with black truffle and parmesan that accompanies the bread. The chef would worry more if you didn't.

**SYDNEY BY AREA**

Rockpool (fish) p74

### Yoshii

*115 Harrington Street, between Essex & Argyle Streets, CBD (9247 2566/ www.yoshii.com.au). CityRail/ferry Circular Quay.* **Open** 6-9.30pm Mon, Sat; noon-2pm, 6-9.30pm Tue-Fri. **$$$**. Licensed. **Japanese**. Map p55 B2 ⑫
Ryuichi Yoshii's dad was a sushi chef, and the genes have run true, with young Yoshii-san himself offering Sydney some of the finest sashimi in the land. Sit at the bar and watch him at work or take a table for cooked treats like the chaud-froid of egg and sea urchin roe. This is serious culinary inventiveness at the cutting edge, and all presented in cosy but utterly civilised surrounds.

### Zeta Bar

*4th Floor, Hilton Sydney, 488 George Street, between Park & Market Streets, CBD (9265 6070/www.zetabar.com.au). CityRail Town Hall/Monorail City Centre.* **Open** 5pm-late Mon-Wed; 3pm-late Thur, Fri; 4pm-late Sat. **Bar**. Map p55 B4 ⑬

Zeta Bar might not be the sort of place that wants to know you personally, but the drinks and service are good – almost good enough to justify the prices. Beware of the snaking queues of suburbanites at weekends.

## Shopping

### Between the Flags

*Opera Quays, East Circular Quay (9241 1603). CityRail/ferry Circular Quay.* **Open** 9am-9pm Mon-Fri; 10am-9pm Sat, Sun. Map p55 B2 ⑭
Thanks to Between the Flags, beach-loving shoppers can have fun on the sands and give something back to those iconic Aussie lifesavers at the same time. That's because ten per cent of the takings from this innovative swimwear shop goes to the Bondi Surf Bathers' Life Saving Club. This Opera Quays outlet boasts some cheerful maritime memorabilia throughout the store. You'll find numerous other branches of BTF throughout Sydney.

## Billabong

*393 George Street, CBD (9262 2878/
www.billabong.com.au). CityRail St
James or Town Hall/Monorail City
Centre.* **Open** 9am-6.30pm Mon-Wed,
Sat; 9am-9pm Thur; 10am-5pm Sun.
**Map** p55 B4 ⑦
Billabong founder Gordon Merchant
was responsible for designing the first
surfboard with a tucked-under edge,
and the first surfboard leg-rope. In
1973, he began producing home-made
boardshorts too. His designs became
overnight favourites with the surfers
in Queensland, before almost instantly
spreading across Australia and, from
there, around the world. Step over the
threshold of Billabong's massive
Sydney store and you'll find yourself
in surfie heaven. There's gear for the
beach – cute bikinis and short shorts
for the girls, and uber-cool board
shorts, tees and more for the guys.

## Borders

*Skygarden, 77 Castlereagh Street, CBD
(9235 2433/www.borders.com.au).
CityRail Martin Place, St James or
Town Hall/Monorail City Centre.* **Open**
9am-7pm Mon-Wed, Fri; 9am-9.30pm
Thur; 9am-6.30pm Sat; 10am-6pm Sat.
**Map** p55 B4 ⑯
Borders, the US monster book chain, is
well represented in Sydney. The shops
are typically capacious and many also
have coffee shops. Their most notable
asset is that they stock Sydney's most
reliably comprehensive selection of
international magazines.
**Other locations:** Westfield Bondi
Junction (9389 2200); Westfield
Parramatta (9687 3388); Westfield
Chatswood (9415 4800); see website for
other suburban locations.

## Chifley Plaza

*2 Chifley Square, corner of Hunter
& Phillip Streets, CBD (9221 6111/
www.chifleyplaza.com.au). CityRail
Martin Place.* **Map** p55 B3 ⑰
Sydney's most chic office workers shop
at this New York-style tower complex,
which stocks designer labels such as
MaxMara, Pierucci and local girl Leona
Edmiston. There's also a food court,

not to mention the excellent Japanese
restaurant Azuma (p75).

## David Jones

*Market Street, at Castlereagh Street;
Elizabeth Street, at Market Street, CBD
(9266 5544/www.davidjones.com.au).
CityRail St James or Town Hall/
Monorail City Centre.* **Open** 9.30am-
6pm Mon-Wed; 9.30am-9pm Thur;
9.30am-7pm Fri; 9am-7pm Sat; 10am-
6pm Sun. **Map** p55 B4 ⑱
Opened in 1838 by its Welsh-born
namesake, DJ's is the world's oldest
department store still trading under its
original name. The flagship city-centre
store is on two sites at the junction of
Market and Castlereagh Streets, linked
by a first-floor walkway. The Market
Street store has three floors of
menswear, plus furniture, homewares
and electrical goods. There's a gourmet
food hall on the lower-ground floor,
with an excellent noodle bar,
Champagne and oyster bar, sushi bar
and much more, as well as a stationers
and a cosmetics section – although the
main one is on the ground floor, along
with jewellery and accessories. Yet
more cosmetics, perfumes, jewellery
and accessories are to be found on the
ground floor of the Elizabeth Street
store. Above them are four floors of
women's fashion, including a good
range of international designers.

## Dinosaur Designs

*Strand Arcade, 412-414 George Street,
between King & Market Streets, CBD
(9223 2953/www.dinosaurdesigns.
com.au). CityRail Martin Place, St
James or Town Hall/Monorail City
Centre.* **Open** 9.30am-5.30pm Mon-
Wed, Fri; 9.30am-8pm Thur; 10am-4pm
Sat; noon-4pm Sun. **Map** p55 B4 ⑲
Three former art students got together
in 1985 to set up local favourite
Dinosaur Designs. The shop sells
home-made bright, glowing resin
bowls, vases, jugs, plates and other
pieces of crockery and household
items. It is also known for its chunky
jewellery, in particular its ranges
inspired by natural forms and
Australian landscapes.

## Galeries Victoria

*500 George Street, at Park Street, CBD
(9265 6888/www.tgv.com.au). CityRail
Town Hall/Monorail Galeries Victoria.*
**Map** p55 B4 ❽⓿
Designed by award-winning Sydney
architects Crone Associates, the
Tokyo-esque four-level Galeries
Victoria is a welcome relief from the
nearby identikit Pitt Street malls. Here
you'll find something different: MNG,
Freedom Furniture and Mooks, plus
cosmetics store Mecca Cosmetica and
Wagamama, the Japanese restaurant
chain. Worth a trip is Kinokuniya,
Sydney's largest cross-cultural book-
shop which stocks titles in English,
Japanese, Chinese, French and German
(find it on level two).

## Gary Castles

*Strand Arcade, 412-414 George Street,
between King & Market Streets, CBD
(9232 6544/www.garycastlessydney.
com). CityRail Martin Place, St James
or Town Hall/Monorail City Centre.*
**Open** 9.30am-6pm Mon-Wed, Fri, Sat;
9.30am-8.30pm Thur; 11am-5pm Sun.
**Map** p55 B4 ❺⓵
Gary Castles sells a great range of
smart and sophisticated ladies' shoes
in some terrific colour combinations.

## Jayson Brunsdon

*The Strand Arcade, Shop 123, 412-
414 George Street, CBD (9233 8891/
www.jaysonbrunsdon.com.) CityRail
Martin Place, St James or Town
Hall/Monorail City Centre.* **Open**
9.30am-5.30pm Mon-Wed, Fri;
9.30am-8pm Thur; 9.30am-4pm Sat.
**Map** p55 B4 ❺⓶
He may seem like the new kid on the
block but Mr Brunsdon has actually
been working in the fashion industry
for 20 years – not all of that designing,
though (he used to be an illustrator and
magazine fashion editor, then creative
director with Morrissey before he
decided to branch out and set up his
own fashion label). Brunsdon likes to
work with bold colours and shapes that
accentuate feminine curves and stand
out in a crowd. The results are real
head-turning event pieces.

## Map World

*280 Pitt Street, between Park &
Bathurst Streets, CBD (9261 3601/
www.mapworld.net.au). CityRail Town
Hall/Monorail Galeries Victoria.* **Open**
9am-5.30pm Mon-Wed, Fri; 9am-6.30pm
Thur; 10am-4pm Sat. **Map** p55 B5 ❻⓷
Road maps for the whole of Australia,
as well as travel guides, atlases and
books about such outdoor activities as
four-wheel-driving and rock climbing.

## Marcs

*Shop 1, Ground Floor, QVB, 455
George Street, between Market & Druitt
Streets, CBD (9267 0823/www.marcs.
com.au). CityRail Town Hall/Monorail
Galeries Victoria.* **Open** 9am-6pm Mon-
Wed, Fri, Sat; 9am-9pm Thur; 11am-
5pm Sun. **Map** p55 B4 ❻⓸
The Marcs label launched in the 1980s
when a couple of designers had the
idea to make men's shirts out of
women's fabrics. Now it's a massively
successful string of men's and
women's clothes shops.

## Midas

*Ground Floor, QVB, 455 George
Street, between Market & Druitt
Streets, CBD (9261 5815/www.midas
shoes.com.au). CityRail Town
Hall/Monorail Galeries Victoria.* **Open**
9am-6pm Mon-Wed, Fri, Sat; 9am-9pm
Thur; 11am-5pm Sun.**Map** p55 B4 ❻⓹
Midas is great for well priced, well
made and gorgeous ladies' footwear. It
also sells bags, belts and scarves.

## MLC Centre

*Martin Place, corner of King &
Castlereagh Streets, CBD (9224
8333/www.mlccentre.com.au).
CityRail Martin Place/Monorail City
Centre.* **Open** 9am-6pm Mon-Wed, Fri,
Sat; 9am-9pm Thur; 11am-5pm Sun.
**Map** p55 B4 ❽⓺
Old-timers still mourn the loss of the
Parisian-style Rowe Street, which was
levelled to make way for this arcade in
the 1970s. It's now the domain of city
slickers who come to splurge on top
designers, such as Cartier and Gucci,
as well as at uber-boutique Belinda.
The Theatre Royal is also part of the
complex and there's a good food court.

# Views from the top

Sydney is awash with great views, and the best are from on high. The Harbour Bridge is *the* place to start by joining the famous **BridgeClimb** (p63), a three-and-a-half-hour adventure along catwalks and up ladders to the summit of the bridge, 134 metres (440 feet) above the harbour. Once at the top, drink in the 360-degree views of the Pacific Ocean to the east, the Blue Mountains to the west and the harbour city surrounds.

Celebrating its 40th birthday in 2008, the 165-metre (541-foot) high **Summit restaurant** (p75) is perched on level 47 of one of Sydney's most beautiful skyscrapers – Harry Seidler's Australia Square. The restaurant itself revolves at one metre (3.5 feet) per minute and is the largest revolving restaurant in the world.

The floor-to-ceiling windows open out on to a gradually revolving 360-degree panorama, which takes in the entire city skyline in 105 minutes.

Sydney Tower's famed **Skywalk** (p64) is Sydney's highest open-air attraction – at 260 metres (853 feet) above the city, a 45-minute walk on the glass-floored viewing platform, attached to a safety harness, is a real buzz. The Skywalk is twice the height of the Harbour Bridge and the same height as the Eiffel Tower. Guides point out landmarks – but most Skywalkers are happy just to take in the high-altitude atmosphere as they crawl like bugs across the roof under the clouds.

Over in the Domain, next door to the Royal Botanic Gardens, **Mrs Macquarie's Chair** (p56) was carved out of a rock ledge for Governor Lachlan Macquarie's wife, Elizabeth, who loved the panoramic view of the harbour from here. You too can enjoy great views west to the Harbour Bridge and the Blue Mountains. Looking north and east, you can see Kirribilli House, Pinchgut Island and the Navy dockyards based at Woolloomooloo.

For a lesser-known lookout, head to the **Sydney Observatory** (p63). Set on Observatory Hill, the site became an astronomical observation point during the 19th century. Today star-gazing through telescopes draws crowds, but a stroll in the gardens also makes for a great day out. There is a magnificent view of the Harbour Bridge, which many locals believe to be far superior to that afforded by Mrs Macquarie's Chair.

## Myer

*436 George Street, at Market Street, CBD (9238 9111/www.myer.com.au). CityRail St James or Town Hall/ Monorail City Centre.* **Open** 9am-6pm Mon-Wed, Sat; 9am-9pm Thur; 9am-7pm Fri; 10am-6pm Sun. **Map** p55 B4 ⑰

In 2004, Sydney institution Grace Bros changed its name to Myer in one of the biggest-ever rebrandings in Australian history (it had been owned by Coles Myer since 1983). Sidney Myer was a penniless Russian immigrant who opened his first store in Bendigo, Victoria. Now, along with David Jones, Myer is one of the leading department stores in the country. You'll find a good range of clothes, homewares, electrical goods and cosmetics.

## Paxtons

*285 George Street, at Hunter Street, CBD (9299 2999/www.paxtons.com.au). CityRail Wynyard.* **Open** 8am-6pm Mon-Wed, Fri; 8am-8pm Thur; 9am-4pm Sat; 10am-3.30pm Sun. **Map** p55 B3 ⑱

Sydney's largest independent camera retailer stocks a very good selection of digital cameras, video cameras, lenses, digital audio gear and more.

## RM Williams

*389 George Street, between King & Market Streets, CBD (9262 2228/ www.rmwilliams.com.au). CityRail Martin Place, St James or Town Hall/Monorail City Centre.* **Open** 8.30am-6pm Mon-Wed, Fri; 8.30am-9pm Thur; 9am-5pm Sat; 11am-5pm Sun. **Map** p55 B4 ⑲

Reginald Murray Williams started out as a 'bush outfitters' in southern Australia in the 1930s. These days his clothes are more likely to be seen on urban cowboys than the jackaroos they were designed for. Boots are the staple and the shirts and shorts are popular.

## Queen Victoria Building (QVB)

*455 George Street, between Market & Druitt Streets, CBD (9264 9209/ www.qvb.com.au). CityRail Town Hall/ Monorail Galeries Victoria.* **Map** p55 B4 ⑳

The elegant, airy Victorian halls of this historic building have always pulled in the tourist dollar, although clued-up Sydneysiders shop here as well. You'll find designer labels, fashion chain stores, shoe shops, chocolate shops and florists on the ground floor, and arts, antiques and Australiana on level two. The lower-ground level links through to the Town Hall Square station and shops, along with the Galeries Victoria shopping centre.

## Red Eye

*66 King Street, between George & York Streets, CBD (9299 4233/www.redeye. com.au). CityRail Wynyard.* **Open** 9am-6pm Mon-Wed, Fri; 9am-9pm Thur; 9am-5pm Sat; 11am-5pm Sun. **Map** p55 A4 ㉛

The biggest of the indie shops, Red Eye has an excellent selection of Australian bands and labels, as well as a good selection of imports.

## Rip Curl

*61-63 Market Street, CBD (9264 6777/ www.ripcurl.com). CityRail St James or Town Hall/Monorail City Centre.* **Open** 9am-7pm daily (6pm in winter). **Map** p55 B4 ㉜

Stock up on boards, boardies and everything else a surfer could wish for.

## Rocks Market

*North Precinct, George Street & Playfair Street, The Rocks (Sydney Harbour Foreshore Authority 1300 655 995/www.rocksmarket.com). CityRail/ferry Circular Quay.* **Open** 10am-5pm Sat, Sun. **Map** p55 B2 ㉝

Quality arts, crafts, homewares, antiques and collectibles, including a lot of stalls selling indigenous crafts and souvenirs.

## Strand Arcade

*412-414 George Street, between King & Market Streets, CBD (9232 4199/ www.strandarcade.com.au). CityRail Martin Place, St James or Town Hall/ Monorail City Centre.* **Map** p55 B4 ㉞

This beautiful arcade is as historic as the QVB, but a hundred times cooler. There are touristy shops such as Haigh's Chocolates and Strand Hatters

David Jones p77

on the ground floor, but venture upwards and you'll discover all the darlings of the Australian fashion scene, including Leona Edmiston, Lisa Ho, Wayne Cooper, Third Millennium, Bettina Liano, Zimmermann, Little Joe by Gail Elliott, Terry Biviano and Dinosaur Designs. The prices continue to escalate as you move up again – check out the divine Alex Perry and sleek Jayson Brunsdon.

### Strand Hatters

*Strand Arcade, 412-414 George Street, between King & Market Streets, CBD (9231 6884/www.strandhatters. com.au). CityRail Martin Place, St James or Town Hall/Monorail City Centre.* **Open** 8.30am-6pm Mon-Wed, Fri; 8.30am-8pm Thur; 9.30am-4.30pm Sat; 11am-4pm Sun. **Map** p55 B4 ⑨⑤
While Aussie icon Akubras pull the crowds in, you can also buy authentic panamas or fedoras at the Hatters – or even a replica of the pith helmet worn by dapper soldiers at Rorke's Drift in 1879.

## Nightlife

### ArtHouse Hotel

*275 Pitt Street, between Park & Market Streets, CBD (9284 1200/ www.thearthousehotel.com.au). CityRail St James or Town Hall/Monorail Galeries Victoria.* **Open** *Verge Bar, Gallery Bar & Dome Lounge* 11am-midnight Mon-Thur; 11am-3am Fri; 5pm-6am Sat. *Attic Bar* 5pm-late Wed-Sat. *Saturday sessions* **Admission** $25. **Map** p55 B4 ⑨⑥
This former 19th-century school of art, which has also been a theatre and a chapel in its time, is transformed into a 21st-century club with attitude for its Saturday Sessions nights. But all that glamour doesn't come cheap – the admission price is every bit as loft as the mile-high stilettos that the wannabe model clubbers teeter in on. The ArtHouse is definitely a place to make an effort – dress up, dress funky and praise be for all those dark corners to hide in – this is a young and very glamourous crowd.

## Basement

*29 Reiby Place, off Pitt Street, Circular Quay (9251 2797/ www.thebasement. com.au). CityRail/ferry Circular Quay.* **Open** noon-late Mon-Fri; 7pm-late Sat, Sun. **Admission** $12-$60. **Map** p55 B3 ㊲

One of the hippest clubs on the scene, this hugely popular jazz and blues venue near Circular Quay boasts a supper-club-style setting with tables, an adjacent 'blue room' and a bistro for cheap eats.

## Slip Inn

*111 Sussex Street, at King Street, CBD (8295 9911/www.merivale.com.au). CityRail Town Hall or Wynyard.* **Open** *Slip Bar* noon-midnight Mon-Thur; noon-2am Fri; 5pm-2am Sat. *Sand Bar* noon-midnight Mon-Thur; noon-3am Fri; 5pm-3am Sat. *Garden Bar* noon-midnight Mon-Fri; 5pm-midnight Sat. *Chinese Laundry* 10pm-4am Fri; 10.30pm-4am Sat. *Cave* 11pm-4am Fri, Sat. **Admission** $10-$15 Fri; $15-$25 Sat. **Map** p55 A4 ㊳

The Slip Inn – now forever famous locally as being the place where Aussie estate agent Mary Donaldson met her future husband, the Prince of Denmark – houses no less than three bars (Slip, Sand and Garden) and two clubs (Chinese Laundry and the smaller Cave). Chinese Laundry splits itself into two nights: Break Inn on Fridays, and the pricier, pumped-up Laundry on Saturdays. Currently seriously popular is the Garden Bar – a huge, sun-filled courtyard at the rear of the building that hosts a buzzing outdoor day club every Sunday.

## Tank

*3 Bridge Lane, off Bridge Street, between George & Pitt Streets, CBD (9240 3000/www.tankclub.com.au). CityRail Circular Quay or Wynyard/ ferry Circular Quay.* **Open** 10pm-6am Fri, Sat. **Admission** $20 Fri; $25 Sat. **Map** p55 B3 ㊴

This high-columned uber-club is the closest thing you'll get to a Studio 54 experience in Sydney. The music has settled into comfortable funky/jazzy house on Friday and a chunkier sound on Saturdays, with plenty of visiting international DJs.

# Arts & leisure

## Andrew (Boy) Charlton Pool

*Mrs Macquarie's Road, The Domain (9358 6686/www.abcpool.org). Bus 411.* **Open** 6am-7pm *(non-daylight saving)*, 6am-8pm *(daylight saving)* daily. **Admission** $5.50; $3.60-$3.80 reductions. **Map** p55 C3 ⓿

A $10-million refurbishment has made this harbourside pool *the* place for inner-city swimming. It was a popular bathing spot long before the British arrived, and public sea baths first opened here in 1860. In the early 1920s, famous Aussie swimmer Andrew 'Boy' Charlton achieved many triumphs here – including, aged just 16, beating European champ Arne Borg, setting a new world record in the process. Today there's an eight-lane, heated 50m pool, a sundeck and café. The pool's edges are glazed, offering unparalleled views across the sparkling bay.

## City Recital Hall

*Angel Place, near Martin Place, CBD (admin 9231 9000/box office 8256 2222/www.cityrecitalhall.com). CityRail Martin Place.* **Admission** $5.50; $3.60-$3.80 reductions. **Map** p55 B3 ⓿

The 1,200-seat City Recital Hall in the centre of the CBD gives Sydney's orchestras room to roam, as well as hosting international names (including one David Helfgott). The pitch-perfect acoustics are said to match Amsterdam's Concertgebouw.

## Dendy Opera Quays

*2 East Circular Quay, Circular Quay (9247 3800/www.dendy.com.au). CityRail/ferry Circular Quay. Screens 3.* **Admission** $14; $6.50-$10.50. **Map** p55 B2 ⓿

A stone's throw from the Opera House, with great views across to the Harbour Bridge, this luxurious complex tends to offers a mix of middlebrow and art-house fare, and is fully licensed.

## Greater Union George Street

*505-525 George Street, between Bathurst & Liverpool Streets, CBD (9273 7431/www.greaterunion.com.au). CityRail Town Hall/Monorail World Square. Screens 17.* **Admission** $16; $7-$12.50 reductions; $9 Tue. **Map** p55 A5 ⓚ

The sprawling cinema complex shows virtually every new commercial movie release as soon as it opens. Located in the heart of George Street's garish entertainment strip, it attracts throngs of noisy kids and can get a little edgy at night, so guard your valuables. The state-of-the-art auditoria with digital surround sound and comfy, if a tad narrow, seats are especially popular with teens and out-of-towners, as you'll see from the queues.

## OpenAir Cinema

*Mrs Macquarie's Chair, The Domain, CBD (1300 366 649/www.stgeorge.com.au/openair). CityRail Circular Quay or Martin Place/ferry Circular Quay.* **Open** Early Jan-mid Feb. **Admission** $23-$25; $22-$23 reductions. **Map** p55 C3 ⓚ

Part of the Sydney Festival (p34), this is the ultimate outdoor moviegoing experience, with the Harbour Bridge and Opera House in the background. You get several Sydney premieres of mainstream movies, as well as a pick of current and classic fare. Films start at 8.30pm, but the gates open from 6.30pm – as do the stylish onsite bar and restaurant. The cinema can seat around 1,700 people.

## State Theatre

*49 Market Street, between Pitt & George Streets, CBD (9373 6852/www.state theatre.com.au). CityRail St James or Town Hall/Monorail City Centre.* **Admission** $50-$135. Production prices vary. **Map** p55 B4 ⓚ

Designed at the dawn of talking pictures, the impossibly over-the-top State is Australia's only example of true rococo. All plaster and all fake, the State hosts rare theatre pieces too supersized to belong elsewhere. It's a

good cinema and average sit-down music venue, but not particularly great for live theatre.

## Sydney Theatre

*22 Hickson Road, opposite Pier 6/7, Walsh Bay (9250 1999/www.sydney theatre.org.au). CityRail/ferry Circular Quay then 15min walk.* **Admission** $59-$79; $40-$67 reductions. Production prices vary. **Map** p55 A2 ⓚ

Very nicely designed, the Sydney Theatre represents the city's lust for a well done playhouse. After numerous rallying calls to secure one, the Sydney public finally got their theatre – with seating for nearly 900. Because it's programmed by the Sydney Theatre Company (see also box p67), the space doesn't depend on the whims of commercial producers for its varying productions. It often features good drama, and occasionally good dance. Beware: its acoustic construction means you can't walk out before the interval without making a great deal of noticeable noise.

## Wharf Theatres

*Pier 4/5, Hickson Road, Walsh Bay (9250 1777/www.sydneytheatre.com.au). CityRail/ferry Circular Quay then 15min walk.* **Open** Early Jan-mid Feb. **Admission** $48-$79; $42-$67 reductions (not Fri, Sat). Production prices vary. **Map** p55 A1 ⓚ

This converted wharf and warehouse on the western side of the Harbour Bridge is near the Sydney Theatre (see above). It's surrounded by very swanky residential redevelopments and houses the Sydney Theatre Company's artistic, management and production staff, a rehearsal space and lovely restaurant, as well as two theatres: Wharf 1 and Wharf 2. The Sydney Dance Company, Australian Theatre for Young People and Bangarra perform here. The complex boasts Sydney's best foyer – on a summer's night, a G&T here is well worth the view, if perhaps not the price. Get off at Circular Quay, walk through the Rocks and under the bridge, and even before the show you'll experience aesthetic magic.

**SYDNEY BY AREA**

Chinese Garden of Friendship p86

# Darling Harbour & Chinatown

Head west from the CBD and you'll hit touristy **Darling Harbour** and its neighbouring concourse **King Street Wharf**, a great melee of contemporary architecture that is considered to be something of a mixed blessing by locals. This reclaimed waterfront is awash with so-so restaurants and also home to the **Australian National Maritime Museum**, **Chinese Garden of Friendship**, **Sydney Aquarium**, **Sydney Wildlife World** and a clutch of hotels. In the evening during summer there's usually a noisy programme of free events, such as concerts, and fireworks, launched from a podium in the Darling Harbour water. Twentysomethings

queue late at night around popular nightclub **Home** or gather for drinks further round the boardwalk at **Cargo Bar** and you can catch ferries from here to Circular Quay or across the water to Balmain. But while it's all very buzzy, there's still an unavoidable air of artificiality.

For a bit more soul, head to the **Chinese Garden of Friendship** at Darling Harbour and beyond it, to the ever-growing sprawl of **Chinatown**. Here you'll find Chinese shops and restaurants – even a Chinese cinema. The huge **World Square Tower** has the feel of a Hong Kong development and, together with its attached shopping centres on the edge of Chinatown, is extending the

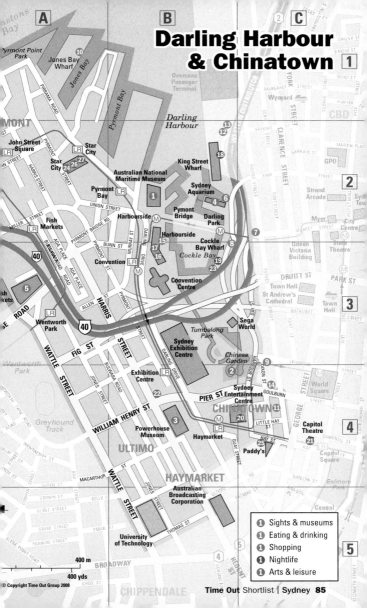

# Darling Harbour & Chinatown

**Map labels:**

Winstons Bay
Pyrmont Point Park
Pyrmont Point Park
Jones Bay Wharf
Jones Bay
Pyrmont Bay
Overseas Passenger Terminal
Darling Harbour
YORK STREET
Wynyard
MARGARET STREET
ERSKINE STREET
CLARENCE STREET
CBD
HUNTER STREET
BOND ST
BRIDGE ST
GPO
BARRACK ST
MARTIN PLACE
PITT STREET
PYRMONT
PIRRAMA ROAD
John Street Square
Star City
Star City
PYRMONT STREET
HARRIS STREET
MILLER STREET
Australian National Maritime Museum
Pyrmont Bay
UNION STREET
King Street Wharf
Sydney Aquarium
Pyrmont Bridge
Darling Park
Harbourside
Strand Arcade
Myer
Market City
City Centre
Fish Markets
Harbourside
Cockle Bay Wharf
Cockle Bay
Queen Victoria Building
Queen Victoria Building
State Theatre
PITT STREET
GEORGE STREET
Convention
DRUITT ST
PARK ST
Convention Centre
Town Hall
St Andrew's Cathedral
BATHURST STREET
BUNN ST
ADA PLACE
Wentworth Park
Fish Markets
PYRMONT BRIDGE RD
DARLING DRIVE
MURRAY ST
PYRMONT STREET
HARRIS STREET
ALLEN STREET
FIG ST
WATTLE STREET
Town Hall
Sega World
Tumbalong Park
Sydney Exhibition Centre
Chinese Garden
Exhibition Centre
PIER ST
Sydney Entertainment Centre
Liverpool
World Square
GEORGE STREET
CHINATOWN
GOULBURN STREET
Wentworth Park
Greyhound Track
WILLIAM HENRY ST
JONES STREET
BULWARRA ROAD
Powerhouse Museum
Haymarket
LITTLE HAY ST
Capitol Theatre
BAY ST
ULTIMO
Paddy's
CAMPBELL ST
Capitol Square
Belmore Park
HAYMARKET
MACARTHUR ST
JONES STREET
THOMAS ST
QUAY STREET
Central
Australian Broadcasting Corporation
WATTLE STREET
GLEBE POINT ROAD
University of Technology
BROADWAY
CHIPPENDALE
REGENT STREET
ELIZABETH STREET

400 m
400 yds
© Copyright Time Out Group 2008

| | |
|---|---|
| ❶ | Sights & museums |
| ❶ | Eating & drinking |
| ❶ | Shopping |
| ❶ | Nightlife |
| ❶ | Arts & leisure |

borders of this Asian-inspired pocket of town further still.

On the other side of Darling Harbour is **Pyrmont**, a former wharf area now converted and boasting the glitzy **Star Casino** at its heart. The **Powerhouse Museum** and recently added, and very popular, **Ian Thorpe Aquatic Centre** lie beyond on Harris Street. Further west is the wonderful **Sydney Fish Market**.

## Sights & museums

### Australian National Maritime Museum

*2 Murray Street, Harbourside, Darling Harbour (9298 3777/www.anmm. gov.au). Ferry Darling Harbour or Pyrmont Bay/LightRail Pyrmont Bay/Monorail Harbourside/bus 443.* **Open** 9.30am-5pm daily (6pm in Jan). **Admission** free; $15-$30 for special exhibits & vessels. **Map** p85 B2 ❶
An exhibition at the Maritime Musuem traces the history of the Royal Australian Navy, but the biggest attractions by far for visitors are the vessels themselves, among them an 1888 racing yacht *Akarana*, a 1950s naval destroyer HMAS *Vampire* and a traditional Vietnamese junk *Tu Duo* ('Freedom'), which sailed into Darwin in 1977 with 39 refugees.

### Chinese Garden of Friendship

*Corner of Pier & Harbour Streets, Darling Harbour (9281 6863/ www.chinesegarden.com.au). CityRail Central or Town Hall/Monorail Paddy's Markets or World Square/LightRail Paddy's Markets.* **Admission** $6; $3 reductions. **Open** 9.30am-5pm daily. **Map** p85 B4-C4 ❷
Designed in Sydney's sister city, Guangzhou in China, to commemorate the 1988 bicentenary, the Garden of Friendship in Darling Harbour is a symbol of the bond between the two twinned cites. Its dragon wall features two dragon heads, one in gold for Guangzhou, one in blue for NSW, with

a pearl connecting the two. There are waterfalls, weeping willows, pretty water lilies, 'wandering galleries' and wooden bridges. Head up to the tea-room balcony, order a cup of shui-hsien tea and enjoy the best view of all: the entire park reflected in the Lake of Brightness, stuffed full of chubby carp.

### Powerhouse Museum

*500 Harris Street, between William Henry & Macarthur Streets, Ultimo (9217 0111/www.phm.gov.au). CityRail Central/Monorail/LightRail Paddy's Markets.* **Open** 10am-5pm daily. **Admission** $10; $5-$6 reductions. **Map** p85 B4 ❸
This former power station opened as a fun and funky museum in 1988 and is the largest museum space in Australia, with a collection of 385,000 objects, 22 permanent and five temporary display spaces, and more than 250 interactive exhibits. The displays cover science, technology, creativity, decorative arts and Australian popular culture, and exhibitions can be on such diverse themes as Tokyo street style or child-hood memories of migration.

### Sydney Aquarium

*Aquarium Pier, Wheat Road, Darling Harbour (8251 7800/www.sydney aquarium.com.au). Ferry Darling Harbour/CityRail Town Hall/Monorail Darling Park.* **Open** 9am-10pm daily. Seal sanctuary 9.30am-sunset daily. **Admission** $28.50; $14.50-$19.50 reductions. **Map** p85 B2 ❹
This fantastic aquarium is made up of a main exhibit hall, two giant floating oceanariums – one dedicated to the Great Barrier Reef (with the largest collection of sharks in captivity), the other a seal sanctuary – plus two touch pools. Watch out for the saltwater crocs in the northern river section and those elusive platypuses in the south-ern river section. Underwater viewing tunnels mean visitors can watch sharks and rays gliding past, and seals frolicking close by. The new Shark Explorer ride, in a glass-bottomed boat, is another way to get up-close-and-personal and raise your heartbeat.

## Sydney Fish Market

*Corner of Pyrmont Bridge Road &
Bank Street, Pyrmont (9004 1100/
www.sydneyfishmarket.com.au).
LightRail Fish Market/bus 501.* **Open**
7am-4pm daily. **Map** p85 A3 ❺
This working fishing port – which has
trawlers in Blackwattle Bay, wholesale
and retail fish markets, shops, a great
variety of indoor and outdoor eateries,
and picnic tables on the outdoor deck
– is well worth the trek to Pyrmont. It's
the largest market of its kind in the
southern hemisphere, and you won't
find more varieties of fish on sale anywhere outside Japan: the market trades
more than 100 species a day and over
15 million kilos of fish a year.

## Sydney Wildlife World

NEW *Aquarium Pier, Wheat Road,
Darling Harbour (9333 9288/
www.sydneywildlifeworld.com.au).
Ferry Darling Harbour/CityRail Town
Hall/Monorail Darling Park.* **Open** 9am-
10pm daily. **Admission** $28.50; $14.50-
$19.50 reductions. **Map** p85 B2 ❻
There are over 100 Australian animal
species on site at Wildlife World and
Sydney's largest variety of unique and
bizarre indigenous plants and animals.
It's a clever and well-executed space
and you can see the rainforest canopy
from outside the building. The ethos of
the park is to tell each species' story on
an evolutionary timeline within its own
habitat, while highlighting Aboriginal
dreamtime and conservation issues.
Koalas are, of course, top of the hit list
here, but the butterfly collection has to
be seen to be believed.

## Eating & drinking

## Chinta Ria Temple of Love

*201 Sussex Street, Cockle Bay Wharf
(9264 3211/www.chintaria.com).
CityRail Town Hall/ferry Darling
Harbour/Monorail Darling Park.* **Open**
noon-2.30pm, 6-11pm daily. **$$**.
Licensed/BYO. **Asian**. **Map** p85 C2 ❼
The gigantic laughing Buddha statue
in the middle of the room dominates
Chinta Ria and all the furniture is 1950s
diner. Dishes such as beef rending,

chicken satay skewers and gado gado,
washed down with Tiger beer, make
this a popular spot with post-work
twenty- and thirtysomethings.

## Coast

*Roof Terrace, Cockle Bay Wharf,
Darling Harbour (9267 6700/
www.coastrestaurant.com.au).
CityRail Town Hall/ferry Darling
Harbour/Monorail Darling Park.* **Open**
noon-2.30pm, 6-10pm Mon-Fri;
6-10pm Sat. **$$$**. Licensed. **Italian**.
**Map** p85 B2 ❽
Coast boasts traditional Italian food in
stunning, breezy surrounds high above
Darling Harbour. Enjoy the likes of
bright green asparagus with poached
egg and almonds, and give something
back at the same time – the restaurant
is an active member of the Streetsmart
charity which aims to help Sydney's
homeless people.

## East Ocean Restaurant

*88 Dixon Street, at Liverpool Street,
entrance at 421-429 Sussex Street,
Haymarket (9212 4198/www.east
ocean.com.au). CityRail Central/
Monorail Paddy's Markets or World
Square/LightRail Capitol Square
or Paddy's Markets.* **Open** 10am-
midnight Mon-Fri; 9am-2am Sat, Sun.
**$$**. Licensed/BYO. **Cantonese**.
**Map** p85 C3 ❾
At this slick Hong Kong restaurant, the
salt-and-pepper squid is particularly
good, as are the baby abalone steamed
with ginger and spring onion. And the
yum cha – diverse and fresh – is also
among the city's finest, so be prepared
to queue at weekends.

## Flying Fish

*Lower Deck, Jones Bay Wharf, 19-21
Pirrama Road, Pyrmont (9518 6677/
www.flyingfish.com.au). LightRail Star
City/bus 443.* **Open** 6.30-10.30pm Mon;
noon-2.30pm, 6.30-10.30pm Tue-Fri;
6-10.30pm Sat; noon-3.30pm Sun. **$$$**.
Licensed. **Seafood**. **Map** p85 A1 ❿
It's all about the crab at Flying Fish.
The mighty Queensland mud crab
comes with Sri-Lankan style curries,
raw fish dishes and some of the best
chips in town.

## Golden Century

*393-399 Sussex Street, between Goulburn & Hay Streets, Haymarket (9212 3901). CityRail Central/Monorail World Square/LightRail Capitol Square.* **Open** noon-4am daily. **$$**. Licensed/BYO. **Chinese**. Map p85 C4 ⑪

Although the printed menu at Golden Century is fine, most regulars bypass it completely and simply flag down a member of the famously surly staff for steamed fish with ginger and spring onion, salt-and-pepper prawns and the top-notch signature Peking duck. After 10pm, the restaurant switches down a gear, offering a set of cheaper, one-bowl meals for night owls, drunks, chefs and other miscreants.

## Loft

*3 Lime Street, King Street Wharf (9299 4770/www.theloftsydney.com). CityRail Wynyard/ferry Darling Harbour/Monorail Darling Park.* **Open** 4pm-1am Mon-Wed; noon-3am Thur-Sun. **Bar**. Map p85 B2 ⑫

The Loft's Baghdad Iced Tea – made with cucumber, Smirnoff Blue voddy, Plymouth gin, apple, mint, lime and jasmine tea – is a great early-evening refresher in hot weather. The carved Moorish-style ceilings, lots of squishy leather loungers, verandas opening on to water views across Darling Harbour all conspire to keep punters smiling, and the great tapas are served late.

## Malaya

*39 Lime Street, King Street Wharf (9279 1170/www.themalaya.com.au). CityRail Town Hall/ferry Darling Harbour/Monorail Darling Park.* **Open** noon-3pm, 6pm-late Mon-Sat; 6-9pm Sun. **$$**. Licensed. **Malaysian**. Map p85 B2 ⑬

The Malaya looms large in the recent history of Sydney restaurants, having been responsible – over the course of 30-odd years and several changes of location – for introducing locals to galangal, lemongrass and other Asian flavours. It might not be at the cutting edge for food any more, but the laksa and fish curry still delight in this airy establishment boasting water views.

## Red Chilli

*Shop 3/51 Dixon Street, Haymarket (9211 8122/www.redchillirestaurant. com.au). CityRail Central/LightRail Capitol Square.* **Open** 11.30am-3pm, 5-11pm daily. **$$**. Licensed/BYO. **Chinese**. Map p85 C4 ⑭

It's Sichuan, it's spicy and it's cheap. Try the tasty pumpkin fried in duck egg yolk or the 'very hot and spicy chicken' – where you'll pick through a mountain of dried chilli for little bites of chook, which, weirdly, aren't spicy.

## Zaaffran

*Level 2, 345 Harbourside Shopping Centre, Darling Harbour (9211 8900/ www.zaaffran.com.au). CityRail Town Hall/ferry Darling Harbour/Monorail Harbourside.* **Open** noon-2.30pm, 5.30-9.30pm Mon-Thur, Sun; noon-2.30pm, 5.30-10.15pm Fri, Sat. **$$$**. Licensed. **Indian**. Map p85 B2 ⑮

Free-range chickens issuing from the tandoor, semolina-crusted barramundi with turmeric, lime, ginger and chilli – this is an Indian restaurant, but not as you know it. And while you might not want to hit Darling Harbour expressly to visit it, should you find yourself there already, it's a superior option.

# Shopping

## Gavala Aboriginal Cultural Centre

*Harbourside Centre, Darling Drive, Darling Harbour (9212 7232/ www.gavala.com.au). CityRail Town Hall/ferry Darling Harbour/Monorail Harbourside.* **Open** 10am-9pm daily. Map p85 B3 ⑯

Established in 1995, Gavala is Aboriginal-owned and staffed, and a top spot to buy arts and crafts made by Aboriginal artists. Visit for jewellery, boomerangs and didgeridoos, plus paintings in the attached art gallery.

## Harbourside

*Darling Drive, Darling Harbour (9281 3999/www.harbourside.com.au). CityRail Town Hall/ferry Darling Harbour/Monorail Harbourside.* Map p85 B3 ⑰

# The real national game

**Star City Casino**

Feeding the ever-hungry pokie machines in Sydney's gambling venues may be about to become a little less prevalent if Australian prime minister Kevin Rudd has his way. In a war on compulsive gambling, he is betting that a ban on ATMs in pokie joints will be an important weapon in tackling the problem. He also wants to see the pokies' spin rates reduced.

And prominent anti-gambling activist the Reverend Tim Costello thinks Mr Rudd is deadly serious about addressing the issue. 'Rudd has shown he is moving on a number of issues, such as binge drinking, and I think pokies are next on the list,' Costello says.

Rudd himself has commented that he thinks pokie machines are 'wrong'. 'I don't want to promise the world', he has said, 'but I know we have a problem.'

A late-night walk through **Star City Casino** (p91) at Pyrmont is a salutary experience – the sheer number of bodies relentlessly feeding the slot machines is truly alarming. The Australian Bureau of Statistics reports that 21 per cent of the world's poker machines

operate in Australia and 70 per cent of problem gambling is associated with poker machines.

In Australia alone, there are 333,000 problem gamblers, spending an average of $12,000 a year. Sydney's only casino, Star City, sparked controversy early in 2008 with plans to build a $3.9 million outdoor gaming area. The proposed alfresco leisure zone will contain 130 poker machines – and reportedly be targeted at young people, aged 18-35.

But it seems that Rudd might be able to count on celebrities with a conscience to help him out in his battle. Actor Russell Crowe and businessman Peter Holmes à Court are the co-owners of the South Sydney football club, and the pair are putting forward a radical proposal of their own.

The duo have gone on record as saying that they want to get rid of their club's 160 poker machines. 'It's an incredible social cost when you're in an area like we are in Redfern, which is trying to transform itself' Holmes à Court has said.'It's just not appropriate for us to be supporting gambling.'

The very glitzy Harbourside shopping centre on the Pyrmont side of Darling Harbour has been refurbished and now offers a slick fresh food precinct and food court. The shops, including a good clutch selling Australian products, are open until 9pm daily with the aim of attracting as many tourists as possible in to the centre at the end of a day's sightseeing – but don't expect too many discounts or bargains. The new entertainment floor includes a 20-lane Kingpin Bowling Lounge (www.king-pinbowling. com.au) and Australia's first Boeing 737-800 flight simulator, the Flight Experience (www.flight experience.com.au). Shoppers get two hours' free parking if they spend $40 at any of the shops in the centre.

## Nightlife

### Cargo Bar

*52-60 The Promenade, King Street Wharf, Darling Harbour (9262 1777/ www.cargobar.com.au). CityRail Wynyard/ ferry Darling Harbour/ Monorail Darling Park.* **Open** *Bar* 11am-late daily. *DJs* 6pm-late Thur-Sun. **Map** p85 B2 ⑱
Cargo works hard to earn its cred. It may not attract the coolest crowd by any means, but it does boast some impressive views out overlooking the water. It's a bar most of the time, with DJs shifting it into club mode towards the end of the week. Also hosts the occasional band night, usually taking place on a Sunday.

### Home

*Cockle Bay Wharf, Darling Harbour (9266 0600/www.homesydney.com). CityRail Town Hall/Monorail Darling Park/ferry Darling Harbour.* **Open** *Bar* 11am-late daily. *Club* 11pm-7am Fri; 11pm-6.30am Sat. **Admission** *Club* $25 Fri, Sat. No credit cards. **Map** p85 B3 ⑲
Home is one of Sydney's few old-school large-scale clubbing experiences. It sprawls over three levels and four bars, and includes chillout areas, space-age lighting and a great view over Darling Harbour. Sublime on Friday night

spills over with everything from house to trance to drum 'n' bass and throws its finger at critics by remaining the longest running club night in the city. Future Music's Famous rocks up on Saturday, and the club also hosts the self-explanatory Homesexual.

### Sydney Entertainment Centre

*35 Harbour Street, between Hay & Pier Streets, Darling Harbour (admin 9320 4200/www.sydentcent.com.au). CityRail Central or Town Hall /Monorail/ LightRail Paddy's Markets.* **Admission** prices vary. **Map** p85 B4-C4 ⑳
This 12,500-seater complex in Darling Harbour presents more A-list acts than any other. Built in 1983, it's a typical aircraft hangar that can accommodate crowds easily and safely and is conve-nient for transport and accommoda-tion. Like most venues this size, though, it falls short on atmosphere, with heavy-handed security. Beyoncé, Bob Dylan, the Cure and the like play to packed houses.

## Arts & leisure

### Capitol Theatre

*13 Campbell Street, between Pitt & George Streets, Haymarket (box office 1300 136166/admin 9320 5000/ www.capitoltheatre.com.au). CityRail Central/LightRail Capitol Square. Box office 9am-5pm Mon-Fri.* **Admission** $45-$112.90. Production prices vary. **Map** p85 C4 ㉑
Completed in 1893, the interior of the Capitol (originally known as the Hippodrome) was designed by an American theatre specialist to create the illusion of sitting outdoors under stars. Sadly though, like most illusions, it generally fails. Once reduced to being a seedy oversized porn cinema and subsequently left practically derelict for years, the Capitol was expensively and extensively restored just as the fashion for gargantuan long-running musicals was at its peak. It's deeply kitsch and at the time of writing seems to be the perfect venue for *Billy Elliot The Musical.*

## Ian Thorpe Aquatic Centre

NEW *458 Harris Street, Ultimo (9518 7220/www.itac.org.au). CityRail Central/LightRail Convention/Monorail Convention.* **Open** 6am-9pm Mon-Fri (gym till 10pm); 6am-8pm Sat, Sun. **Admission** *All facilities* $16; $8.50 reductions. *Pool only* $6; $3.70-$4.40 reductions. **Map** p85 B4 ㉒

This $40-million facility, opened at the end of 2007, has provided the residents of Ultimo with a truly fantastic sports centre. There are three indoor pools – one of them Olympic-sized – alongside a range of aquatic education services, a spin and fitness studio with classes galore, a steam room, sauna and a separate spa. There's also parking on site, and the whole thing is housed in a fabulous Harry Seidler-designed white, wave-like building.

## IMAX Sydney

*31 Wheat Road, southern end of Darling Harbour (9281 3300/ www.imax.com.au). CityRail Town Hall/ferry Darling Harbour/Monorail or LightRail Convention.* **Admission** $25-$18; $13-$21 reductions. **Map** p85 B3 ㉓

The giant, eye-shaped IMAX theatre sticks out on the water in touristy Darling Harbour. The 540-seat theatre claims to have the world's largest screen – some eight storeys high – and screens around 12 films a day from 10am to 10pm. Expect a mixed bag of 2D and 3D affairs, with documentaries a common feature. Hardly essential viewing, although the sheer impact of seeing a 3D film makes it a worthy stop for the uninitiated.

## Lyric Theatre

*Star City Casino, 80 Pyrmont Street, between Jones Bay Road & Union Street, Pyrmont (9777 9000/bookings 1300 795 267/www.starcity.com.au). LightRail Star City/ferry Darling Harbour/bus 443.* **Admission** prices vary. **Map** p85 A2 ㉔

Designed for Lloyd-Webber musicals and the like, the Lyric is a modern, state of the art theatre that, like the Capitol, is generally home to Sydney's big-budget musicals.

## Reading Cinemas

*Market City, 9-13 Hay Street, entrance on Thomas Street, Haymarket (9280 1202/www.readingcinemas.com.au). CityRail Central/LightRail or Monorail Paddy's Markets. Screens 5.* **Admission** $15.50; $9-$12.50 reductions; $9 Tue. **Map** p85 C4 ㉕

A youngish pup in the local market, the Reading's five screens are directly above Paddy's Market in Chinatown. Appropriately enough, the listings favour Asian movies which are shown in Cantonese with English subtitles. All screens have Dolby digital sound.

## Star City Casino

*80 Pyrmont Street, at Foreshore Road, Pyrmont (9777 9000/www.starcity. com.au). LightRail Star City/Monorail Harbourside/bus 443, 449.* **Open** 24hrs daily. **Admission** free. **Map** p85 A2 ㉖

It's easy to get lost at this huge casino – although that's probably a deliberate ruse to keep you gambling. Opened in 1997, Star City is both slick and tacky – marble toilets, cocktails, Champagne, fine dining, alongside fish and chips, beer and miles of pokies. There are 1,500 slot machines, a huge sports betting lounge and bar, and some 200 gaming tables featuring everything from blackjack to roulette. Elsewhere are invitation-only private gaming rooms for the high-rollers, many of whom fly in from Asia. The Astral restaurant offers great views alongside its French food, and the revamped deluxe hotel, with its impressive spa, means you don't even have to leave (see also box p89).

## Star Theatre

*Star City Casino, 80 Pyrmont Street, between Jones Bay Road & Union Street, Pyrmont (9777 9000/booking 1300 795 267/www.starcity.com.au). LightRail Star City/ferry Darling Harbour/bus 443.* **Admission** prices vary. **Map** p85 A2 ㉗

It's big, it's brassy but at least you get bar service during the entertainment. Star City's 950-seat, cabaret-style room recreates some of the tackiness of Las Vegas in the heart of Sydney.

**SYDNEY BY AREA**

Darlinghurst Road

# Kings Cross to Potts Point

Kings Cross, starting at the top of **William Street** under the neon Coca-Cola sign and stretching west along **Darlinghurst Road**, has long been Sydney's sex district and home to a seedier, more edgy, some would say bohemian, lifestyle. That aura still pervades although heavy policing and a genuine local love for the noise and tackiness of the Cross strip means that any danger for tourists is more perceived than real. Sex is a licensed industry here and very much a part of life in the Cross. But there's a lot more as well. At night this place buzzes with all kinds of life and a mass of clubs, bars and massage joints. By day it's just like any other suburb with its coffee shops and bakeries. Backpackers tend to flock to the Cross – if you're one of their number, choose your lodging carefully as some places are well past their sell-by date.

Carry on past the **Alamein Fountain** and Darlinghurst Road becomes **Macleay Street**. The architecture suddenly becomes more elegant – a mix of art deco mansion blocks and Victorian houses. This is **Potts Point** and fast becoming one of Sydney's more chic suburbs. Turn right into **Greenknowe Avenue** and it gets even more swish. **Elizabeth Bay** is home to some of the city's most impressive deco houses and blocks and water views to boot.

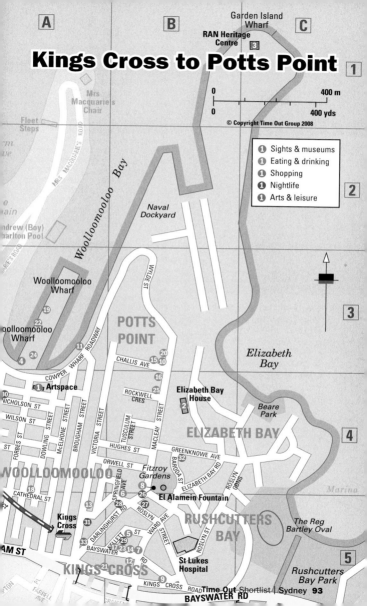

# Kings Cross to Potts Point

Garden Island Wharf

RAN Heritage Centre **3**

0        400 m

0        400 yds

© Copyright Time Out Group 2008

- **1** Sights & museums
- **1** Eating & drinking
- **1** Shopping
- **1** Nightlife
- **1** Arts & leisure

Mrs Macquaries Chair

Fleet Steps

Woolloomooloo Bay

Naval Dockyard

Woolloomooloo Wharf

ndrew (Boy) harlton Pool

**19**

**22**
oolloomooloo Wharf

**4** **24**

**11**

POTTS POINT

WHOLE ST

CHALLIS AVE

**20**
**15** **10**

ROADWAY

COWPER WHARF

**1** Artspace

**30**

NICHOLSON ST

WILSON ST

FORBES ST

ST

McELHONE STREET

DOWLING STREET

BROUGHAM STREET

VICTORIA STREET

ROCKWELL CRES

TUSCULUM STREET

MACLEAY STREET

**16**

**25**

Elizabeth Bay House
**2**

Elizabeth Bay

Beare Park

**ELIZABETH BAY**

HUGHES ST

ORWELL ST

Fitzroy Gardens

SPRINGFIELD AVE

WOOLLOOMOOLOO

**18**

CATHEDRAL ST

Kings Cross

**13**

**31**

DARLINGHURST RD

KELLETT ST

BAYSWATER

**33**

**21**

**KINGS CROSS**

AM ST

**8**

**26**

**27**

El Alamein Fountain

ROSLYN ST

ROSLYN AVE

WARD AVE

ROSLYN STREET

BARODA ST

GREENKNOWE AVE

**32**

ELIZABETH BAY RD

ROSLYN GDNS

Marina

RUSHCUTTERS BAY

The Reg Bartley Oval

**5** **6**
**14**
**23** **29**

**12**

St Lukes Hospital

**9** KINGS CROSS ROAD

BAYSWATER RD

Rushcutters Bay Park

**Elizabeth Bay House**

To the east of Potts Point is **Woolloomooloo Bay** where the Royal Australian Navy's fleet is moored. The area's Aboriginal roots are celebrated in several colourful murals, although it doesn't have the best reputation for safety so wander with care. Jutting into the bay is **Woolloomooloo Wharf** (or Cowper Wharf), built in 1910 as a wool and cargo handling facility and now converted into a hotel, apartments and a boardwalk of superbly appointed eateries.

## Sights & museums

### Artspace

*The Gunnery, 43-51 Cowper Wharf Road, Woolloomooloo (9356 0555/ www.artspace.org.au). CityRail Kings Cross then 10min walk/bus 311.* **Open** 11am-5pm Tue-Sat. **Admission** free. **Map** p93 A4 ❶
This government-funded modern art gallery presents edgy, experimental and challenging work. There are five galleries and 12 studios (for local and international artists) housed in the historic Gunnery building.

### Elizabeth Bay House

*7 Onslow Avenue, Elizabeth Bay (9356 3022/www.hht.net.au). CityRail Kings Cross/bus 311, 312.* **Open** 9.30am-4pm Fri-Sun. **Admission** $8; $4 reductions. **Map** p93 B4 ❷
No expense was spared on this handsome Greek Revival villa, designed by John Verge for NSW colonial secretary Alexander Macleay in 1839. Over the years the grand old house was vandalised, partly demolished and finally divided into 15 studio flats. The gardens have long since gone to property developers, but the house still breathes noblesse, wealth and good taste.

### Royal Australian Navy Heritage Centre

*Garden Island (9359 2003/www.navy. gov.au/ranhc). Ferry Garden Island.* **Open** 9.30am-3.30pm daily. **Admission** free. *Exhibition Gallery* $5; children free. **Map** p93 C1 ❸
For close on a century, Garden Island, home to the Royal Australian Navy, has been strictly off-limits to the general public. In late 2005, the very tip of the one-time island was reopened, with the only access via a five-minute ferry ride from Circular Quay. The view from the former Main Signal Building is spectacular and the Heritage Centre includes a range of items providing insight into Navy life.

## Eating & drinking

### Aki's

*1 Woolloomooloo Wharf, Cowper Wharf Road, Woolloomooloo (9332 4600/www.akisindian.com.au). CityRail Kings Cross then 10min walk/bus 311.* **Open** noon-3pm, 6-10pm Mon-Fri, Sun; 6-10pm Sat. **$$$**. Licensed. **Indian**. **Map** p93 A3 ❹
Sydney's Indian dining scene doesn't have the sophistication of London's but it does have Sydney Harbour, as seen from Aki's. Enjoy artfully presented

(mostly Southern) Indian food as waves lap at the edge of the wharf.

## Aperitif

*7 Kellett Street, Kings Cross (9357 4729). CityRail Kings Cross.* **Open** 5.30pm-3am Mon, Wed-Sat; 5.30pm-midnight Sun. **Bar. Map** p93 B5 **5**

With a courtyard set under a massive old fig tree and dotted with rickety tables lit by candles, this is balmy Sydney summer sipping at its best. Ex-MG Garage sommelier Charles Leong tends the bar, doing a mean trade in wonderful aperitifs such as Amer Picon.

## Bay Bua

*Ground Floor, 2 Springfield Avenue, Potts Point (9358 3234/ www.baybua.com.au).* **Open** 5.30-10.30pm Mon-Thur; 5.30-11pm Fri-Sun. **$$.** Licensed. **Vietnamese. Map** p93 B5 **6**

Affordable fine dining from Sydney restaurateur Mai Tran is on offer at Bay Bua. Try the delectable boneless chicken stuffed with pork and sweet little rice cakes topped with pork mince.

## Bayswater Brasserie

*32 Bayswater Road, Kings Cross (9357 2177/www.bayswaterbrasserie.com.au). CityRail Kings Cross.* **Open** 5pm-late Mon-Thur; noon-late Fri; 5-10pm Sun. **$$$.** Licensed. **Mod Oz. Map** p93 B5 **7**

In the 1980s, the Bayz was better known as 'the Office'. And while the zenith of the expense-accounts days may have passed, the Harry's-esque bar at the back still retains a whiff of that three-o'clock-be-damned spirit, staffed by informed bartenders and stocked with a notable selection of tequilas. Enjoy great oysters and other French brasserie classics in the restaurant at the front or opt for luxe bar snacks – foie gras on toast, say – at the back.

## Bourbon

*24 Darlinghurst Road, at Macleay Street, Kings Cross (9358 1144/ www.thebourbon.com.au). CityRail Kings Cross.* **Open** 10am-6am Mon-Fri; 9am-6am Sat, Sun. Licensed. **Pub. Map** p93 B4 **8**

The Bourbon & Beefsteak opened in the 1960s to cater to the tastes of visiting US sailors. It remains very broad in the scope of drinkers it attracts, and is a fine last resort for any night in the Cross.

## Café Hernandez

*60 Kings Cross Road, between Ward Avenue & Roslyn Street, Kings Cross (9331 2343/ www.cafehernandez.com.au). CityRail Kings Cross.* **Open** 24hrs daily. Unlicensed. **Café. Map** p93 B5 **9**

A favourite among Sydney's devoted band of strong coffee drinkers, this Spanish-inflected, 24-hour establishment just off the Kings Cross strip is one of the few places where you'll find non-alcoholic entertainment after the witching hour.

## Fratelli Paradiso

*12-16 Challis Avenue, at Macleay Street, Potts Point (9357 1744). CityRail Kings Cross.* **Open** 7am-11pm Mon-Fri; 7am-5pm Sat, Sun. **$$$.** Licensed. **Italian. Map** p93 B3 **10**

It's an all-Italian menu and an all-Italian wine list at the Paradiso. When this busy restaurant overflows with punters, the waiter will stand out front and recite the menu to the waiting throng.

## Harry's Café de Wheels

*Cowper Wharf Road, opposite Brougham Street, Woolloomooloo (9357 3074/www.harryscafe dewheels.com.au). CityRail Kings Cross/bus 222, 311.* **Open** 8.30am-2am Mon-Thur; 8.30am-4am Fri; 9am-4am Sat; 9am-12.30am Sun. Unlicensed. **Café. Map** p93 A3 **11**

This famous and historic snack van is a true Sydney institution. Harry's has been supplying late-night meat pies with gravy, mash and mushy peas to a succession of devoted locals, curious tourists, sailors, peckish cabbies, A-list celebrities and drunks for more than 50 years. See also box p98.

**SYDNEY BY AREA**

## Hugo's Lounge

*Level 1, 33 Bayswater Road, between Ward Avenue & Kellett Street, Kings Cross (9357 4411/www.hugos.com.au). CityRail Kings Cross.* **Open** 7pm-3am Thur-Sat; 8pm-3am Sun. Licensed. **Bar/pizza**. Map p93 B5 ⑫

Most people come to Hugo's for the drinks such as the peerless fresh mango daiquiris. Downstairs is Hugo's separate pizza and pasta restaurant.

## jimmy liks

*186-188 Victoria Street, Potts Point (8354 1400/ www.jimmyliks.com). CityRail Kings Cross.* **Open** 5-11pm daily. **$$$**. Licensed. **South-east Asian**. Map p93 A5 ⑬

jimmy liks has had its fair share of dissatisfied customers in the past but its full-flavoured South-east Asian street food is beyond reproach. The mussaman curry of veal shank with peanut betel leaf is inspired.

## Lincoln

*36 Bayswater Road, Kings Cross (9331 2311/www.thelincoln.com.au). CityRail Kings Cross.* **Open** 6pm-midnight Wed; 6pm-3am Thur; 5pm-3am Fri; 6pm-3am Sat; 4pm-midnight Sun. **Bar**. Map p93 B5 ⑭

Take a classic cocktail, give it a twist and you have an inspired drink, Lincoln-style. It also does a beaut line in bar snacks.

## Lotus

*22 Challis Avenue, at Macleay Street, Potts Point (9326 9000/www.merivale. com). CityRail Kings Cross.* **Open** 6-10.30pm Tue-Sat. **$$$**. Licensed. **Mod Oz**. Map p93 B3 ⑮

The cocktails at Lotus are the stuff of legend but Lauren Murdoch's smart Mod Oz menu is reason to stay the course. Check out the Florence Broadhurst wallpaper lining the bar.

## Macleay Street Bistro

*73 Macleay Street, at Challis Avenue, Potts Point (9358 4891). CityRail Kings Cross.* **Open** 6-11pm daily. **$$$**. BYO. **Mod Oz**. Map p93 B4 ⑯

It's the bistro to the stars – actor David Wenham's been spotted here along with plenty of other A-listers. Sit outside if it's a nice evening and order the spatchcock with pea ragu.

## Melt Bar

*Level 3, 12 Kellett Street, at Bayswater Road, Kings Cross (9380 6060/ www.meltbar.com). CityRail Kings Cross.* **Open** 8pm-late Thur-Sat; 9pm-late Sun. **Bar**. Map p93 B5 ⑰

The Melt Bar's walls are covered in murals, the lighting is virtually non-existent, tatty couches and milk crates make up the furnishings and DJs mix together some cool tunes.

## Old Fitzroy Hotel

*129 Dowling Street, at Cathedral Street, Woolloomooloo (9356 3848/ www.oldfitzroy.com.au). CityRail Kings Cross/bus 200.* **Open** 11am-midnight Mon-Fri; noon-midnight Sat; 3-10pm Sun. No credit cards. **Pub/South-east Asian**. Map p93 A4 ⑱

Even without the cheap Asian noodle soups, this pub has a rollicking charm all too rare for this neck of the woods.

## Otto

*8 Woolloomooloo Wharf, Cowper Wharf Road, Woolloomooloo (9368 7488/ www.otto.net.au). CityRail Kings Cross then 10min walk/bus 311.* **Open** noon-3pm, 6pm-late daily. **$$$$**. Licensed. **Italian**. Map p93 A3 ⑲

If you can fight your way through the air-kissing and attract the attention of the charming but wildly inconsistent waiters, you might be in for some outstanding *cucina moderna*. Or you might not – it's that sort of place.

## Oy

*71A Macleay Street, at Challis Avenue, Potts Point (9361 4498). CityRail Kings Cross.* **Open** noon-3pm, 6pm-late Tue-Sun. **$$**. Licensed. **Thai**. Map p93 B3 ⑳

This blink-and-you-miss-it diner is a relative of Sailor's Thai (p74) and does dishes like pad thai and caramelised pork hock, but also such exotica as braised squid and pork with flat rice noodles and gravy and a great sweet but sour chicken curry topped with crisp noodles.

## Penny's Lane

**NEW** *Corner of Penny's Lane & Kings Cross Road, Darlinghurst (9356 8177/ www.pennyslane.com.au).* CityRail Kings Cross. **Open** 7am-3pm, 6-10pm daily. **$$**. Licensed. **Italian**. **Map** p93 B5 ㉑

Simple, pared-back bistro fare in the heart of the Cross. The confit chicken leg with cavolo nero is perfectly executed and the wine list is well priced.

## Salon Blanc

**NEW** *2-6 Cowper Wharf Road, Woolloomooloo (9356 2222/www.salon blanc.com.au).* CityRail Kings Cross then 10min walk/bus 311. **Open** noon-3pm, 6-11pm Mon-Sat; noon-4pm, 6-9pm Sun. **$$$**. Licensed. **Mod Oz**. **Map** p93 A3 ㉒

This newcomer to the Woolly eating strip has become a favourite with the it-crowd. It blends French, Spanish and Italian flourishes with fresh Australian produce. Try the yabbi ravioli with caramelised figs.

## Uliveto

*33 Bayswater Road, between Kellett Street & Ward Avenue, Kings Cross (9357 7331).* CityRail Kings Cross. **Open** 7am-5pm Mon-Sat; 8am-5pm Sun. BYO. No credit cards. **Café**. **Map** p93 B5 ㉓

Uliveto occupies a nice slice of Bayswater Road between a gym and a strip club. In addition to fine breakfast staples it does a wonderful heart-starter smoothie that's ideal if you're feeling a little dented after a hard night out in the Cross.

## Water Bar @ Blue

*Blue, Woolloomooloo Wharf, 6 Cowper Bay Road, opposite Forbes Street, Woolloomooloo (9331 9000).* CityRail Kings Cross then 10min walk/bus 311. **Open** 4-10pm Mon, Sun; 4pm-midnight Tue-Sat. **Bar**. **Map** p93 A3 ㉔

A trendy dark hangout in Blue hotel. Talk to the bartenders and let them show you what they can do.

## Zinc

*Corner of Macleay Street & Rockwall Crescent, Potts Point (9358 6777).*

**Bayswater Brasserie p95**

CityRail Kings Cross. **Open** 7am-4pm Mon; 7am-4pm, 6.30-10pm Tue-Sat; 8am-4pm Sun. Licensed/BYO. **Café**. **Map** p93 B4 ㉕

Perhaps Zinc's popularity with the beautiful people is connected to the prominent role that mirrors play in its design. Or maybe it's just that the city's lovelies have a taste for just-squeezed blood orange juice, good coffee and lovely, fresh Italianate salads.

# Nightlife

## Bourbon

*24 Darlinghurst Road, at Macleay Street, Kings Cross (9358 1144/ www.thebourbon.com.au).* CityRail Kings Cross. **Open** 10pm-6am Fri-Sun. **Admission** $15. **Map** p93 B5 ㉖

There's something a little sad about the sleaze of Sydney giving way to the schmooze of style. The old Bourbon & Beefsteak, once the rowdy headquarters of sailors on shore leave, is now simply the Bourbon, and has been transformed into a slick outfit

# Sydney's other famous Harry

SYDNEY BY AREA

Architect Harry Seidler may be synonymous with Sydney and its stylish skyscape but he isn't the only famous Harry in town. Harry 'Tiger' Edwards may have started from humble origins, pushing a food cart through Sydney's streets back in the 1930s, but these days he's a local legend. Harry's business continues to thrive, his original cart is proudly displayed at the Powerhouse Museum (p86) and his many devotees over the years have included Frank Sinatra, Elton John and Olivia Newton-John.

And perhaps that's the key to understanding the pull of this historic takeaway cart, now permanently nestled on Cowper Wharf Road in Woolloomooloo (p95). It draws together all ages and classes for that single human need to comfort eat at the end of the night. Since 1938, politicians and coppers have stood shoulder to shoulder with sailors and soldiers, cabbies and bookies,

all queueing for the famous pie 'n' pea floaters or the classic mushy pea and potato pasty.

The original Harry's first van was actually an old army ambulance. In 1945, he swapped it for a caravan (the exhibit that is now on display at the museum).

It was a post-war council ruling that carts must move at least 30 centimetres (12 inches) a day and Harry's has had to move several times in the past 55 years. Many customers hail from the nearby Garden Island Naval Dockyard, even though Harry was once a thorn in the Navy's side, his punters blocking the yard gates.

The current cart is owned by Michael Hannah, with the pies made at Hannah's Pies in Ultimo.

A piping hot pie, a mound of mash, a bag brimming with gravy and a plastic fork – and all in the best late-night company that Sydney has to offer.

with its own club, the Cross. Leather ottomans seat a sleek clientele, there to groove on R&B and relaxed sexy house on Sundays.

### Lady Lux
*2 Roslyn Street, between Darlinghurst Road & Ward Avenue, Kings Cross (9361 5000/www.ladylux.com.au). CityRail Kings Cross.* **Open** 10pm-5am Fri, Sat; 10pm-6am Sun. **Admission** $20. No credit cards. **Map** p93 B5 ㉗
Lady Lux runs the gamut of what's happening in Sydney, aimed squarely at the MySpace crowd. Friday nights are Bread and Butter deep house favourites. Dark lighting, bordello-style wallpaper and leather seating all keep it warm, funky and intimate.

### Moulin Rouge
*39 Darlinghurst Road, at Springfield Avenue, Kings Cross (8354 1711/ www.moulinrougesydney.com.au). CityRail Kings Cross.* **Open** 10pm-6am Fri, Sat; 9.30pm-6am Sun. **Admission** $10-$20. **Map** p93 B5 ㉘
The look is gaudy and red. It's a bit like having a nightclub with a cabaret edge in your lounge, where you can drink absinthe while listening to laidback funky breaks and disco.

### Sapphire Suite
*2 Kellet Street, Kings Cross (9331 0058/www.sapphiresuite.com.au). CityRail Kings Cross.* **Open** 8pm-6am Thur-Sun. **Admission** after 9pm Fri-Sun $15. **Map** p93 B5 ㉙
In a vain attempt to bring a touch of Tank-style glamour to the Cross, Sapphire's interior designers have gone all-out with a sapphire-inspired rock wall behind the long bar, with water trickling down its crevices. Acid jazz on Saturday and retro funk on Sunday. Arrive early on Thursday and Friday for complimentary champagne.

### Tilbury Hotel
*12-18 Nicholson Street, Woolloomooloo (9368 1955). CityRail Kings Cross then 10min walk/bus 222, 311.* **Open** 8am-11.45pm Mon-Fri; 9am-11.45pm Sat; 10am-9.45pm Sun. **Admission** free. **Map** p93 A4 ㉚

Come on a Sunday afternoon and evening, and you'll find the upstairs bar at the Tilbury swarming with a very fashionable crowd of gay men. The best place to soak it all up is on the outdoor veranda.

### Yu at Soho Bar
*Soho Bar, 171 Victoria Street, between Darlinghurst Road & Orwell Street, Potts Point (9358 6511/ www.yu.com.au). CityRail Kings Cross.* **Open** *Bar* 10am-4am Mon-Thur, Sun; 10am-6am Fri, Sat. **Admission** $10-$20. **Map** p93 A5 ㉛
Friday nights attract the shiny young set at Fight Night, while Saturday brings a Trashbags night, often with international DJs. Prince Harry caused a stir when he dropped in during a trip to Sydney a few years back.

## Arts & leisure

### Darlinghurst Theatre
*19 Greenknowe Avenue, at Baroda Street, Elizabeth Bay (8356 9987/ www.darlinghursttheatre.com). CityRail Kings Cross/bus 311, 312.* **Admission** $35; $30 reductions. **Map** p93 B4 ㉜
The 111-seat Darlo is located on the edge of Kings Cross, and has comfortable, individually sponsored seats and excellent sight lines. The theatre co-produces a variety of new work and updated classics in collaboration with a range of local and touring companies. One of Sydney's best-value theatres, with a happily eclectic programme.

### Ginseng Bathhouse
*1st Floor, Crest Hotel, 111 Darlinghurst Road, off Victoria Street, Kings Cross (9356 6680/www.ginseng bathhouse.com.au). CityRail Kings Cross.* **Open** 9.30am-9pm Mon-Fri; 9am-9pm Sat, Sun. **Admission** varies according to treatment. **Map** p93 A5 ㉝
This traditional Korean bathhouse is a sanctuary for foot-sore, weary tourists, offering relaxing steam treatments, restorative ginseng baths, reviving scrubs and masterly massage. There are separate baths for men and women.

**Oxford Street**

# Darlinghurst to Surry Hills

Urbanites who seek out Sydney's gritty, arty edge – it does have one lurking beneath all that outdoor glamour – gravitate to east Sydney, on the edge of the city, Darlinghust ('Darlo') and the super-creative Surry Hills. It is here that you'll find the one-off fashion stores, the tattoo parlours and piercing joints, the more quirky art galleries and design spaces, the uber-cool bars and restaurants and a melee of Sydney tribes.

The main strips in Darlinghurst are **Victoria Street** for its busy cafés – many with pavement tables or courtyards at the back – and **Oxford Street**, which is the centre of gay Sydney. In Surry Hills,

**Crown Street** has some great pubs, restaurants, cocktail bars and shops, while the more recent **St Margaret's Development** on **Bourke Street** is developing into a chic haven for cashed-up dinks and singletons. Some of the best restaurants are on **Stanley Street** and **Liverpool Street**.

## Sights & museums

### Brett Whiteley Studio

*2 Raper Street, off Davies Street, Surry Hills (9225 1740/recorded info 9225 1790/1800 679 278/www.brett whiteley.org). CityRail Central then 10min walk/bus 301, 302, 303, 352.* **Open** 10am-4pm Sat, Sun. **Admission** free. **Map** p101 B5 ❶

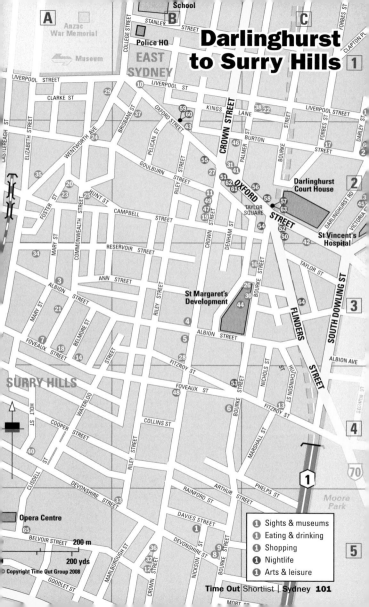

**A**

Anzac
War Memorial

Museum

**B** School

STANLEY STREET

Police HQ

**C**

CLAPTON PL

FORBES ST

EAST
SYDNEY

COLLEGE STREET

LIVERPOOL STREET

CLARKE ST 29

10 LIVERPOOL ST

KINGS LANE 38 22

LIVERPOOL STREET

37

BRISBANE ST

OXFORD STREET 59 60 43

BURTON STREET

FORBES ST

DARLEY ST

**2**

6

WENTWORTH AVE

24

PELICAN STREET

55

46 PALMER

BOURKE STREET

17

ELIZABETH STREET

LAS LEREAGH ST

35

GOULBURN STREET

RILEY STREET

31 41

OXFORD

51
61 56

CROWN STREET

STREET

57

Darlinghurst
Court House

45

DARLINGHURST RD

VICTORIA S

20

HUNT ST

25

11

49
47
19

TAYLOR
SQUARE

63

STREET 58

62

52
50

54

St Vincent's
Hospital

FOSTER

23

CAMPBELL STREET

DENHAM ST

42

MARY ST

COMMONWEALTH ST

RESERVOIR STREET

CROWN ST

TAYLOR ST

**3**

34

ANN STREET

16

SOUTH DOWLING ST

3

ALBION

RILEY STREET

St Margaret's
Development

26
30

BOURKE ST

44

64

FLINDERS

ALBION AVE

21

BELMORE ST

4

5

ALBION STREET

BECKNOW ST

7

FOVEAUX STREET

18

14

FITZROY ST

23

STREET

**70**

MARY ST

FOVEAUX ST

48

NICHOLS ST

HUTCHINSON ST

53

6

BOURKE ST

13

FITZROY ST

SURRY HILLS

WATERLOO ST

COLLINS ST

RILEY STREET

MARSHALL ST

**4**

40

COOPER STREET

HOLT ST

DEVONSHIRE STREET

RAINFORD ST

ARTHUR STREET

PHELPS ST

**1**

Moore
Park

33

DAVIES STREET

CLISDELL ST

Opera Centre

200 m

BELVOIR STREET

200 yds

65

MARLBOROUGH ST

36

32
12

DEVONSHIRE ST

NICKSON ST

9
8

BOURKE STREET

CROWN STREET

**5**

© Copyright Time Out Group 2008

GOODLET ST

MORT ST

**1** Sights & museums

**1** Eating & drinking

**1** Shopping

**1** Nightlife

**1** Arts & leisure

Brett Whiteley was one of Australia's most exciting artists. In 1985, he bought a warehouse in Surry Hills and converted it into a studio, art gallery and living space. Following Whiteley's death in 1992, the studio was turned into a museum.

## Sydney Jewish Museum

*148 Darlinghurst Road, at Burton Street, Darlinghurst (9360 7999/ www.sydneyjewishmuseum.com.au). CityRail Kings Cross/bus 311, 378, 380, 389.* **Open** 10am-4pm Mon-Thur, Sun; 10am-2pm Fri. **Admission** $10; $6-$7 reductions. **Map** p101 C2 ❷

At the end of World War II, over 30,000 survivors of the Holocaust emigrated to Australia, settling mainly in Sydney and Melbourne. This museum, opened in 1992, is a permanent memorial to victims of both world wars.

## Eating & drinking

### Assiette

*48 Albion Street, at Mary Street, Surry Hills (9212 7979/www.restaurant assiette.com.au). CityRail/LightRail Central.* **Open** noon-3pm Fri; 6-10.30pm Tue-Sat. $$$. Licensed. **French**. **Map** p101 A3 ❸

Marco Pierre White-trained chef Warren Turnbull may dabble a little in the dark arts of progressive cuisine, but for the most part it's solid cooking with some lovely French flavours at excellent prices.

### Bentley Restaurant & Bar

*320 Crown Street, Surry Hills (9332 2344/www.thebentley.com.au). Bus 311, 333, 352, 373, 377, 378, 380, 392, 394, 396.* **Open** noon-4pm, 6-11pm Tue-Sat. $$$. Licensed. **Mod Oz/Spanish**. **Map** p101 B3 ❹

This highly popular restaurant in a heritage pub is the smart work of chef Brent Savage and somellier Nick Hildebrandt. Hildebrandt complements Savage's food with wines from an unbelievably comprehensive wine list including plenty available by the glass. The progressive tapas at the Bentley are well worth investigating.

## Billy Kwong

*355 Crown Street, between Albion & Foveaux Streets, Surry Hills (9332 3300). CityRail/LightRail Central then 10min walk/bus 301, 302, 303, 374, 376, 391.* **Open** 6-10pm Mon-Thur; 6-11pm Fri, Sat; 6-9pm Sun. $$$. Licensed/BYO (wine only). **Modern Chinese**. **Map** p101 B3 ❺

Billy Kwong is loud, you can't book, you eat elbow-to-chopstick with other diners on three-legged stools – and it's all utterly fabulous. Celebrity chef Kylie Kwong takes the food of her Cantonese ancestry and sexes it up, keeping the emphasis on freshness, flavour and lightness then adding her own much-lauded twist. The stir-fries rock, kingfish sashimi sings with sweet freshness and simplicity, while the crisp duck with blood plums has a well deserved local following.

## Bistrode

*478 Bourke Street, between Foveaux & Phelps Streets, Surry Hills (9380 7333). Bus 301, 302, 303.* **Open** 6-10.30pm Tue-Thur, Sat; noon-3pm, 6-10.30pm Fri. $$$. Licensed. **European**. **Map** p101 B4 ❻

To some, Jeremy and Jane Strode's food may seem a little simple, but to others, the cooking at Bistrode is real art on a plate. Dishes like fried duck egg served with sourdough crumbs and pine mushrooms work extremely well and are a good example of how three elements on a plate can often work much better than six.

## Bodega

*Shop 1/216 Commonwealth Street, at Foveaux Street, Surry Hills (9212 7766). Bus 301, 302, 303.* **Open** 6pm-late Mon, Tue, Sat; noon-3pm, 6pm-late Wed-Fri. $$. Licensed. **South American**. **Map** p101 A3 ❼

Young and fun, this neo-tapas bar goes from strength to strength, even if it is very loud. Chefs Elvis Abrahanovitz and Ben Millgate are fresh but hardly green, and after a recent trip to South America have come back with a whole new sack of ammo, including skirt steak with chimmichurri.

SYDNEY BY AREA

## Book Kitchen

*255 Devonshire Street, at Bourke
Street, Surry Hills (9310 1003/
www.thebookkitchen.com.au). CityRail/
LightRail Central then 10min walk/bus
301 303, 355.* **Open** 8am-4pm Mon,
Sun; 8am-4pm, 6.45-10pm Wed-Sat.
Licensed/BYO. **Café**. Map p101 B5 ❽

Browse shelves of new, imported and
secondhand food titles at Book Kitchen
while you wait for your excellent hand-
cut chips or home-made baked beans
cooked with ham hock. The ricotta hot
cakes with honey, roasted rhubarb and
caramelised banana are delicious.

## Bourke Street Bakery

*633 Bourke Street, at Devonshire
Street, Surry Hills (9699 1011).
CityRail/LightRail Central then 10min
walk/bus 301, 303, 355.* **Open** 7am-
6pm Mon-Fri; 8am-5pm Sat, Sun.
Unlicensed. No credit cards. **Bakery/
Café**. Map p101 B5 ❾

It's hard to swing a ciabatta at Bourke
Street Bakery, let alone a cat. Yet this
slightly scruffy corner bakery still
finds room to pack shelves with great
chocolate cookies, pork and fennel
sausage rolls, pastries rich with olive,
and all sorts of wonderful bread.

## Burdekin Hotel

*Corner of Oxford & Liverpool
Streets, Darlinghurst (9331 3066/
www.burdekin.com.au). CityRail
Museum/bus 333, 378, 380.* **Open**
4pm-4am Tue-Thur; 4pm-6am Fri;
5pm-6am Sat; 4pm-midnight Sun. **Bar**.
Map p101 B1 ❿

One of the best Sydney bars of the
early 1990s, the Burdekin may have
aged a bit, but it still has great bone
structure. The upstairs rooms offer a
world of dance options at the weekend,
while the ground-floor bar feels like an
upmarket pub. The tiny tiled art deco
Dugout Bar in the basement, with its
speakeasy cred, is the coolest bet.

## Café Lounge

*277 Goulburn Street, Darlinghurst
(9356 8888). CityRail Museum/bus
333, 378, 380.* **Open** 6pm-late Tue-
Thurs, Sat, noon-3pm, 6pm-late Fri.
**Café/Bar**. Map p101 B2 ⓫

Café Lounge, down an alley off Crown
Street, does great breakfasts. It's also
open sufficiently late for drinking the
headier stuff. Strings of fairy lights,
cobbled stones and big benches make
this one of the darlings of the 'Hurst.

## Café Mint

*579 Crown Street, between Devonshire
& Cleveland Streets, Surry Hills (9319
0848/www.cafemint.com.au). CityRail/
LightRail Central then 10min walk/bus
301, 302, 303.* **Open** 7am-4pm Mon,
Sat; 7am-9.30pm Tue, Wed; 7am-10.30pm
Thur, Fri. **$$**. BYO. No credit cards.
**Mediterranean**. Map p101 B5 ⓬

Cool yet inexpensive (and tiny!) caff-
cum-restaurant Café Mint is down the
uncool end of Crown Street. The food
from chef/owner Hugh Foster is great
– spicy lamb with humous – and the
almond and grapefruit frappé is an
exceptional hangover-buster.

## Cricketers Arms

*106 Fitzroy Street, at Hutchinson
Street, Surry Hills (9331 3301).
CityRail Central then 10min walk/bus
339, 374, 376, 391.* **Open** noon-
midnight Mon-Sat; noon-10pm Sun. No
credit cards. **Pub**. Map p101 C4 ⓭

Aside from being one of the finest
places in Sydney to have a beer, the
Cricketers is everything that's good
about Surry Hills in microcosm – it's
well poised between unreconstructed
flavour (read grime and the occasional
thug) and moving with the times (read
decent grub, a good range of beers and
quality music). The beer garden is the
ideal spot in which to mount a late-
afternoon assault on sobriety.

## Cru 54

*54 Foveaux Street, between Belmont
Street & Bellevue Streets, Surry Hills
(9281 1054). Bus 301, 302, 303.*
**Open** noon-late Tue-Fri. Licensed. **$$**.
**Tapas**. Map p101 A3 ⓮

Sit at the bar and order a few tapas-like
roasted almonds or tortilla Española –
wafer-thin slices of potato captured in
a thick set omelette – or the excellent
and moreish *jamon* croquettes. Great
service and interesting wines too.

**Collect p109**

## Darlo Bar

*Corner of Liverpool Street & Darling-hurst Road, Darlinghurst (9331 3672/www.darlobar.com). CityRail Kings Cross/bus 389.* **Open** *10am-midnight Mon-Sat; noon-midnight Sun.* **Bar. Map** p101 C1 ⑮

The Darlo Bar has been a proper local institution for the past decade: in gay friendly Darlinghurst it's distinguished by its reputation for being the number one straight pick-up joint. Sure, there's plenty of boy-boy, girl-girl action to be had over its pool tables, mismatched op-shop furniture and adequate drinks, but the ease with which happy young heteros also hook up here is almost verging on the freakish. The new roof bar is one of the places in Darlo to be.

## Emmilou

**NEW** *413 Bourke Street, Surry Hills (9360 6991/www.emmilou.com.au). Bus 311, 333, 352, 373, 377, 378, 380, 392, 394, 396.* **Open** *noon-3pm, 6pm-1am Tue-Sat.* **$$$** *Licensed.* **Spanish. Map** p101 C3 ⑯

This new offering on Bourke Street serves up a mix of interesting tasting plates, such as white anchovies and chargrilled octopus, and heftier options such as vongole wrapped in shoelaces of ham or veal sweetbreads. Emmilou is a good choice if you're out late and need a little ballast.

## Forbes & Burton

*252 Forbes Street, Darlinghurst (9356 8788). Bus 311, 333, 378, 380, 389.* **Open** *Café 7am-3.30pm Mon-Fri; 8am-3.30pm Sat; 9am-4pm Sun. Restaurant 6.30-10pm Tue-Sat.* **$$$**. *Licensed.* **Café/Restaurant. Map** p101 C2 ⑰

Forbes & Burton's smooth sandstone interior transforms from cool, laidback café by day to stylish restaurant by night. Dave Pegrum's food is pitched just right for east Sydneyites who come to breakfast on the likes of figs, goat's curd and honey on toast, or to enjoy a dinner of such earthy delights as skate and puy lentils. The kitchen also turns out excellent freshly squeezed juices and very decent coffee.

## Foveaux Restaurant + Bar

**NEW** *65-67 Foveaux Street, between
Commonwealth & Belmore Streets,
Surry Hills (9211 0664/www.foveaux.
com.au). Bus 339, 374, 376, 391.*
**Open** 6pm-late Tue-Thur, Sat; noon-
3pm, 6pm-late Fri. **Bar/Restaurant**.
**Map** p101 A3 🔞
Darrell Felstead makes mean snacks
upstairs while, in the dungeon-like
downstairs cocktail bar, Julian Serna
(ex-Hemmesphere) mixes mean drinks
to go with them. The menu constantly
changes as Felstead experiments with
miniature toffee apples, popcorn and
pork in all its guises while maintaining
a baseline of solid cooking.

## Gaslight Inn

*278 Crown Street, between Oxford &
Campbell Streets, Surry Hills (9360
6746). Bus 311, 333, 352, 373, 377,
378, 380, 392, 394, 396.* **Open** noon-
midnight Mon, Tue; noon-1.30am Wed,
Thur; noon-3am Sat; noon-10pm Sun.
No credit cards. **Bar**. **Map** p101 B2 🔞
Prop up the bar downstairs at the
Gaslight Inn for some peace and quiet
and a well poured schooner, or stake a
claim at one of the tables in the upstairs
little-known courtyard.

## Hotel Hollywood

*Corner of Foster & Hunt Streets,
Surry Hills (9281 2765/www.hotel
hollywood.com.au). CityRail Central or
Museum/bus 301, 302.* **Open** 11am-
midnight Mon-Wed; 11am-3am Thur,
Fri; 6pm-3am Sat. No credit cards. **Pub**.
**Map** p101 A2 🔞
This Surry Hills stalwart has outlived,
outshone and outsung half the pubs in
the area all the while maintaining bags
more style and all its original fitouts. It
also does a decent cheese plate.

## Kafa

*224 Commonwealth Street, between
Foveaux & Albion Streets, Surry Hills
(9280 2624). CityRail/LightRail
Central.* **Open** 7am-4pm Mon-Fri.
Unlicensed. No credit cards. **Café**.
**Map** p101 A3 🔞
A single large round table fills the
room, and above it hangs an enormous
chandelier constructed of large bucket-

like… buckets. Just the thing to ponder
while you knock off breakfast treats
from the better-than-average menu.

## Kings Lane Sandwiches

*28 Kings Lane, between Palmer &
Bourke Streets, Darlinghurst (9360
8007). CityRail Museum/bus 311, 373,
377, 378, 380, 392, 394, 396, 399.*
**Open** 8am-2.30pm Mon-Fri; 10am-2pm
Sat. Unlicensed. No credit cards.
**Sandwich bar**. **Map** p101 C1 🔞
A longtime favourite which inevitably
has queues snaking outside at
lunchtime for its gigantic sarnies.

## La Sala

*23 Foster Street, between Hunt &
Campbell Streets, Surry Hills (9281
3352/www.lasala.com.au). CityRail
Central or Museum/LightRail Central.*
**Open** 6-11pm Mon-Wed, Sat; noon-
3pm, 6-11pm Thur, Fri. **$$$**. Licensed.
**Italian**. **Map** p101 A2 🔞
An Italian restaurant with a hint of the
British Isles on its menu in the shape
of bone marrow served with parsley
and caper salad or corned beef brisket.
You'll also find Italian staples such as
risotto and crudités of crisp raw veg
with smooth aïoli on the side.

## Lo Studio

*53-55 Brisbane Street, Surry Hills
(9212 4118/www.lostudio.com.au).
CityRail Central or Museum/LightRail
Central.* **Open** noon-3pm, 6pm-late
Mon-Fri; 6pm-late Sat. **$$$**. Licensed.
**Italian**. **Map** p101 A2 🔞
Surry Hills asked for another Italian,
and Lo it was good: the old Paramount
Studios building is a fittingly deco
home for this paean to chic 1950s Italy.
Think *The Talented Mr Ripley*, only
with better food and cocktails (the
Corleone with fresh nectarine is an
offer you can't refuse).

## Longrain

*85 Commonwealth Street, at Hunt
Street, Surry Hills (9280 2888/
www.longrain.com). CityRail Central or
Museum/LightRail Central.* **Open** noon-
2.30pm, 6-11pm Mon-Fri; 6-11pm Sat;
5.30-10pm Sun. **$$$**. Licensed. **Thai**.
**Map** p101 A2 🔞

The restaurant's hip and gorgeous and so is the crowd sat lined up along its trendy communal tables. Longrain's peanut curry of wagyu beef with chilli and Thai basil is curry gone glam and its much-celebrated dish of betel leaves with prawn, peanuts and pomelo is frequently imitated, seldom bettered. The bar is a must-visit too.

## Lumiere

NEW *Shop 13, 425 Bourke Street, Surry Hills (9331 6184). Bus 311, 333, 373, 377, 378, 380, 392, 394, 396, 397, 399, L94.* **Open** 7.30am-5pm Mon-Fri; 8am-5pm Sat, Sun. Unlicensed. **Café/ Patisserie**. Map p101 B3 26
Sit outside with Sunday brunch aand the papers at this smart joint in the St Margarets development, popular with a cool crowd dressed in designer tees.

## Mad Mex

NEW *Shop 2, 241-247 Crown Street, between Oxford & Crown Streets, Surry Hills (9331 7788/www.madmex. com.au). Bus 311, 333, 352, 373, 377, 378, 380, 392, 394, 396.* **Open** 6-11pm Mon-Thur; 6-11.20pm Fri-Sun. $. Licensed. **Mexican**. Map p101 B2 27
Latching on to the growing love for Mexican in Sydney is this new addition to Crown Street. It's cheap, it's fun, there's a chandelier hanging in the middle of the room made out of empty Corona bottles and they serve great $8 margaritas and hot Mexican faves.

## Marque

*Shop 4/5, 355 Crown Street, between Albion & Foveaux Streets, Surry Hills (9332 2225/www.marquerestaurant. com.au). CityRail/LightRail Central then 10min walk/bus 301, 302, 303, 374, 376, 391.* **Open** 6.30-10.30pm Mon-Sat. $$$$. Licensed/BYO.
**French**. Map p101 B3 28
Chef Mark Best trained with France's finest and now has one eye on the pioneering work of Spain's gastro wizards – yet the food at his quietly luxe restaurant still manages to be both at the bleeding edge and utterly his own. Beetroot tart (almost a *tatin*) with horseradish foam sits cheek by

jowl with sweetbreads, sea urchin roe and samphire on one of the country's most exciting menus.

## Mars Lounge

*16 Wentworth Avenue, between Oxford & Goulburn Streets, Surry Hills (9267 6440/ www.marslounge.com.au). CityRail Museum/bus 333, 378, 380.* **Open** 5pm-midnight Wed, Thur; 5pm-3am Fri; 7pm-3am Sat; 7pm-1am Sun. **Bar**. Map p101 A1 29
Sunday night is the new Saturday. Or at least it is in this neighbourhood. Fed up with Oxford Street being overrun by suburbanites on Fridays and Saturdays, many locals now save much of their partying for Sundays. Foremost among the Sunday-nighters, the dark and spacious red and black Mars Lounge is famed for its mixed crowd and extensive selection of ultra premium vodkas. Food comes courtesy of platters, pizzas and snacks.

## Pizza Mario

*417-421 Bourke Street, Surry Hills (9332 3633/www.pizzamario.com.au). Bus 311, 333, 352, 373, 377, 378, 380, 392, 394, 396.* **Open** 6pm-late daily. $$. Licensed. **Pizza**. Map p101 C3 30
These guys have the Verace Pizza Napoletana stamp of approval – a licence to make pizza (and pretty much everything else Italian) properly, the way it is in the old country. The Pizza Mario kitchen does a killer potato, sea salt and rosemary pizza as well as some excellent antipasti.

## Rambutan

*96 Oxford Street, between Crown & Palmer Streets, Darlinghurst (9360 7772/www.rambutan.com.au). Bus 311, 333, 352, 373, 377, 378, 380, 392, 394, 396.* **Open** 6pm-late daily. $$. Licensed. **Thai**. Map p101 B2 31
Rambutan is quite possibly one of the most promising restaurants to have opened on the Pink Strip in ages. Menu highlights include the wagyu shin with ribbons of wide rice noodles, and tea smoked quail. Make sure you head to the downstairs bar for a cocktail before you hit the nosh pit.

## Red Lantern

*545 Crown Street, between Lansdowne & Cleveland Streets, Surry Hills (9698 4355/www.redlantern.com.au). Bus 301, 302, 303.* **Open** 12.30-3pm, 6.30-10.30pm Tue-Fri; 6.30-10.30pm Sat, Sun. **$$**. Licensed. **Vietnamese**. Map p101 B5 ㉜

The chef might be a white guy, but the combination of his skills and the knowledge and experience of the restaurant's young Vietnamese owners raises Red Lantern above most other purveyors of the cuisine, while the funked-up look and democratic prices give it an uncommon edge.

## Shakespeare

*200 Devonshire Street, at Riley Street, Surry Hills (9319 6883). CityRail Central/LightRail Central.* **Open** 10am-midnight Mon-Sat; noon-10pm Sun. **$**. Licensed. **Oz**. Map p101 B5 ㉝

A notorious pub for actors and journos, the Shakey has sadly lost its beer garden but still does the most excellent $10 lunches and dinners, such as the 400g T-bone or pork ribs. Go on a rainy night for a quiet ale and cheap feed.

## Single Origin

*60-64 Reservoir Street, between Elizabeth & Mary Streets, Surry Hills (9211 0665/www.singleorigin.com.au). CityRail Central/LightRail Central.* **Open** 7am-4pm Mon-Fri. Unlicensed. No credit cards. **Café**. Map p101 A3 ㉞

Suffice it to say that the guys who work the bean down at the Single O are trippers. On caffeine, that is. You might visit for the selection of cakes and muffins, but you stay for the coffee (the beans are roasted in a behemoth machine that they call Boris the Roaster). Coffee fans can choose from a standard flat white or a properly heart-starting ristretto.

## Spice I Am

*90 Wentworth Avenue, between Campbell & Commonwealth Streets, Surry Hills (9280 0928/www.spiceiam.com). CityRail Central or Museum/LightRail Central.* **Open** 11.30am-3.30pm, 6-10pm Tue-Sun. **$$**. BYO. **Thai**. Map p101 A2 ㉟

# Policing the gay beat

Mardi Gras, Sydney's gay night of nights, is all about fun, but in 2008, there was a more sombre item on the agenda. Leading out the parade were Craig Gee and Shane Brennen, victims of a brutal beating at the hands of gay bashers. The couple made headlines following the vicious attack, which happened while they were walking hand-in-hand along Crown Street, in the midst of the gay strip. Gee, 27, suffered a broken leg, fractured jaw and smashed eye socket.

The 2008 Mardi Gras intended to throw a spotlight on such violence. 'While I think it will take some time to break the existing culture at Surry Hills [police station], at least steps are being taken to create a more compassionate and sympathetic culture,' said Gee at the time.

And positive action is being taken. The community, with the help of Sydney's Mayor Clover Moore, has proposed an initiative whereby local businesses display a sticker in their windows encouraging victims of assault to approach them and access support. Trained community workers, known as the Generation Q Street Angels, also patrol the gay beat on Friday and Saturday night. And local police now provide a service where a victim of a hate crime can ask to see a Gay and Lesbian Liaison Officer (GLLO), if they are not comfortable talking to a general police officer.

Spice it certainly is: this unremarkable bolt-hole on, appropriately enough, a fume- and backpacker-laden street, serves the most authentic Thai food in Sydney. If you want to dice with some serious chilli, just ask your waitress to take your order down in Thai. That way the kitchen will do your green mango salad, your mussel and chilli pancakes and sour curries without any concession to local tastes.

## Tabou

*527 Crown Street, between Devonshire & Lansdowne Streets, Surry Hills (9319 5682). Bus 301, 302, 303.* **Open** noon-2.30pm, 6.30-10pm Mon-Fri; 6-10.30pm Sat, Sun. **$$.** Licensed/BYO (wine only Mon-Thur, Sun). **French**. Map p101 B5 ❸

A French bistro with all the trimmings – steak-frites, moules, wooden chairs and long glass mirrors with the menu scribbled elegantly across them.

## Uchi Lounge

*15 Brisbane Street, between Goulburn & Oxford Streets, Surry Hills (9261 3524). CityRail Museum.* **Open** 6.30-11pm Mon-Sat. **$$**. Licensed/BYO (wine only). **Japanese**. Map p101 B1 ❸

Downstairs will get you some edamame or spiced almonds and a sake cocktail, upstairs will get you the likes of lightly seared salmon sushi blocks and aubergine with sweet soy paste topped with parmesan. For dessert you can't look past the green tea and cinnamon crème brûlée.

## Universal

NEW *Republic, 2 Courtyard, Palmer Street, between Burton & Liverpool Streets, Darlinghurst (9331 0709/ www.universalrestaurant.com).* **Open** 6-10pm Mon-Thur, Sat; noon-3pm 6-10pm Fri. **$$**. Licensed. **Mod Oz**. Map p101 C1 ❸

Sydney star chef Christine Manfield is back after a stint in London and she's come out with all guns blazing at this new, small-plates-only establishment. The flavours are big and often Asian-inspired – think jasmine tea-soaked duck and turmeric lemongrass broth.

The crowd is cool, the cocktails potent and the fitout gloriously technicolour.

## Victoria Room

*Level 1, 235 Victoria Street, between Liverpool & William Streets, Darlinghurst (9357 4488/www.thevictoriaroom.com). CityRail Kings Cross.* **Open** 6pm-midnight Tue-Thur; 6pm-2am Fri; 2pm-2am Sat; 1pm-midnight Sun. **Bar/ Restaurant**. Map p101 C2 ❸

Victoria Street goes sexy Victorian with this hip space harking back to the Raj. There's plenty to like by way of the Tom Collinses and old-school, long, tall drinks but no shortage of ginger and vanilla martinis and their ilk, should you decide to travel back to the future. There's also a Mediterranean/ Middle East-inflected restaurant.

## Vini

*3/118 Devonshire Street, at Holt Street, Surry Hills (9698 5131). CityRail Central/LightRail Central.* **Open** noon-midnight Tue-Fri; 5pm-midnight Sat. **Bar/Restaurant**. Map p101 A4 ❹

There's an old shipping container on one side of Vini's miniature space that doubles as its wine bar, or there's the main enoteca – large enough to swing a kitten (just) – which offers an all-Italian wine list and simple, well executed dishes, such as pastas and risottos, to match.

## Shopping

### Aussie Boys

*102 Oxford Street, between Crown & Palmer Streets, Darlinghurst (9360 7011/www.aussieboys.com.au). Bus 352, 378, 380, 333.* **Open** 10am-6pm Mon-Wed, Fri, Sat; 10am-9pm Thur; 11am-5pm Sun. **Map** p101 B2 ④
A fun, friendly and fabulous shop that sells beach towels from the very cute Aussie Boys label, alongside Dolce & Gabbana bathers and Bonds T-shirts. There's also a hair stylist downstairs, making this place pretty much a one-stop shop for all that the smart gay man needs in order to kit himself out before hitting the beach.

**Supper Club p112**

### Bookshop Darlinghurst

*207 Oxford Street, between Flinders & South Dowling Streets, Darlinghurst (9331 1103/www.thebookshop.com.au). Bus 352, 378, 380.* **Open** 10am-10pm Mon-Wed; 10am-11pm Thur; 10am-midnight Fri, Sat; 11am-11pm Sun. **Map** p101 C2 ④
This simply named outlet specialises in gay and lesbian literature and stocks a range of rare imported books, as well as mainstream tomes catering to the hip inner-city crowd.

### Central Station Records

*46A Oxford Street, between Hyde Park & Crown Street, Darlinghurst (9361 5222/www.centralstation.com.au). CityRail Museum/bus 373, 377, 378, 380, 333.* **Open** 10am-6pm Mon-Wed, Fri; 10am-9pm Thur; 10am-6pm Sat; noon-5pm Sun. **Map** p101 B2 ④
Central Station's vast basement shop houses the very latest in import and domestic dance, house, hip hop, R&B and Mardi Gras compilations.

### Collect

*Object Gallery, St Margarets, 417 Bourke Street, Surry Hills (9361 4511/www.object.com.au). Bus 371, 373, 377, 380, 396.* **Open** 11am-6pm Tue-Sun. **Map** p101 B3 ④
Located on the ground floor below the Object Gallery, which showcases the work of Australian designers, this innovative shop sells collectable glass and ceramics and unique Australia-made homewares and jewellery.

### Provedore Pelagios

*235 Victoria Street, between Liverpool & Surrey Streets, Darlinghurst (9360 1011). CityRail Kings Cross/bus 311, 389.* **Open** 9am-8pm Mon-Sat; 10am-7pm Sun. **Map** p101 C2 ④
Established in 1926, this traditional Italian grocer prides itself on its very knowledgeable and enthusiastic staff. The bread is divine and it also does salads, cold cuts, cheeses, organic veg and gourmet pasta. The chocolate counter at the checkout is especially tempting at Easter – but there's plenty to tempt your tastebuds here no matter what time of year you visit.

## Raw by Anthony Nader

*30 Burton Street, Darlinghurst (9380 5370/www.rawhair.com.au). Bus 222, 311, 373, 377, 378, 380, 392, 394, 396, 397, 399.* **Open** 10am-5pm Tue, Wed; 10am-8pm Thur; 10am-9pm Fri; 10am-6pm Sat. **Map** p101 B2 ⓪

There's good reason why the A-list wait in line for Anthony Nader, the founder of this chic salon – Nader is a man who really knows about hair. He specialises in sophisticated, natural styling and the salon is a genuine delight to visit with its chandeliers, dramatic native flora and candelit basement. After this, the barber's will never quite cut it again.

## Route 66

*255-257 Crown Street, at Goulburn Street, Darlinghurst (9331 6686/ www.route66.com.au). Bus 301, 302, 303, 352.* **Open** 10.30am-6pm Mon-Wed, Fri, Sat; 10.30am-8pm Thur; noon-5pm Sun. **Map** p101 B2 ⓪

Route 66 is rockabilly heaven selling a huge range of secondhand Levi's, 1950s chintz frocks and more Hawaiian shirts than you can shake a lei at.

## Surry Hills Market

*Shannon Reserve, Corner of Crown & Forveaux Streets, Surry Hills (9310 2888). CityRail/Light Rail Central.* **Open** 10am-5pm 1st Sat of mth. **Map** p101 B4 ⓪

Surry Hills still boasts the hippest of all of the city's many weekend markets. There's lots to catch the eye in the form of clothes, accessories and good junk. This is also where you'll find retro revivals before anyone else realises they are fashionable.

## Wheels & Doll Baby

*259 Crown Street, at Goulburn Street, Darlinghurst (9361 3286/www.wheels anddollbaby.com). CityRail Museum/bus 373, 374, 377, 378, 380.* **Open** 10am-6pm Mon-Wed, Fri, Sat; 10am-8pm Thur; 11am-5pm Sun. **Map** p101 B2 ⓪

Melanie Greensmith started her vampy fashion label in 1987. Her clothes became synonymous with all things rock when Michael Jackson came in browsing for a customised leather jacket for his Bad tour. Now rockers such as Deborah Harry and the Black Crowes all wear her styles on stage. Greensmith has recently launched two 'baby shops' in LA and London's Harvey Nichols, creating a whole new set of celebrity fans in the shape of Kate Moss and Gwen Stefani.

# Nightlife

## Arq Sydney

*16 Flinders Street, between Oxford & Taylor Streets, Darlinghurst (9380 8700/www.arqsydney.com.au). Bus 311, 333, 352, 373, 377, 378, 380, 392, 394, 396.* **Open** 9pm-late Thur-Sun. **Admission** (after 10pm) $20 Fri; $25 Sat; $5 Sun. No credit cards. **Map** p101 C2 ⓪

Arq is *the* quintessential gay club par excellence. The main action takes place over two levels, with a flesh-friendly vibe about the whole thing. Weekends remain the gay-focused nights, while weekdays tend to be more mixed.

## Colombian Hotel

*117-123 Oxford Street, corner of Oxford & Crown Streets, Darlinghurst (9360 2151). Bus 311, 333, 352, 373, 377, 378, 380, 392, 394, 396.* **Open** 9am-6am daily. **Map** p101 B2 ⓪

Once a Westpac bank, the Colombian has superseded its neighbour the Stonewall Hotel (p112) to become the hottest gay bar-club on Oxford Street. The bar downstairs looks out on to the strip, while upstairs a generally gay (sometimes mixed) crowd jives to whatever is on offer.

## Flinders Hotel

*63 Flinders Street, off Oxford Street, Darlinghurst (9356 3622). Bus 311, 333, 352, 373, 377, 378, 380, 392, 394, 396.* **Open** 2pm-late Mon-Fri; 3pm-late Sat-Sun. **Map** p101 C2 ⓪

The Flinders is great for a quiet bevvy in the afternoon, and hosts a number of different functions for Sydney's gay community in the evenings. It's the home of the Harbour City Bears on Friday nights, and plays host to great monthly lesbian events . There's also a very good restaurant midweek, which sells quality, affordable food.

## Hopetoun Hotel

*416 Bourke Street, at Fitzroy Street, Surry Hills (9361 5257/www.myspace. com/hopetounhotel). Bus 301, 302, 303.* **Open** 2pm-midnight Mon-Sat; noon-10pm Sun. **Admission** $10-$20. No credit cards. **Map** p101 B4 ⑤

The Hopetoun showcases live local talent every week. It's intimate and tends to book Sydney's more leftfield acts. The hotel's basement bar is open throughout the weekend to cater for musos taking an audio break, plus there's an upper level dining area providing lunchtime snacks.

## Middle Bar

*Kinselas Hotel, 383-387 Bourke Street, at Taylor Square, Darlinghurst (9331 3100). Bus 311, 333, 352, 373, 377, 378, 380, 392, 394, 396.* **Open** *Hotel* 9am-6am daily. *Bar* 9pm-4am Fri, Sat. **Map** p101 C2 ⑤

Looking for a more upmarket drinking experience? Middle Bar, located on the upper level of the Kinselas Hotel, may be just the ticket. With an outdoor deck overlooking Taylor Square, it's the place to be on a hot summer night and attracts a dressy crowd encompassing straight, gay and lesbian punters.

## Midnight Shift

*85 Oxford Street, between Riley & Crown Streets, Darlinghurst (9360 4319). CityRail Museum/bus 311, 333, 352, 373, 377, 378, 380, 392, 394, 396.* **Open** *Ground-floor video bar* noon-late Mon-Fri; 2pm-late Sat, Sun. *Top-floor nightclub* 11pm-late Fri, Sat. No credit cards. **Map** p101 B2 ⑤

Midnight Shift is a Sydney legend – and this one's really only for the boys. The Shift is actually two clubs in one: at street level, it's a dark but friendly video bar with a wide range of punters and pool tables out the back. Upstairs is the packed dance club, which has an entry fee and a crowd of wall-to-wall men, who bump and grind both on and off the dancefloor.

## Oxford Art Factory

*38-46 Oxford Street, Darlinghurst (9332 3711/www.oxfordart factory.com). Bus 373, 377, 378, 380, 382, 391, 394, 396.* **Open** 9pm-late Thur-Sun. **Admission** (after 10pm) $10 Fri; $20 Sat; $10 Sun. No credit cards. **Map** p101 C2 ⑤

The hippest venue on Oxford Street, Art Factory favours big-name DJs and bands, with a nod to club nights (notably Kink, formerly at ArtHouse). The venue is sleek, simple and roomy, with a no-frills attitude inside and out.

## Oxford Hotel

*134 Oxford Street, at Taylor Square, Darlinghurst (9331 3467). Bus 311, 333, 352, 373, 377, 378, 380, 392, 394, 396.* **Open** *Main bar* 24hrs daily. *Basement bar* 10pm-10am Fri, Sat. *Will & Toby's Supper Club* (level 1) 7pm-late Wed-Sun. *Polo Lounge* (level 2) 6pm-3am Tue-Sun. **Map** p101 C2 ⑤

A mainstay of the Golden Mile for about as long as anyone can remember, the Oxford has undergone a few changes in recent years. The ground-floor pub used to be a bit dark and cloistered, but recent renovations have opened it up considerably. A wooden veranda now enables outdoor drinking over Taylor Square, which is very welcome in the warmer months. But the best things about the place haven't changed: the main area is still pretty much a 24-hour bar, and an almost universally gay male venue. Upstairs at Will and Toby's, two sophisticated and rather ritzy lounge bars have found their new home.

## Palms on Oxford

*124 Oxford Street, at Taylor Square, Darlinghurst (9357 4166). Bus 311, 333, 352, 373, 377, 378, 380, 392, 394, 396.* **Open** 8pm-midnight Thur; 8pm-3am Fri, Sat; 8pm-midnight Sun. **Map** p101 C2 ⑤

Let's not beat around the bush: Palms on Oxford is most likely gay Sydney's most tragically fun venue. Don't go expecting cutting-edge music and hip-per-than-hip lighting effects, but do expect lots of Kylie/disco diva remixes and a friendly crowd out for a good time. Located a few doors down from the popular Oxford Hotel (p111), Palms feels a bit like a 1980s gay bar – and that's just the way its regular crowd of devoted punters seem to prefer it.

## Q Bar
*Exchange Hotel, Level 3, 34-44 Oxford Street, between Riley & Liverpool Streets, Darlinghurst (9360 1375). CityRail Museum/bus 311, 333, 352, 373, 377, 378, 380, 392, 394, 396.* **Open** 10pm-late Wed-Sun. **Admission** $15 Fri; $20 Sat. **Map** p101 B1 🟠
The big, busy Q Bar has become Oxford Street's seedy after-party joint for pretty much anyone and everyone, be they hipsters or gangstas, gay or straight. There's a dancefloor that swirls with funk and house, becoming the burlesque club 34b on Friday nights, with a 'VIP area' for members offering ping pong and lounges. The bar is housed within the multi-level Exchange Hotel, a popular gay venue, which also boasts the Phoenix club (for more dancing), and Spectrum (for live music, see below).

## Spectrum
*Exchange Hotel, 34-44 Oxford Street, between Riley & Liverpool Streets, Darlinghurst (9331 1936/www.pash presents.com). Bus 311, 371, 373, 377, 378, 380, 392, 394, 396, 397, 399, 890, X39.* **Open** 8pm-late Sat; 8pm-midnight Sun. **Admission** $5-$20. **Map** p101 B1 🟠
Bringing live music screaming on to the Pink Strip, this intimate club has succeeded in showcasing hot new bands and attracting established talent who want a central location that isn't a barn. Spectrum is set within the four-level Exchange Hotel, also home to the Q Bar (see above) .

## Stonewall Hotel
*175 Oxford Street, Darlinghurst (9360 1963/www.stonewallhotel.com). Bus 311, 333, 352, 373, 377, 378, 380, 392, 394, 396.* **Open** 9.30am-5am Mon-Fri; 9.30am-7am Sat, Sun. No credit cards. **Map** p101 B2 🟠

A large, three-level pub and dance venue, much loved and always busy. The crowd tends to lean towards younger gay men (wearing the latest-season fashions and spiky quiffs) and those who fancy them. The street-level bar has a chatty, pub-style atmosphere, with drag shows, the occasional talent quest, a small dancefloor and sexy male dancers atop the bar at weekends. Upstairs, there are two lounge areas with more bars. The crowds pack in for Wednesday's Malebox night, at which everyone is assigned a number, and messages can be left for punters who you like the look of. Tuesday's Karaoke night is another Stonewall institution.

## Slide
*41 Oxford Street, between Crown & Bourke Streets, Darlinghurst (8915 1899). Bus 311, 333, 352, 373, 377, 378, 380, 392, 394, 396.* **Open** 7pm-3am Wed-Sun (open Mon, Tue for private functions only). **Map** p101 B2 🟠
The very slick Slide opened its doors in 2005. In the early evening it often functions as a top-notch restaurant, but the party mood kicks in as the night wears on. Admission prices apply for special shows on different nights.

## Supper Club
NEW *Will & Toby's, Taylor Square, 134 Oxford Street, Darlinghurst (9331 3467/www.willandtobys.com.au). Bus 378, 343, 309, 376, 392, 397, L94.* **Open** 8pm-late Thur-Sat; 7pm-late Sun. **Admission** varies. **Map** p101 C2 🟠
This classy Taylor Square hangout run by celebrated Sydney restaurateur brothers Will and Toby Osmond includes a lavishly decorated 200-capacity supper club. The club features sophisticated music, comedy acts and cabaret and serves sharing plates, impressive cocktails and good wines.

## Taxi Club
*40-42 Flinders Street, between Taylor & Short Streets, Darlinghurst (9331 4256). Bus 311, 333, 352, 373, 377, 378, 380, 392, 394, 396.* **Open** 10am-2am Mon-Thur, 10am-6am Fri-Sun. No credit cards. **Map** p101 C3 🟠

**Belvoir Street Theatre**

When everything else is closed at the weekend, fear not – there's always the Taxi. This is the venue for night owls, serious drinkers or a combination of the two. It provides the cheapest drinks in queer Sydney and is open until 6am on weekends. Which is why it's a favourite both with drag queens – who stop here after a night's work – and some extremely intoxicated out of towners who end up rolling in here at the end of a long night on the tiles.

## Arts & leisure

### Belvoir Street Theatre

*25 Belvoir Street, at Clisdell Street, Surry Hills (9699 3444/www.belvoir. com.au). CityRail/LightRail Central.* **Box office** 9.30am-6pm Mon, Tue; 9.30am-7.30pm Wed-Sat; 2.30-6pm Sun. **Tickets** Company B productions $54; $25-$45 reductions. Production prices vary. **Map** p101 A5 ⑥⑤
This one-time tomato sauce factory, now owned by a non-profit consortium of performers, actors, writers and their supporters, is home to the innovative Company B, which has exclusive use of the brilliantly intimate 350-seat Upstairs Theatre. The even more bijou 80-seat Downstairs space hosts Belvoir's B Sharp fringe season. Belvoir Street attracts Sydney's most discerning and loyal theatregoers, who can often be found maintaining their passion in the foyer bar (served by the city's best arts bar staff).

### Zen Day Spa

*116-118 Darlinghurst Road, between William & Liverpool Streets, Darlinghurst (9361 4200/www.zendayspa.com.au). CityRail Kings Cross.* **Open** 9am-9pm Mon-Fri; 8am-8pm Sat; 10am-7pm Sun. **Map** p101 C2 ⑥⑥
Serenity is the name of the game at this day spa, a sanctuary in the heart of bustling Darlinghurst. The list of tempting treatments includes massage, aromatherapy sessions, and facials using Dermalogica products, plus there are waxes, manicures and pedicures to get you beach- and bikini-ready.

SYDNEY BY AREA

Centennial Park p116

# Paddington to Woollahra

These days, it's hard to believe that chic Paddington was once one of Sydney's worst slums. Its quaint Victorian terraces, with their iron lace balcony balustrades, have been renovated to within an inch of their tin rooves, boasting glass floor-to-ceiling rears opening out on to bijou lap pools and tiny terraces. Pokey rooms have been knocked through to create open-plan stylish living areas, their period details retained for good measure. And in between the terraces (which now fetch more than a million a pop), modern apartment blocks house the party set who live here.

Paddington is flanked by **Moore Park** with the **Sydney Cricket Ground** and **Sydney Football Stadium**, **Fox Studios** and the **Entertainment Quarter** of cinemas and shops; glorious **Centennial Park** with its majestic bridlepaths and cycle ways; old-money Woollahra and, heading back towards the city, **Darlinghurst's gay strip**.

The shops in Paddington and Woollahra are fashion and design central and there are more cafés than you can shake a lightly toasted Turkish loaf at. At Five Ways – the meeting of five winding roads – in Paddington's heart, restaurants, a pub, pavement cafés, galleries and designer shops tumble into each other. And just in the distance you can see the blue of the harbour down in Rushcutters Bay. Very Sydney!

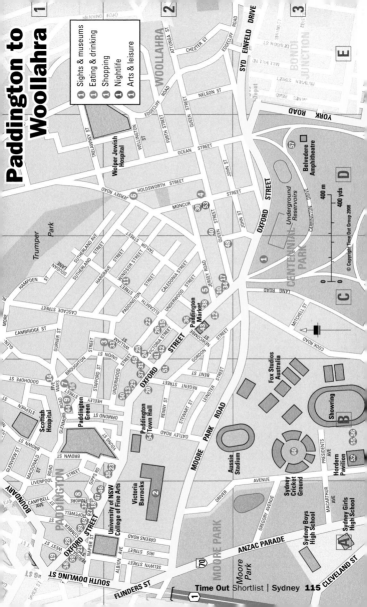

# Paddington to Woollahra

**Key**
- 1 Sights & museums
- 1 Eating & drinking
- 1 Shopping
- 1 Nightlife
- 1 Arts & leisure

Wolper Jewish Hospital

WOOLLAHRA

Trumper Park

Scottish Hospital

Paddington Green

Paddington Town Hall

Victoria Barracks

University of NSW College of Fine Arts

PADDINGTON

Paddington Market

Fox Studios Australia

Aussie Stadium

Sydney Cricket Ground

Hordern Pavilion

Showring

CENTENNIAL PARK

Underground Reservoirs

Belvedere Amphitheatre

Moore Park

Sydney Boys High School

Sydney Girls High School

BONDI JUNCTION

© Copyright Time Out Group 2008

400 m
400 yds

Flat White

## Sights & museums

### Centennial Park

*Between Oxford Street, York, Darley, Alison & Lang Roads, Paddington (9339 6699/www.cp.nsw.gov.au). Bus 333, 352, 355, 378, 380.* **Open** 24hrs daily. *Vehicles* Sunrise-sunset daily. Car-free days last Sun in Mar, May, Aug, Nov. **Admission** free. **Map** p115 C3-D3 ❶

A weekend trip to Centennial Park affords visitors a fine example of Sydneysiders at their leisure best. All kinds of fitness fiend, from walkers to joggers, cyclists to in-line skaters, are on show here. There's an outdoor gym and you can hire skates and bikes or go horse riding. It's very pretty with its ponds, statues and native Australian flowers, plus there's a fantastic café.

### Victoria Barracks

*Oxford Street, between Greens & Oatley Roads, Paddington (9339 3170). Bus 352, 378, 380, L82.* **Open** *Museum* 10am-3pm Sun. *Tour,* 10am Thur. Closed Christmas holidays. **Admission** *Museum* $2. *Tour* free. **Map** p115 A2 ❷

Built in the 1840s, the Regency-style Victoria Barracks were designed by Lieutenant-Colonel George Barney, who also built Fort Denison. Nowadays, the barracks are used as a military administration centre. The museum is housed in the former jail, also home to a ghost, Charlie the Redcoat, who hanged himself while incarcerated for shooting his sergeant. Well worth a visit.

## Eating & drinking

### Alimentari

*2 Hopetoun Street, Paddington (9358 2142). Bus 333, 352, 378, 380.* **Open** 7am-6pm Mon-Fri; 8am-5pm Sat. Unlicensed. **Café**. **Map** p115 C2 ❸

Tucked away at the end of William Street, under the frangipani trees, is this little slice of Italy in Paddo. Don't miss the rich coffee and paninis.

### Bistro Moncur

*Woollahra Hotel, corner of Moncur & Queen Streets, Woollahra (9363 2519/ www.woollahrahotel.com.au). Bus 378, 380, 389.* **Open** 6-10.30pm Mon; noon-3pm, 6-10.30pm Tue-Sun. **$$$**. Licensed. **French**. **Map** p115 D2 ❹

Damien Pignolet is the god of (seemingly) simple things done well. Try bistro classics such as Provençal fish soup with rouille, pork sausages with Lyonnaise onions and sirloin steak.

### Buzo

*3 Jersey Road, Woollahra (9328 1600). Bus 333, 352, 378, 380, 389.* **Open** 6.30pm-late Mon-Sat. **$$$**. Licensed. **Italian**. **Map** p115 C2 ❺

The atmosphere of this classy osteria in Woollahra is fostered by the rustic simplicity of the blackboard menu, the relatively modest pricing and the crush of locals who storm the place.

### Flat White

*98 Holdsworth Street, at Jersey Road, Woollahra (9328 9922). Bus 200, 389.* **Open** 7am-4pm Mon-Sat; 8am-4pm Sun. BYO **Café**. **Map** p115 D2 ❻

Gruyère and ham brioche toastie? Yes please. The space isn't huge (and, between you and me, neither are the portions), but everything here is skewed towards the perfectly formed.

### Gusto Deli Café
*Corner Broughton & Heeley Streets Paddington (9361 5640). Bus 389.* **Open** 7am-7.30pm daily. Unlicensed. **Café**. **Map** p115 B1 ❼
A Paddington institution with limited seating inside but a number of tables outside precariously perched on the Five Ways hills. Coffee is excellent but most come for the healthy salads and more substantial rolls and sandwiches.

### Jackie's
*1C Glenmore Road, Paddington (9380 9818). Bus 352, 378, 380, 333.* **Open** 7.30am-3.30pm daily; 6-11pm Wed-Sat. Licensed. **Café**. **Map** p115 A1 ❽
This is a great place for a pre-shopping breakfast of vanilla ricotta pancakes or scrambled eggs and Turkish toast. For lunch, there's angel hair pasta with chilli and prawns, plus sushi.

### L'Etoile
*211 Glenmore Road, Paddington (9332 1577/www.letoilerestaurant.com.au). Bus 389.* **Open** 6pm-late Mon-Thur; noon-3pm, 6pm-late Fri; 10am-3pm, 6pm-late Sat-Sun. **$$$**. Licensed. **French**. **Map** p115 B1 ❾
Classic, ultra-French food in the civilised surrounds of Paddington. A dish of scallops with boudin noir arrives as plump, bouncy scallops perched on rounds of rich sausage, while the roast garlic and hazelnut soup is creamy, smooth and soothing.

### Light Brigade
*2A Oxford Street, Woollahra (9331 2930/www.lightbrigade.com.au). Bus 333, 352, 378, 380, 389.* **Open** noon-late daily (downstairs); 5pm-late Tue-Sat (upstairs). **Pub**. **Map** p115 C2 ❿
On the one hand a beautiful old pub, on the other, as its name suggests, it's also something of a battleground. In the trenches (ie downstairs), owner Dean Haritos is going more for a blaring sports bar than a lounge bar. But over the top (ie upstairs), it's all about plush privacy, original features and cocktails. Head bartender Percy Small mixes

playful concoctions like his Apple and Grapefruit Sling. Chaaarge!

### Lucio's
*Corner of Windsor & Elizabeth Streets, Paddington (9380 5996/www.lucios. com.au). Bus 380, 382, 389.* **Open** 12.30-3pm, 6.30-11pm Mon-Sat. **$$$$**. Licensed. **Italian**. **Map** p115 C2 ⓫
Love art and food? Lucio's – where the myth of the starving artist is exploded – is the answer. The restaurant's walls are festooned with works by many of the foremost Australian painters of the past 50 years, while the plates come adorned with 20 years worth of Italian cooking. Head chef David Dale plates up traditional Ligurian fare such as duck neck filled with its own liver.

### Max Brenner
*437 Oxford Street, Paddington (9357 5055/www.maxbrenner.com). Bus 352, 378, 380, 333.* **Open** 9am-11pm Mon-Thur; 9am-midnight Fri, Sat; 10am-10.30pm Sun. **Café**. **Map** p115 C2 ⓬
Drink frozen chocolate cocktails, thick steaming cups of hot choc, or gorge on strawberries dipped in sinful chocolate fondue at this specialist chocolatier.

### Micky's
*268 Oxford Street, Paddington (9361 5157/www.mickyscafe.com.au.) Bus 352, 378, 380, 333.* **Open** 8am-midnight daily. BYO. **Café**. **Map** p115 B2 ⓭
Micky's serves up BLTs, nachos, big hangover breakfasts with freshly whipped frappés and shakes, plus there's coffee and cookies.

### Royal Hotel
*237 Glenmore Road, at Five Ways, Paddington (9331 2604/www.royal hotel.com.au). Bus 389.* **Open** 10am-midnight Mon-Sat; 10am-10pm Sun. Licensed. **Mod Oz**. **Map** p115 B1 ⓮
The Royal's three levels of well heeled conviviality comprise the ground-floor bar, the quite reasonable Mod Oz restaurant on the first floor, and the top floor's Elephant Bar, which is stuffed with pachyderm knick-knacks and young upwardly mobiles enjoying their cosmopolitans and caipiroskas.

### Sugo

*10 Elizabeth Street, Paddington (9331 2962). Bus 333, 352, 378, 380.* **Open** noon-3pm, 6-10.30pm Mon-Sat. **$$**. Licensed/BYO (wine only). **Pizza**. **Map** p115 C2 ⑮

Traditional wood-fired pizza in Paddo, including a very good margherita and a spicy sausage-topped number.

### Wasavie

*8 Heeley Street, Paddington (9380 8838). Bus 333, 352, 378, 380, 389.* **Open** 6-10pm Mon-Thur; noon-3pm, 6-10pm Fri-Sun. **$$$**. BYO. **Japanese**. **Map** p115 B1 ⑯

This minimal little local is living proof that good, cheap Japanese food isn't a paradox. Sear slices of raw fish on a hot stone for a bit of theatre or enjoy sticky braised pork belly with hot mustard.

## Shopping

### Akira Isogawa

*12A Queen Street, Woollahra (9361 5221/ www.akira.com.au). Bus 352, 378, 380, 333.* **Open** 10.30am-6pm Mon-Wed, Fri; 10.30am-7pm Thur; 10am-6pm Sat; 11am-4pm Sun. **Map** p115 C2 ⑰

Akira is known for his romantic other-worldly multi-layering of transparent fabrics and bold colours and his garments are now sold in all the world's fashion epicentres.

### Alannah Hill

*118-120 Oxford Street, Paddington (9380 9147/www.alannahhill.com.au). Bus 352, 378, 380, 333.* **Open** 10am-6pm Mon-Wed, Fri, Sat; 10am-8pm Thur; 11am-6pm Sun. **Map** p115 A1 ⑱

Melbourne designer Alannah Hill has cornered flirty feminine style. The vintage-doll-like shop assistants look like they are having as much fun trying on the rich fabrics, velvet trims, lace and feathered hats as the customers.

### Ariel

*42 Oxford Street, Paddington (9332 4581/www.arielbooks.com.au). Bus 352, 378, 380, 333.* **Open** 9am-midnight daily. **Map** p115 A1 ⑲

Situated opposite the NSW University College of Fine Art, Ariel stocks a lot of gorgeous hardback (and therefore expensive) art, design, photography, fashion and contemporary culture books, which the laidback staff are happy for you to leaf through for as long as you like.

### Ben Sherman

*255C Oxford Street, Paddington (9360 3770/www.bensherman.com). Bus 352, 378, 380, 333.* **Open** 10am-5.30pm Mon-Wed, Fri, Sat; 10am-8pm Thur; 11am-5pm Sun. **Map** p115 B2 ⑳

The Brit Mod-inspired designer brings his unique brand of shirts and jackets to Sydney in a large and always busy funky flagship store.

### Berkelouw Books

*19 Oxford Street, Paddington (9360 3200/www.berkelouw.com.au). Bus 352, 378, 380, 333.* **Open** 9am-11pm Mon-Thu, Sun; 9am-midnight Fri, Sat. **Map** p115 A1 ㉑

Berkelouw has an intriguing selection of new and antique Australiana and assorted rare tomes.

### Calibre

*398 Oxford Street, Paddington (9380 5993/www.calibreclothing.com.au). Bus 352, 378, 380, 333.* **Open** 9.30am-6pm Mon-Wed, Fri, 9.30am-8pm Thur; 10am-6pm Sat; 11am-5pm Sun. **Map** p115 C2 ㉒

Started from one shop in Melbourne, Calibre is a stylish menswear store boasting its own popular label as well as international brands.

### Charlie Brown

*178 Oxford Street, Paddington (9360 9001/ www.charliebrown.com.au). Bus 352, 378, 380, 333.* **Open** 10am-6pm Mon-Wed, Fri, Sat; 10am-8pm Thur; 11am-5pm Sun. **Map** p115 B2 ㉓

American-born Charlie Brown sells flamboyant, innovative clothes for women who are tired of the stick-insect sizes provided by other designers.

### Collette Dinnigan

*33 William Street, Paddington (9360 6691/www.collette dinnigan.com.au). Bus 352, 378, 380, 333.* **Open** 10am-6pm Mon-Sat; noon-5pm Sun. **Map** p115 C2 ㉔

Models tying the knot and celebs in need of a sensational red-carpet gown love Dinnigan's exquisite beading and sensual embroidery.

## Corner Shop

*43 William Street, Paddington (9380 9828). Bus 352, 378, 380, 333.* **Open** 10am-6pm Mon-Wed, Fri, Sat; 10am-7pm Thur; 10am-5.30pm Sun. **Map** p115 C2 ㉕

The team behind this eclectic fashion venture scours the world's fashion fairs to bring back the hippest and brightest designs they can find from the globe's up-and-coming designers. The Corner Shop is also a good place to catch the newest Aussie names.

## Easton Pearson

*18 Elizabeth Street, Paddington (9331 4433/www.eastonpearson.com). Bus 352, 378, 380, 333.* **Open** 10am-6pm Mon-Sat. **Map** p115 C2 ㉖

Beautiful fabrics and unusual textiles are the go with dynamic design duo Pamela Easton and Lydia Pearson, who take their influences – and a lot of their materials – from India, Africa, Mexico and Polynesia. Their attention to the smallest details – buttons, stitching – is what defines their special style.

## Ed Hardy

*108 Oxford Street, Paddington (9357 3150/www.edhardy.com.au). Bus 352, 378, 380, 333.* **Open** 10am-7pm Mon-Wed, Fri, Sat; 10am-9pm Thur; 10am-6pm Sun. **Map** p115 A1 ㉗

A favourite with rock stars around the world, Christian Audigier's tees and jeans, based on the tattoo art of Ed Hardy, are all over the party people. The store also sells children's clothes.

## Family Jewels

*46 Oxford Street, Paddington (9331 6647/www.thefamilyjewels.com.au). Bus 352, 378, 380, 333.* **Open** 10am-6pm Mon-Wed, Fri, Sat; 10am-7.30pm Thur; 11am-5.30pm Sun. **Map** p115 A1 ㉘

Family Jewels stocks silver pieces from all over the world, plus fun designs from hot local designers and various items of sparkly costume jewellery.

## Folkways Music

*282 Oxford Street, between Underwood & William Streets, Paddington (9361 3980). Bus 352, 378, 380, 333.* **Open** 9am-6pm Mon-Wed, Fri, Sat; 9am-8pm Thur; 11am-6pm Sun. **Map** p115 B2 ㉙

Browse the wide selection at Folkways, Sydney's standard bearer for folk and ethnic music.

## Jones the Grocer

*68 Moncur Street, Woollahra (9362 1222/www.jonesthegrocer.com). Bus 389.* **Open** 7.30am-5.30pm Mon-Sat; 9am-5pm Sun. **Map** p115 D2 ㉚

Known for fine cheeses, sausages, cakes and high quality groceries, Jones is also a great place to simply hang out and sip a coffee.

## Just William

*4 William Street, Paddington (9331 5468/www.justwilliam.com.au). Bus 352, 378, 380, 333.* **Open** 10am-6pm daily. **Map** p115 B2 ㉛

This diminutive store is filled to the rafters with chocolate-coated delights. A chocaholic's fantasy.

## Kirrily Johnston

*6 Glenmore Road, Paddington (9380 7775/www.kirrilyjohnston.com). Bus 352, 378, 380, 333.* **Open** 10am-6pm Mon-Wed, Fri, Sat; 10am-7pm Thur; 11am-5pm Sun. **Map** p115 A1 ㉜

Kirrily's bold sassy use of colour and lush fabrics blend effortlessly with her genuinely comfortable designs. All of which means you don't have to be a stick insect to wear her clothes. Before you rejoice, though, watch out – the price tags can carry quite a sting.

## Leona Edmiston

*88 William Street, Paddington (9331 7033/www.leonaedmiston.com.au). Bus 352, 378, 380, 333.* **Open** 10am-6pm Mon-Fri; 10am-5pm Sat; noon-4pm Sun. **Map** p115 C2 ㉝

Leona Edmiston is all about fun and flirty collections of pretty frocks and fabulous accessories. Chic and cheeky femininity is the thing here and locals love her use of delicate prints and ultra-flattering cuts.

# Sydney style

**Sass & Bide**

In a country where much of the population lives in shorts and thongs (flip-flops), it is perhaps ironic that fashion is booming. But head to design central Paddington and you'll see a bevy of fashion savvy girls and guys all shopping for the latest threads. Sydney's annual Spring/Summer Fashion Week in April and May attracts buyers from around the world and there's no denying that there's a buzz around Australian designs.

It all started as a murmur many years back when the likes of **Collette Dinnigan** (p118), **Lisa Ho** (p121) and **Sass & Bide** (p122) cracked both London stores and the Hollywood A-list – but the explosion of young talent that has followed has nonetheless been astonishing. Being still babes in the arms of global couture, local designers wear their innocence on their sleeves. Their clothes are at best groundbreaking, at worst a poor copy of a Stella McCartney or Miuccia Prada, and generally fall somewhere between the two.

Where Australian fashionistas do excel is in their diverse fabric choice and, in Sydney especially, their exciting use of colour. Best of all, though, their clothes are beautifully suited to the climate – easy to wear, light and layered and always with a flirty edge. Unlike their Euro and US counterparts, most of Sydney's young designers set up on their own straight out of college, and it is in the boutiques of Paddington that you'll find them. Start at **Corner Shop** (p119) or **Parlour X** (p122) and look for Alice McCall's boho creations, Lover jeans, Josh Goot knits, Ruby Smallbone's cute tops, Anna & Boy swimwear and Michelle Jank jewellery. Some young designers, like **Kirrilly Johnston** (p119) and **Easton Pearson** (p119), already have their own shops. Admittedly, the clothes aren't cheap, but they're uniquely Aussie.

## Lisa Ho

*Corner of Oxford & Queen Streets,*
*Woollahra (9360 2345/www.lisaho.*
*com.au). Bus 352, 378, 380, 333.*
**Open** 10am-6pm Mon-Wed, Fri; 10am-
8pm Thur; 10am-6pm Sat; 11am-5pm
Sun. **Map** p115 C2 ③④

Stretch fabrics, silk and sheer chiffon
are beaded and pleated with gorgeous
results at Lisa Ho. Great swimwear too.

## Mecca Cosmetica

*126 Oxford Street, Paddington (9361*
*4488/www.meccacosmetica.com.au).*
*Bus 352, 378, 380, 333.* **Open** 10am-
6pm Mon-Wed, Fri, Sat; 10am-8pm
Thur; 11am-5pm Sun. **Map** p115 B2 ③⑤

Mecca is a chic cosmetic boutique
sporting overseas brands such as Nars,
Stila and Philosophy.

## Mimco

*436 Oxford Street, Paddington (9357*
*6884/www.mimco.com.au). Bus 352,*
*378, 380, 333.* **Open** 10am-6pm Mon-
Wed, Fri, Sat; 10am-8pm Thur; 11am-
5pm Sun. **Map** p115 C2 ③⑥

Try Mimco for highly original funky
bags, luggage, fantastic sunhats and
up-to-the-minute jewellery and wallets.

## Mollini

*302 Oxford Street, Paddington (9331*
*1732/www.mollini.com.au). Bus 352,*
*378, 380, 333.* **Open** 10am-6pm Mon-
Wed, Fri; 10am-8.30pm Thur (8pm in
winter); 9.30am-6pm Sat; 11am-5pm
Sun. **Map** p115 B2 ③⑦

Head to Mollini for wedges, flats,
round-toes, point-toes, boots, kitten
heels, high heels and stilettos from the
four corners of the globe.

## Morrissey

*372 Oxford Street, Paddington (9380*
*7422/www.morrissey.net.au). Bus 352,*
*378, 380, 333.* **Open** 9.30am-5.30pm
Mon-Wed, Fri, Sat; 9.30am-8pm Thur;
11am-5pm Sun. **Map** p115 C2 ③⑧

Peter Morrissey started out working
with Leona Edmiston (see p119), and
together, they created the Morrissey
Edmiston label, a hit for 14 years.
Today Morrissey is owned by Oroton
and his designs reflect the latter's
classic styling and vibrant colours.

## Napoleon Perdis
## Make-up Academy

*74 Oxford Street, Paddington (9331*
*1702/www.napoleoncosmetics.com). Bus*
*352, 378, 380, 333.* **Open** 9am-6pm
Mon-Sat; 10am-5pm Sun. **Map** p115 A1 ③⑨

Set up by an Aussie-born Hollywood
make-up artist, this shop has its own
cosmetics brand and in-house experts.

## Nicola Finetti

*92 Queen Street, Woollahra (9362*
*1685/www.nicolafinetti.com). Bus 352,*
*378, 380, 333.* **Open** 10am-6pm Mon-
Wed, Fri, Sat; 12pm-7pm Thur; 11am-
5pm Sun. **Map** p115 D2 ④⓪

Italian-born Nicola lived in Argentina
before settling in Australia and a Latin
flair pulsates through his (yes, Nicola
is a he!) sensual designs.

## Nine West

*308 Oxford Street, Paddington (9331*
*8481/www.ninewest.com.au). Bus 352,*
*378, 380, 333.* **Open** 9.30am-6pm
Mon-Wed, Fri, Sat; 9.30am-8pm Thur;
10am-5pm Sun. **Map** p115 C2 ④①

The US shoe and bag chain came to
Australia in 1995 and now boasts 45
stores nationwide. Its reasonable prices
are very attractive in a city where
shoes often seem to cost way too much.

## Opus Designs

*344 Oxford Street, Paddington (9360*
*4803/www.opusdesign.com.au). Bus 352,*
*378, 380, 333.* **Open** 10am-6pm Mon-
Wed, Fri; 10am-7.30pm Thur; 9am-6pm
Sat; 11am-5pm Sun. **Map** p115 C2 ④②

Try Opus for funky ashtrays, photo
frames, beach bags, clocks and drag-
queen greetings cards, plus kitchen-
ware and stylish furniture too.

## Paddington Market

*Paddington Uniting Church, 395*
*Oxford Street, Paddington (9331 2923/*
*www.paddingtonmarkets.com.au). Bus*
*352, 378, 380, 333.* **Open** 10am-4pm
Sat. **Map** p115 C2 ④③

This market is at the heart of Paddo
shopping on a Saturday. Many a big-
name fashion designer made their
name here. There are lots of jewellery
makers and artisans selling their
wares, plus multicultural food stalls.

**SYDNEY BY AREA**

## Parlour X

*213 Glenmore Road, at Five Ways,
Paddington (9331 0999/www.parlourx.
com.au). Bus 389.* **Open** 10am-6pm
Mon-Wed, Fri; 10am-7pm Thur; 10am-
5pm Sat, Sun. **Map** p115 B1 ㊹
Eva Galambos has a knack for picking
out the best pieces from local rising
stars while also stocking top-end
labels. *The* place for fashionistas.

## Rose & Ruby

*5 William Street, Paddington (9357
6414/www.roseandruby.com). Bus 352,
378, 380, 333.* **Open** 9.30am-6pm
Mon-Wed, Fri, Sat; 9.30am-7pm Thur;
11am-4pm Sun. **Map** p115 B2 ㊺
This fashion boutique is as pretty as a
picture. Cream furniture, floorboards
and chandeliers are as tasteful as the
ethereal designs of sisters-in-law duo
Rebecca Reeves-Saunders and Karah
Tarran-Wilson.

## Sass & Bide

*132 Oxford Street, Paddington (9360
3900/www.sassandbide.com.au). Bus
352, 378, 380, 333.* **Open** 10am-6pm
Mon-Wed, Fri, Sat; 10am-8pm Thur;
11am-5pm Sun. **Map** p115 A1 ㊻
Sarah-Jane 'Sass' Clarke and Heidi
'Bide' Middleton started out selling
clothes on London's Portobello Road.
They struck gold when they made
international headlines with their sexy,
skinny low-rise jeans.

## Scanlan & Theodore

*122 Oxford Street, Paddington (9380
9388/www.scanlantheodore.com.au).
Bus 352, 378, 380, L82.* **Open** 10am-
6pm Mon-Wed, Fri; 10am-8pm Thur;
10am-5.30pm Sat; noon-5pm Sun.
**Map** p115 A1 ㊼
If you only have time to take in one
Aussie designer, make it Scanlan
& Theodore. Gary Theodore and Fiona
Scanlan work with seriously luxurious
fabrics and creative, classy colours.

## Simon Johnson
## Quality Foods

*55 Queen Street, Woollahra (9328
6888/www.simonjohnson.com). Bus
389.* **Open** 10am-6.30pm Mon-Fri; 9am-
5pm Sat; 10am-4pm Sun. **Map** p115 C2 ㊽

Esteemed foodie Simon Johnson is the
nation's leading provider of Australian
and imported gourmet foods.

## Sweet Art

*96 Oxford Street, Paddington (9361
6617/www.sweetart.com.au). Bus 352,
378, 380, 333.* **Open** 10am-5pm daily.
**Map** p115 A1 ㊾
Cake creation at its best. Check out the
window displays of sculptured cakes,
made to whatever design you desire.

## Toni & Guy

*255 Oxford Street, Paddington (9380
2299/www.toniandguy.com.au.) Bus
352, 378, 380, 333.* **Open** 9am-6pm
Mon-Wed; 9am-8pm Thur; 9am-9pm
Fri; 9am-5.15pm Sat. **Map** p115 B2 ㊿
The global chain is well established in
Oz and a good place to get a quality cut.

## Zimmermann

*387 Oxford Street, Paddington (9357
4700/www.zimmermannwear.com). Bus
352, 378, 380, 333.* **Open** 10am-6pm
Mon-Wed, Fri, Sat; 10am-8pm Thur;
10am-5pm Sun. **Map** p115 B2 ㉑
Launched by sisters Nicole and Simone
Zimmermann in the 1990s, this highly
successful swimwear range is among
Sydney's most stylish.

# Nightlife

## Hordern Pavilion

*Driver Avenue, Moore Park (9921
5333/www.playbillvenues.com.au).
Bus 339, 373, 374, 376, 377, 393,
395, 396.* **Admission** prices vary.
**Map** p115 B3 ㉒
This barn of a venue retains a relaxed
vibe while seating 5,500. Big-name
local acts (Powderfinger, John Butler
Trio) and overseas artists play here.

## Woollahra Hotel

*Corner of Moncur & Queen Streets,
Woollahra (9327 9777/www.woollahra
hotel.com.au). Bus 389.* **Open** noon-
midnight Mon-Sat; noon-10pm Sun.
**Admission** free. **Map** p115 D2 ㉓
Not an ideal venue, but the musical
servings can still surprise. Jazz Juice
sessions every Sunday (6.30-9.30pm)
and Thursday (7.45-10.45pm).

# Arts & leisure

### Chauvel

*Paddington Town Hall, Paddington (9361 5398/www.chauvelcinema. net.au). Bus 352, 378, 380, 333. Screens 2.* **Admission** *$15.50; $9-$12.50 reductions; $8 Tue.* **Map** p115 B2 ③④
Named after Australian film pioneer Charles Chauvel, this grand cinema is much loved by locals and has reopened after a period of closure.

### Cinema Paris

*Bent Street, Entertainment Quarter, Driver Avenue, Moore Park (9332 1633/www.hoyts.com.au). Bus 355, 371, 372, 391, 392, 393, 394, 395, 396, 397, 399, 890. Screens 4.* **Admission** *$15.50; $8.50-$12.50 reductions; $9 Tue.* **Map** p115 B3 ⑤⑤
Unassuming art-house cinema within Fox Studios' Entertainment Quarter, with a total seating capacity of 600. Hosts several annual events including the Bollywood Film Festival.

### Hoyts EQ

*Bent Street, Entertainment Quarter, Driver Avenue, Moore Park (9332 1300/www.hoyts.com.au). Bus 355, 371, 372, 391, 392, 393, 394, 395, 396, 397, 399, 890. Screens 12.* **Admission** *$15.50; $8.50-$12 reductions; ($9 Tue $8 reductions).* **Map** p115 B3 ⑤⑥
Located in the Fox Studios complex, this vast pseudo-retro site boasts huge screens, stadium seating for 3,000 and clean facilities.

### Moonlight Cinema

*Belvedere Amphitheatre, Centennial Park, Woollahra (1300 511 908/ www.moonlight.com.au). Bus 378, 380, 333.* **Open** *Early Dec-mid Mar.* **Admission** *$15-$17; $11-$14 reductions.* **Map** p115 D3 ⑤⑦
The Moonlight's outdoor programme focuses on mainstream releases and customary classics such as *Grease* and *Breakfast at Tiffany's* on Valentine's Day. Films kick off at sunset and entry is via Woollahra Gate (Oxford Street) only. Bring a picnic, cushions and insect repellent and arrive early.

**Paddington Market**

### Palace Academy Twin Cinema

*3A Oxford Street, Paddington (9361 4453/www.palacecinemas.com.au). Bus 352, 378, 380, 333. Screens 2.* **Admission** *$15.50; $9-$12.50 reductions; $9.50 Mon.* **Map** p115 A1 ⑤⑧
One of Sydney's oldest art cinemas, the Academy Twin has seen better days. It hosts the Mardi Gras Film Festival.

### Palace Verona Cinema

*17 Oxford Street, Paddington (9360 6099/www.palacecinemas.com.au). Bus 352, 378, 380, 333. Screens 4.* **Admission** *$15.50; $9-$12.50 reductions; $9.50 Mon.* **Map** p115 A1 ⑤⑨
The Palace's screens are small but the mix of quirky and foreign films appeals.

### Sydney Cricket Ground

*Driver Avenue, Moore Park (1800 801 155/9360 6601/tours 1300 724 737/ www.sydneycricketground.com.au). Bus 372, 373, 374.* **Open** *Tours* 10am, 1pm Mon-Fri; 10am Sat. **Admission** *$25; $17 reductions; $65 family.* **Map** p115 B3 ⑥⓪
Book ahead for a one-and-a-half-hour tour of the hallowed SCG.

**Bondi Beach**

# Bondi to Coogee

The stretch of ocean beaches in Sydney's east starts at iconic Bondi and can be covered in the hugely popular Bondi to Coogee walk. Once a working-class suburb, Bondi has been transformed and continues to grow, thanks to the constant nagging addition of yet more glass and steel palaces – mostly chic apartment blocks for the very well heeled. The beach, too, has had an overhaul. Cleaned up pre- and post-Olympics it is now more pristine than it has ever been. Today's Bondi is supremely hip, and from the in-line skaters and skateboarders, to the surfing dudes, power-walking babes and early-morning outdoor yoga tribes, life is all about hanging on, or around, the sands. Come midday, the cafés, bars and restaurants swell with pretty people – and in the evening it's party central. Bondi also boasts some fine eateries – notably **Icebergs Dining Room** (p126), **North Bondi Italian Food** (p129)

and **Sean's Panaroma** (p129) – and while beer is the chosen beverage for the backpackers who still unite here, cocktails are the signature of the new hip crowd.

Head south around the corner from Bondi, and the next beach along is **Tamarama**. Swimming is dangerous here because of the rocks, but sunbathers (yes, ozone layer hole be damned, Sydneysiders do still love a tan) flock to this 100-metre (328-foot) sheltered cove, with volleyballers gathering for games at the back of the sand.

In the next bay, at the foot of a steep hill, is **Bronte**, backed by a grassy park and a stretch of increasingly chi-chi eateries, packed with yummy mummies and their broods. The outdoor **Bronte baths** are the preserve of kids.

Further still around the coast, beyond **Waverley Cemetery** (arguably one of the world's most picturesque burial sites) and past Burrows Park, is one of Sydney's

most idyllic spots – **Clovelly Beach**. A favourite with locals and as yet relatively undiscovered by tourists, this long inlet of calm water surrounded by a boardwalk and a concrete promenade is *the* place to swim and snorkel. Sitting on the rocks here watching the waves crash in is quite a treat.

The final stop on the walk is family swimming beach **Coogee**, which has old-fashioned pools carved into the rocks at both ends. Coogee is always busy and a tourist hub. Fast-food outlets line the promenade and pubs such as the **Coogee Bay Hotel** can get pretty rowdy at night. The softer side of Coogee can be seen on the Bay's northern headland – renamed **Dolphin Point** in 2003 – where two plaques commemorate the six Coogee Dolphin Rugby League players killed in the Bali bombings.

## Eating & drinking

### Blue Orange

*49 Hall Street, Bondi Beach (9300 9885/www.blueorangerestaurant. com.au). CityRail Bondi Junction then bus 333, 380, 381, 382, 333/bus 380.* **Open** 7.30am-4pm, 6.30pm-midnight Wed-Fri; 7am-4.30pm, 6.30pm-midnight Sat, Sun. Licensed/BYO (wine only). **Café. Map** p125 B1 ❶

Intimate and woody, Blue Orange is a sultry restaurant by night, but its day-time incarnation as a café offers the most mileage. If a ricotta and passion fruit soufflé isn't your cup of tea first thing, then the smoked salmon pancakes are also a good bet.

### Churrasco

*240 Coogee Bay Road, between Arden & Brook Streets, Coogee (9665 6535/ www.churrasco.com.au). Bus 372, 373.* **Open** 6-10.30pm Mon-Sat; noon-4pm, 6-10.30pm Sun. **$$**. Licensed. **Brazilian. Map** p125 A5 ❷

Here are six words for barbecue fans with a healthly appetite: All. You. Can. Eat. Brazilian. Barbecue. At Churrasco,

everything from sausages to hunks of lamb are skewered on giant sword-like constructs and cooked over hot coals. It's too loud for sensible conversation, so concentrate on the carnivorous carnage and drink a mojito.

### Coogee Bay Hotel

*Corner of Arden Street & Bay Road, Coogee (9665 0000/www.coogeebay hotel.com.au). Bus 372, 373, 374.* **Open** *Beach Bar* 9.30am-3am daily. *Sports Bar* 9am-4am Mon-Thur; 9am-6am Fri, Sat; 9am-10pm Sun. *Arden Bar & Arden Lounge* noon-1am daily (summer only). *Nightclub* 9pm-late Thur-Sat. No credit cards. **Pub. Map** p125 A5 ❸

Seating 500 punters (most of them visiting from the UK) the Coogee Bay's beer garden is truly a sight to behold. Other bars within the pub itself – which is enormous – offer sport, top-40 DJs, pool tables, a brasserie with cook-your-own steaks, and live music, all of which are attractions but none of which come close to supplanting the allure of the outdoor areas.

### Drift

*Ravesi's, 118 Cambell Parade, at Hall Street, Bondi Beach (9365 4422/ www.ravesis.com.au). CityRail Bondi Junction, then bus 333, 380, 381, 382/bus 333, 380.* **Open** 5pm-1am Mon-Fri; 3pm-1am Sat; 3pm-midnight Sun. **Pub. Map** p125 B1 ❹

This incredibly popular drinking haunt opened in late 2007 and has been over-flowing with pretty-somethings ever since. Upstairs at Ravesi's hotel (p176), slap bang on Campbell Parade, Drift is a chic glass and soft furnishings hang-out. Guests fight for the seats at the front with views across to the beach. Cocktails are the go, but so is lager, Mexican beer… whatever your tipple.

### Icebergs Dining Room

*1 Notts Avenue, Bondi Beach (9365 9000/www.idrb.com). CityRail Bondi Junction then bus 333, 380, 381, 382/bus 333, 380.* **Open** noon-3pm, 6.30-10.30pm Tue-Sat; noon-3pm, 6.30-9pm Sun. **$$$$**. Licensed. **Mediterranean. Map** p125 C2 ❺

# Beach safety

Stay out of strife in the surf.

Each year Sydney's surf lifesavers carry out countless rescue operations. A number of these involve tourists who have under-estimated the rips (currents) in the surf. Waves at Sydney's ocean beaches can reach up to four metres (13 feet) high and conceal powerful rips. To be safe, always swim between the red and yellow flags planted in the sand. If you stray outside them, the lifesavers will blow whistles and scream at you through megaphones. And don't think shallow water is completely safe. Dumpers are waves that break with force, usually at low tide in shallow water. Finally, remember that alcohol and water don't mix – most adults who drown in NSW are under the influence. If you do get caught by a rip and you're a confident swimmer, try to swim diagonally across it. If not, stay calm, put your hand in the air and float until rescued.

## Sharks

There was a fatal attack in NSW in 2008 but shark attacks are very rare. It's true that more sharks have been spotted in the waters around Sydney in recent years, but this is only because better sewage methods have left the ocean cleaner and more palatable to sharks. Many beaches are shark-netted to prevent them from establishing a habitat too close to shore. If you *do* see one while swimming, try not to panic. It's easier said than done, of course, but sharks are attracted to jerky movements, so try your best to swim calmly to shore. Scared? Remember it hardly ever happens.

## Stingers

Two kinds of jellyfish are common in summer. The jimble is box-shaped with four pink tentacles and often found on harbour beaches. In the ocean you're more likely to come across bluebottles, which have long blue tentacles.

Jimbles can deliver a painful sting but are not dangerous; bluebottles are nastier, causing an intense pain. If you are stung by a jimble, wash the affected area with vinegar (lifesavers keep stocks of it) – or, if you can, pee on it – and gently remove any tentacles with tweezers. If stung by a bluebottle, leave the water immediately and apply an ice pack or anaesthetic spray.

# Perfect picnic spots

**Clovelly Beach**

Even though Sydney is bursting with great places to eat, it's well worth joining the locals in the all-time favourite Aussie summer pastime: the spontaneous picnic.

All the delis in Sydney are picnic friendly, selling home-cooked rolls and loaves of bread, a multitude of cheeses and hams, olives and dips. A trip to the fish shop for a bucket of prawns (make sure you get ice as well and put them in an esky, the obligatory Aussie picnic carrier), and perhaps to the bottle shop for some chilled chardy and you're off! If you're planning to hit the barbecue (most beaches have them), don't forget to take a pair of tongs and kitchen paper to clean the grill down after use.

Bondi boasts a grassy picnicking slope that delivers on every count – panoramic ocean views, a whole swag of barbecues, plus toilets in the nearby elegant Bondi Pavilion.

If you're looking for rocks to lay your spread out on, try Tamarama, which has a secluded beach, picnic area and plenty of flat rocks to set up on. Supplement your picnic with refreshing power juices from the beach's Tama Café.

Bronte is the jewel in the crown, with its exquisite stretch of sand and tempting sea pool. There's plenty of shade on offer under the sandstone rocks, plus covered picnic benches (some with inlaid chessboards) and barbecues.

Swathed in natural beauty, Clovelly is an idyllic picnic spot. Barbecue pavilions and picnic tables abound, with amazing views of the ocean ahead. There's also a good café, Seasalt, which serves quality coffee and ice-creams.

Or, for an excellent family-friendly swimming beach boasting old-fashioned pools carved into the rocks, Coogee is hard to beat. The grassy picnic area behind the sand has barbecues and cafés. Beware of the pigeons and seagulls who will join you, looking for a handout.

Bondi Beach-flavoured eye-candy and visiting celebs are the order of the day at this crisply chic dining room, styled by the seriouly talented Maurice Terzini. Happily, the food more than matches the stellar location. Melt-in-the-mouth ox fillet, tender salt-crusted suckling lamb, delicate crab and soft polenta – it's all excellent. The Icebergs bar, with its top-tier views across the sweeping curve of Bondi's sands, is perfect for a drink at dusk, and the building also houses the famous Icebergs swimming club (see p130).

## North Bondi Italian Food

*118-120 Ramsgate Avenue, at Campbell Parade, North Bondi (9300 4400/ www.idrb.com). CityRail Bondi Junction then bus 333, 380, 381, 382/bus 333, 380.* **Open** 5-10.30pm Mon, Tue; noon-4pm, 6.30-10.30pm Wed-Sat; noon-4pm, 6.30-10pm Sun. **$$$**. Licensed. **Italian**. Map p125 C1 ❻

Yes, North Bondi Italian Food can get a bit noisy; no, you can't book a table and nope, it isn't as cheap as the menus printed on disposable paper place mats might suggest either. But this place, run by Icebergs restaurateur Maurice Terzini, is fabulous – fabulously busy, fabulously simple, a fabulously stylish osteria by the beach. It's all suitably rustic, which means Coopers Pale Ale and red wine on tap and hearty mains such as tripe with sausage, borlotti beans and peas. Pasta standouts include spaghetti arrabbiata with crab, cooked in a paper bag, and farfalle with braised game and porcini.

## Oceanic Thai

*309 Clovelly Road, at Walker Street, Clovelly (9665 8942/www.oceanicthai. com.au). CityRail Bondi Junction then bus 360/bus 339, X39.* **Open** 6-10pm Tue-Sat. **$$**. Licensed. **Thai**. Map p125 B4 ❼

Sexier than your average Thai diner, Oceanic Thai is in a great spot by the water. Max Mullin plied his trade at the stylish Sailors Thai in the Rocks; here his menu is designed to be eaten in small amounts over several courses. Try the *miang* of prawns, served with pomelo, the cashew salad, laced with chilli and kaffir lime, or the hot and heavenly stir-fried salted beef.

## Pompei

*Corner of Roscoe & Gould Streets, Bondi Beach (9365 1233). CityRail Bondi Junction then bus 333, 380, 381, 382/bus 333, 380.* **Open** 3-11pm Tue-Thur; 11am-11pm Fri-Sun. **$$**. Licensed/BYO (wine only). **Pizza**. Map p125 B1 ❽

It's a matter of fierce debate among locals: is the greatest thing about Pompei the creamy, all-natural gelato that comes in a range of seriously good flavours? Or is it the pizza, Naples-thin and served topped with everything from seasonal delights – such as the pizza bianco with fresh artichoke – to a timeless margherita?

## Sean's Panaroma

*270 Campbell Parade, at Ramsgate Avenue, Bondi Beach (9365 4924/ www.seanspanaroma.com.au). CityRail Bondi Junction then bus 333, 380, 381, 382, 333/bus 380.* **Open** 6.30-9.30pm Wed-Thur; noon-3pm, 6.30-9.30pm Fri, Sat; noon-3pm Sun. **$$$**. Licensed/BYO. **Mod Oz**. Map p125 C1 ❾

Sean's Panaroma is Sydney at its gourmet best – as long as you set foot in the place happy to pay top dollar for three (sometimes even just two) elements on a plate. The fact is that you're paying for what chef Sean Moran has the good sense to leave off. His dishes, such as linguine with chilli, rocket and lemon, showcase good quality ingredients, treated with care.

# Shopping

## Big Swim

*74 Campbell Parade, Bondi Beach (9365 4457/www.bigswim.com.au). CityRail Bondi Junction then bus 333, 380, 381, 382.* **Open** 9.30am-6pm daily (5pm in winter). Map p125 B1 ❿

An Aladdin's cave of bikinis, tankinis and one-pieces in loads of different styles and cup sizes. Perhaps Sydney's best swimwear shop for women. Also sells bags, sarongs amd towels.

## Bondi Beach Market

*Bondi Beach Public School, corner of Campbell Parade & Warners Avenue, Bondi Beach (9315 8988/ www.bondi markets.com.au). CityRail Bondi Junction then bus 333, 380, 381, 382, 333/bus 380.* **Open** 10am-5pm Sun. **Map** p125 C1 ⓫

This market can get crowded but it's worth it for new and vintage clothes, plus there's an excellent flower stall.

## Ksubi

*82 Gould Street, Bondi Beach (9300 8233/www.ksubi.com). CityRail Bondi Junction then bus 333, 380, 381, 382, 333/bus 222, 380.* **Open** 10am-6pm Mon-Wed, Fri, Sat; 10am-8pm Thur; 11am-6pm Sun. **Map** p125 B1 ⓬

Sydney surfer boys Dan Single, George Gorrow and Gareth Moody launched Ksubi (originally Tsubi) at Australian Fashion Week in 2001. Having caused a stir with their quirky catwalk shows ever since, they've made a name for themselves in ultra-cool jeans and tees.

## Mambo

*80 Campbell Parade, Bondi Beach (9365 2255/www.mambo.com.au). CityRail Bondi Junction then bus 380, 381, 382, 333/bus 222, 380, 333.* **Open** 9am-7pm daily. **Map** p125 B1 ⓭

This radical surf/skate label has long been a Sydney icon. Reg Mombassa of Aussie band Mental As Anything spun the brand's trademark designs.

## Paablo Nevada

*140 Curlewis Street, Bondi Beach (9365 0165). CityRail Bondi Junction then bus 333, 380, 381, 382, 333/bus 380.* **Open** 11am-6pm daily. **Map** p125 B1 ⓮

A Sydney label combining urban chic streetwear with a little bit of country.

## Nightlife

### Beach Road Hotel

*Corner of Beach Road & Glenayr Avenue, Bondi Beach (9130 7247). CityRail Bondi Junction then bus 380, 381, 333/bus 380, 333.* **Open** *Club nights* 7-11.30pm Tue-Thur; 7pm-1am Fri, Sat; 4-10.30pm Sun. **Admission** free. **Map** p125 B1 ⓯

While you have to wear more than a bikini top at the Beach Road Hotel, this Bondi institution is one of the few places where thongs (flip-flops) get through the door. Early closing during the week keeps the frenzy controlled but it's still a club option for those who want to hop from beach to disco in just a few bounds. Live acts perform on Tuesday, Thursday and Sunday and the hotel shifts to dance mode on Friday and Saturday nights.

## Arts & leisure

### Bondi Icebergs Club

*1 Notts Avenue, Bondi Beach (café 9130 3120/gym 9365 0423/pool 9130 4804/www.icebergs.com.au). CityRail Bondi Junction then bus 333, 380, 381, 382/bus 333, 380.* **Open** *Bar* 10am-late daily. *Café* 10am-10pm Mon-Fri; 8am-10pm Sat, Sun. *Gym* 6am-8.30pm Mon-Fri; 8am-5pm Sat, Sun. *Pool* 6am-6.30pm Mon-Fri; 6.30am-6.30pm Sat, Sun. **Admission** *Gym* $15. *Pool* $4.50; $2.50 reductions. **Map** p125 C2 ⓰

Although most famous for its long-standing all-weather swimming club, Icebergs houses a number of other attractions. Its pool, gym and sauna are all open to the public, plus there's the headquarters of Surf Life Saving Australia and a museum. The stunning Italian restaurant and bar are on the top floor (see p126), but you can get equally good views (and cheaper booze and food) from the Icebergs Club bar and Sundeck Café on the second floor.

### Bondi Openair Cinema

*Bondi Pavilion, Queen Elizabeth Drive, Bondi Beach (9130 1235/www.bondi openair.com.au). CityRail Bondi Junction then bus 380, 381, 382, 333/bus 222, 380, 333.* **Open** Mid Jan-mid Mar. **Admission** $17. **Map** p125 C1 ⓱

Quirky Bondi Openair offers myriad entertainment. Outside the beautiful Bondi Pavilion, the bar offers a local DJ and live bands, plus oceanside dining. When it's time for the main feature, grab a beanbag and head to the lawn or sit in the amphitheatre. All with the waves roaring in the background.

Glebe Market p136

# Glebe, Newtown & Balmain

There was a time when the inner-west area of Sydney was the cheaper, grungier, more real part of town. Devotees of soul over style headed over this way, but these days some of the style is starting to sneak above the parapet. There is still a lot of soul to latch on to out here, mind. Glebe has a warm villagey community feel without any of the quaintness. Despite some very chic apartment developments down on the water and the rising prices of its large Victorian houses, the area still retains a studied shabbiness, clinging on to its hippie-let-live crystal shops and long-standing market. And let's not forget the budget hotels and backpackers that thrive here. The many restaurants along **Glebe Point Road** have remained reasonably priced and the pubs still pack some punch.

Newtown has a very different feel – neo-student meets arty urbanite. Essentially, all shades of society meet here – there's a healthy gay scene, lots of artists, film makers, students and plenty of others besides who just like a bit more edge to their Sydney. Takeaway restaurants abound in the inner-west, and it is the home of the cheap Thai sitdown gaff, all of which are pretty good and all of which attract a devoted pack of regulars. **King Street**, Newtown's main drag, has transformed itself in recent times, exploding with new shops, although many of the newcomers are less quirky and more mainstream than the grungy outlets they replace.

Despite its slum roots, Balmain stands out from Glebe and Newtown as a centre of comfortable living. Along **Darling Street** you'll find great restaurants, cute houses, many with water views, oodles of hip cafés, organic food sellers and clusters of shops selling things you never thought you wanted, but suddenly can't resist.

## Eating & drinking

### Boathouse on Blackwattle Bay

*Blackwattle Bay end of Ferry Road, Glebe (9518 9011/www.boathouse. net.au). Bus 431, 432, 433, 434, 370.* **Open** noon-3pm,6.30-10.30pm Tue-Thur, Sun; noon-3pm, 6-10.30pm Fri, Sat. **$$$**. Licensed. **Seafood**. **Map** p133 C1 ❶

It's all about oysters at the Boathouse. Order lots of them – you'll normally find at least six different kinds on the menu – and splash out on a bottle of quality bubbles while you're at it. Now marvel at the oysters' freshness, their diverse tastes and textures, how well they go with the brown bread and Champagne – and at the unique glory of this most relaxing of top-tier Sydney restaurants. Hungry for more? Don't miss the crab, flown in fresh from the Northern Territory. At the Boathouse it gets the simple treatment it deserves – cracked and tossed in a wok just long enough to bring out just the right amount of seasoning and spring onion to bring out the delicate meat's clean sweetness.

### Courthouse Hotel

*Corner of Australia & Lennox Streets, Newtown (9519 8273). CityRail Newtown.* **Open** 10am-midnight Mon-Sat; 10am-10pm Sun. No credit cards. **Pub/restaurant**. **Map** p135 B2 ❷

Newtown's Courthouse Hotel serves counter meals to go with your fine schooner of beer (the stout on tap is especially good) plus it has one of the nicest courtyards in Sydney. Give the Steak Dianne a bash.

### Fish on Fire

*217A Glebe Point Road, at Bridge Road, Glebe (9660 4212). Bus 431, 434.* **Open** 11am-9pm daily. **$**. Unlicensed. **Fish**. **Map** p133 C3 ❸

Fish on Fire on Glebe Point Road is more of a takeaway hole than an eatery, but there are a couple of tables outside if you want to sit down. The chef does a great beer-battered chip, the fish is succulent and it's all pretty exceptional value.

### Glebe Point Diner

**NEW** *407 Glebe Point Road, between Cook & Forsyth Streets, Glebe (9660 2646). Bus 431, 434.* **Open** 6-9pm Wed, Thur; noon-2.30pm, 6-9pm Fri, Sat; noon-3pm Sun. **$$$**. Licensed. **Mod Oz**. **Map** p133 B2 ❹

Organic roast chook, house-made pasta, Scharer's beer on tap and lip-smackingly fine suckling pig to boot. The Glebe Point Diner is the best that Glebe has to offer.

### Guzman y Gomez

*175 King Street, at O'Connell Street, Newtown (9517 1533/www.guzman ygomez.com). CityRail Newtown.* **Open** 11.30am-10pm Mon-Sat; 11.30am-9pm Sun. **$**. **Mexican**. **Map** p135 C2 ❺

Guzman y Gomez may look like little more than a fast food joint, but don't be fooled. This is the most authentic Mexican food in the city. Its corn chips are legendary and the pork adobado burrito is exceptional.

### Iku Wholefood Kitchen

*25A Glebe Point Road, between Parramatta Road & Francis Street, Glebe (9692 8720/www.iku.com.au). Bus 370, 431, 432, 433, 434.* **Open** 11am-9pm Mon-Fri; 11am-8pm Sat; noon-7.30pm Sun. **$**. BYO. No credit cards. **Vegan**. **Map** p133 C3 ❻

Vegetarians, vegans, macro-eaters and diet-conscious individuals all flock to Iku in search of nourishment that is entirely vegetable in origin.

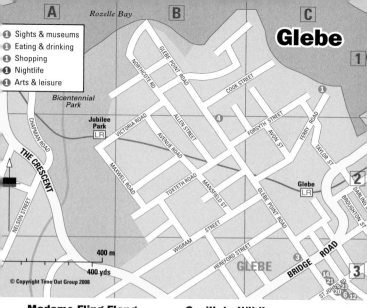

SYDNEY BY AREA

## Madame Fling Flong

*Level 1, 169 King Street, Newtown (9565 2471/www.madameflingflong. com.au). CityRail Newtown or Macdonaldtown.* **Open** 4pm-late daily. No credit cards. **Bar. Map** p135 C1 ❼

In a cosy little room, perched above a dodgy-looking restaurant that at first glance you probably wouldn't cross the street for, hides a bar space odyssey with a fit-out of retro furnishings and tatty chaises longues accommodating a big, padded corner bar. It's pretty easy to see why Madame Fling Flong has become the *bar du jour* for all those resident renaissance slackers in the city's inner-west. Newtown to its skuffed black boot heels and tattooed ankles, Fling Flong likes to keep things reassuringly and suitably eclectic, hosting vintage movie screenings, smooth sounds on Sundays and glass upon glass of crackerjack cocktails all night, every night. If you're looking for the true soul of the inner-west, you'll damn cert find it here.

## Oscillate Wildly

*275 Australia Street, between King Street & Hoffman Lane, Newtown (9517 4700). CityRail Newtown.* **Open** 6-10pm Tue-Sat. **$$**. BYO (wine only). **Mod Oz. Map** p135 B2 ❽

It's not every day you come across a restaurant named after a Smiths track, but it almost makes sense in Newtown. Don't expect the restaurant to share Morrissey's devotion to vegetarianism, however – you'll find the likes of pork belly and fish pie on the menu, alongside duck confit on a white bean purée. Tiny and pitched at diners keen not to drain away their dollars, it's not the most formal and refined of restaurants, but it's got plenty of heart.

## Pastizzi Café

*532 King Street, at Alice Street, Newtown (9519 1063). CityRail Newtown.* **Open** 8am-11pm daily. BYO. **Café. Map** p135 B3 ❾

The Pastizzi Café may be simply laid out, bedecked by bright red and white walls, and with just a few modest wooden tables inside and out, but above the counter are all manner of mouth-watering *pastizzi*. Made to an old family recipe, the crisp and flaky pastries range from bacon and egg, to cheese, chicken and mushroom. Grab one, sit down and enjoy with a coffee or snack on the hoof.

## Peasant's Feast

*121A King Street, between Missenden Road & Elizabeth Street, Newtown (9516 5998/www.peasantsfeast. com.au). CityRail Newtown.* **Open** 6-10pm Tue-Sat. **$$.** BYO. **Pan-European.** Map p135 C1 ⑩

Organic produce is brought to the fore at the Peasant's Feast, but fear not – flavour and presentation haven't fallen foul to the kitchen's staunch idealism. Savour the gnocchi with a tasty ragout of aubergine and mushrooms, or the 100 per cent organic cassoulet. Prices are very reasonable too.

## Pomegranate

*191 Darling Street, between Ann & Stephen Streets, Balmain (9555 5693). Bus 434, 442.* **Open** 5.30-10pm Tue-Thur; 12.30-3pm, 5.30-10pm Fri-Sun. **$$.** Licensed/BYO. **Thai.** Map p137 A2 ⑪

Pomegranate is the best Thai in Balmain, no question. Spoilt for choice on the menu? Its betel leaves with whitebait and the soft shell crab with a side of pomegranate salad are the way to go. Desserts are sweet, salty and true to their authentic Thai roots.

## Restaurant Atelier

*22 Glebe Point Road, between Parramatta Road & Francis Street, Glebe (9566 2112/www.restaurant atelier.com.au). Bus 431, 432, 433.* **Open** 6pm-late Tue-Thur, Sat; noon-2pm, 6pm-late Fri. **$$$.** Licensed/BYO (wine only). **Modern European.** Map p133 C3 ⑫

Glebe Point Road has an unfortunate knack for killing off restaurants that reach for the stars (and sometimes bite off more than they can chew), but let's hope the curse passes the door of this modest-looking eatery with ambition.

Darren Templeman cut his teeth in the Michelin-starred restaurants of the UK, and his command of technique is clear in everything from his Berkshire pork rillettes with pickles to a 'lasagne' of blue swimmer crab, shellfish oil, basil and olives. Long may it stand.

## Restaurant Sojourn

*79 Darling Street, at Duke Street, East Balmain (9555 9764/www.sojourn. com.au). Ferry Balmain or Balmain East/bus 442, 445.* **Open** 6-10.30pm Tue-Sat; noon-3pm , 6-10.30pm Fri. **$$$.** Licensed. **French.** Map p137 C2 ⑬

Perched right near the Balmain wharf, Restaurant Sojourn is a winsome little sandstone restaurant plating up some classic French fare, starched white tablecloths and all. Order the savoury duck terrine or assiette of rabbit. Or, for something with a little more grunt, opt for the pan-fried skate served with braised oxtail.

## Sonoma Café

*215 Glebe Point Road, between Bridge Street & St Johns Road, Glebe (9660 2116/www.sonoma.com.au). Bus 370, 431, 432, 433, 434.* **Open** 8am-4pm Mon-Sat; 9am-2pm Sun. Unlicensed. No credit cards. **Café.** Map p133 C3 ⑭

If you don't try the organic sourdough bread at Sonoma, you're missing out on some of the best buns this side of San Francisco. It also does a decent coffee and a few pastries.

## Town Hall Hotel

*326 King Street, between Newman & Wilson Streets, Newtown (9557 1206). CityRail Newtown.* **Open** 9am-2.30am Mon; 9am-3.30am Tue-Thur; 9am-4.30am Fri, Sat; 10am-midnight Sun. No credit cards. **Pub.** Map p135 B2 ⑮

Popular with students, the pierced, tattooed, dyed and branded, as well as the just plain reckless, the Townie has a kind of mojo at work that sees its two floors of undistinguished wooden furniture and framed train-wreck photos somehow play host to the sort of two-fisted drinking mayhem that makes it a thing of beauty unto itself.

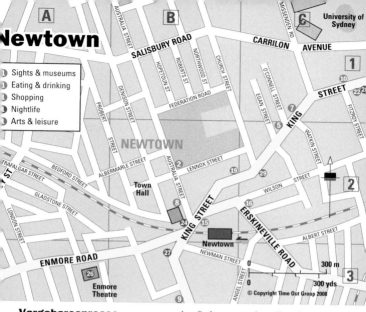

# Newtown

- Sights & museums
- Eating & drinking
- Shopping
- Nightlife
- Arts & leisure

## Vargabarespresso

*Corner of Wilson Street & Erskineville Road, Newtown (9517 1932). CityRail Newtown.* **Open** 7am-6pm Mon-Fri; 8am-5.30pm Sat, Sun. BYO. No credit cards. **Café**. Map p135 C2 🔞

The coolest coffee in Newtown is just off the beaten track. Friendly staff serve interesting American diner-style eats such as meatball sarnies with grilled cheese and the hangover-helping Berocca frappé. The burgers are sensational, but if you're feeling more virtuous, the porridge is good too.

## Shopping

### Balmain Market

*St Andrew's Church, corner of Darling Street & Curtis Road, Balmain (9555 1791/www.balmainmarket.com). Ferry Balmain or Balmain East/bus 442, 445.* **Open** 8.30am-4pm Sat. Map p137 A2 🔞

Artists sell paintings and ceramics in this pretty market in the grounds of a charming 19th-century church. You'll also find very good quality vintage jewellery, hammocks, naturally made cosmetics and organic fruit and veg. A chilled out spot to souvenir shop.

### Dress Me Darling

*305 Darling Street, Balmain (9810 8818). Bus 433, 434, 442, 445.* **Open** 10am-6pm Mon-Sat; 11am-5pm Sun. **Map** p137 A2 🔞

As its name suggests this Balmain boutique is basically an enormous walk-in wardrobe full of decadent buys. There's a well picked selection of undies for those who like their smalls to veer on the cutesy side.

### Fish Records

*261 King Street, between Church & Mary Streets, Newtown (9557 3074/www.fishrecords.com.au). CityRail Newtown.* **Open** 9am-10pm Mon-Sat; 9.30am-6pm Sun. **Map** p135 B2 🔞

Next to the Dendy cinema, this branch of Fish stocks mostly top-40 and dance music, with a good soundtrack section.

## Glebe Market

*Glebe Public School, Glebe Point Road, between Mitchell Street & Parramatta Road, Glebe (4237 7499).* Bus 370, 431, 432, 433, 434. **Open** 10am-4pm Sat. Map p133 C3 **20**

Glebe's selection of Saturday morning stalls used to be the among the most feral in the whole of Sydney, but it is slowly becoming smarter as the area gentrifies. All the same, you can expect second-hand clothing, kooky jewellery and hippie, New-Agey stalls, plus some cracking crafts and bookshops.

## Gleebooks

*49 Glebe Point Road, between Cowper & Francis Streets, Glebe (9660 2333/ www.gleebooks.com.au).* Bus 370, 431, 432, 433 434. **Open** 9am-9pm daily. Map p133 C3 **21**

The highly rated Gleebooks has two branches on Glebe Point Road and a third at the Sydney Theatre. No.191 in Glebe specialises in second-hand and children's books, as well as shelves of more esoteric works on the humanities. This shop at No.49 sells everything else, while the theatre branch only opens around performance times to tout its wares to the luvvies.
**Other locations:** 191 Glebe Point Road, Glebe (9552 2526); Sydney Theatre, 22 Hickson Road, Opposite Pier 6/7, Walsh Bay (9250 1930).

## Goulds

*32 King Street, between Queen & Fitzroy Streets, Newtown (9519 8947/www.gouldsbooks.com.au).* Bus 422, 423, 426, 428, 352. **Open** 8am-midnight daily. Map p135 C1 **22**

Around 3,000m (9,000ft) of bookshelves at Goulds in Newtown make it the largest second-hand bookshop in Sydney. It's a librarian's nightmare, of course, but well worth the rummage – and it's open until midnight if you fancy a post-beer browse. The shop specialises in Australian history and politics, and general Australiana, but you'll find just about anything here from pot-luck fiction to cookbooks to travel guides. A must for backpackers stocking up before hitting the road.

## Sappho Books

*51 Glebe Point Road, between Cowper & Francis Streets, Glebe (9552 4498/ www.sapphobooks.com.au).* Bus 370, 431, 432, 433, 434. **Open** 8am-9pm Mon-Sat; 9am-7pm Sun. Map p133 C3 **23**

A popular, friendly and immaculately catalogued second-hand bookshop that offers something for every bookworm – from Australian first editions and leather-bound tomes, to art books and the latest kiddies' classics. There's also a comfortable café at the rear.

# Nightlife

## Bank Hotel

*324 King Street, between Newman & Wilson Streets, Newtown (8568 1900).* CityRail Newtown. **Open** 10am-late daily. Map p135 B2 **24**

The Bank is one of Newtown's most popular pubs. It draws a smattering of gays and lesbians throughout the week, but traditionally gets overrun with lesbians on Wednesday nights. The three-level venue includes great outdoor areas, casual bars, a quality cocktail lounge and DJs at night. Look out also for the pub's in-house (but outdoor) Thai restaurant, Sumalee Thai.

## Cat & Fiddle Hotel

*456 Darling Street, at Elliot Street, Balmain (9810 7931/www.thecatand fiddle.net).* Bus 432, 433, 434, 445. **Open** 10am-midnight Mon-Sat; noon-10pm Sun. **Admission** $8-$10. No credit cards. Map p137 A2 **25**

Folk, bush, jazz and pop: all do the rounds at this seasoned, ever-reliable venue in Balmain. Out-of-towners pick up work here, while old faves often play low-key shows for the faithful.

## Enmore Theatre

*118-132 Enmore Road, between Simmons & Reiby Streets, Newtown (9550 3666/www.enmoretheatre. com.au).* CityRail Newtown. **Admission** prices vary. Map p135 A3 **26**

The most atmospheric of the inner-city venues, the Enmore's 1,600-seat theatre plays host to established local talent,

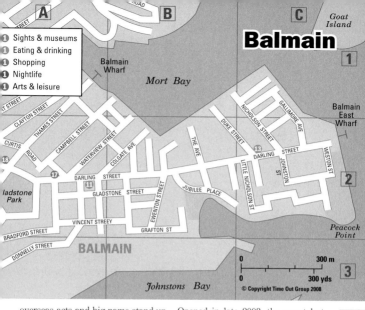

## Balmain

Legend:
- Sights & museums
- Eating & drinking
- Shopping
- Nightlife
- Arts & leisure

0 — 300 m
0 — 300 yds

© Copyright Time Out Group 2008

overseas acts and big-name stand-up and theatre. Queens of the Stone Age, Kings of Leon and the Rolling Stones (doing a bijou club night) have all rocked up and strutted their stuff here.

### Sandringham Hotel

*387 King Street, between Holt & Goddard Streets, Newtown (9557 1254/ www.sando.com.au). CityRail Newtown.* **Open** 10am-midnight Mon-Wed; 10am-2am Thur-Sat; 10am-10pm Sun. **Admission** $5-$15. **Map** p135 B3 ㉗
The Sandringham's upstairs space is small yet cosy and decked out in lots of opulent red. Plenty of undiscovered talent plays to a receptive brigade of young 'uns hungry for fresh sounds.

### Vanguard

*42 King Street, between Queen & Fitzroy Streets, Newtown (9557 7992/www.thevanguard.com.au). Bus 352, 370, 422, 423, 426, 428.* **Open** 5pm-midnight Tue-Sat; 4-10pm Sun. **Admission** $10-$30. **Map** p135 C1 ㉘

Opened in late 2003, the smart but homely Vanguard adds to the inner-west's appeal on the live music front. Expect a range of rock, jazz and blues, in comfy surroundings, plus there's a restaurant for a touch of post- or pre-gig sustenance. Both international and local touring acts regularly grace the stage here.

## Arts & leisure

### Dendy Newtown

*261-263 King Street, between Mary & Church Streets, Newtown (9550 5699/www.dendy.com.au). CityRail Newtown.* Screens 4. **Tickets** $14; $8-$10.50 reductions. **Map** p135 C2 ㉙
The Dendy Newtown offers quality first releases, 562 super-comfortable seats, big screens, digital surround sound and a bar. There's free parking for filmgoers in the Lennox Street car park behind the cinema which is something of a plus for drivers used to too often jam-packed King Street.

North Sydney Olympic Pool

# Kirribilli & Milsons Point

The comfortable north shore starts at Kirribilli and Milsons Point – two tiny suburbs nestled on either side of the Harbour Bridge and offering sweeping dress-circle views of the city and Opera House. The tip of Kirribilli is home to **Kirribilli House**, the official Sydney residence of the prime minister, and **Admiralty House**, home of the governor general.

## Sights & museums

### Luna Park Sydney

*1 Olympic Drive, Milsons Point (9033 7676/www.lunaparksydney.com). CityRail/ferry Milsons Point.* **Open** 11am-6pm Mon-Thur; 11am-11pm Fri; 10am-11pm Sat; 10am-6pm Sun. **Admission** free. Individual rides vary.

Unlimited ride passes $20, $33, $43; free under-85cm (3ft). **Map** p139 A2 ❶

Sydney's venerable funfair is back in full stomach-churning swing after a troubled few decades (see box p140). Attractions include the Big Top, used for concerts, and the revamped Crystal Palace, now a conference hall.

## Eating & drinking

### Catalonia

*31A Fitzroy Street, Kirrribilli (9922 4215/www.catalonia.com.au). CityRail/ ferry Milsons Point.* **Open** 6-10pm Tue-Fri; noon-4pm, 6-10pm Sat, Sun. **$$$**. Licensed. **Spanish**. **Map** p139 B1 ❷

There's an all-Spanish wine list at Catalonia where dishes include a deep-fried egg with runny saffron yolk. The *churros* (doughnuts) are exceptional.

# Kirribilli & Milsons Point

## Garfish

*Corner of Burton & Broughton Streets, Kirribilli (9922 4322/www.garfish. com.au). CityRail/ferry Milsons Point.* **Open** 8-11am, noon-3pm, 6-9.30pm Mon-Sat; 9-11am, noon-3pm, 6-8.30pm Sun. **\$\$\$.** Licensed/BYO (wine only). **Seafood. Map** p139 B1 ❸
The guys at Garfish work hand-in-fin with one of Sydney's leading seafood suppliers, so the focus really is on freshness. Try the likes of aromatic kingfish curry or choose from the daily catch, chalked up on the blackboard.

## Shopping

### Kirribilli Market

*Bradfield Park, Alfred Street, Milsons Point (9922 4428/www.kncsydney.org). CityRail/ferry Milsons Point.* **Open** 7am-3pm 4th Sat of mth; also 1st & 3rd Sat in Dec. **Map** p139 A1 ❹
This monthly market specialises in bric-a-brac and antiques, but you'll also find vintage dress stalls and jewellery.

## Arts & leisure

### Ensemble Theatre

*78 McDougall Street, Kirribilli (9929 0644/www.ensemble.com.au). CityRail Milsons Point/ferry Kirribilli.* **Admission** \$46-\$62; \$22 reductions. **Map** p139 B1 ❺
A beautifully run theatre with one of Sydney's best foyers.

### North Sydney Olympic Pool

*4 Alfred Street South, Milsons Point (9955 2309/www.northsydney.nsw. gov.au). CityRail/ferry Milsons Point.* **Open** 5.30am-9pm Mon-Fri; 7am-7pm Sat, Sun. **Admission** *Pool* \$5.50; \$2.80-\$4.50 reductions. *Sauna, spa & swim* \$16. **Map** p139 A2 ❻
This unique outdoor pool, set between the Harbour Bridge and Luna Park, opened in 1936 and was hailed as the 'wonder pool of Australasia'. Today a slick 25m-indoor pool, gym, spa and sauna have been added to the famed 50m-heated outdoor pool. The views are nothing short of stupendous.

# Ticket to ride

A faceless facelift, a tragic fire and disgruntled local residents have all threatened to thwart the existence of Sydney's iconic amusement park over the past 70 years. But this grand old dame was built on solid foundations – the ones used to construct the Harbour Bridge – and having survived the war, not to mention ghastly plans to turn her into a high-rise tower block, **Luna Park** (p138) is still standing.

The park opened in 1935 on the former site of the Dorman Long Workshop which was used for the construction of the Harbour Bridge. Luna Park was based on the success of its Victorian elder sister in St Kilda, Melbourne. Another less successful sibling, in Glenelg, South Australia, would donate its rides to the fledgling Sydney park. Built in just over three months by 800 structural

workers, the original entrance fee was 6d, 3d for children. War cast an inevitable shadow over the fun and the lights of Luna Park were 'browned', but it remained a magnet for courting couples.

In its heyday, the park was closed each winter to overhaul the rides. When maintenance engineer and later park manager Ted 'Hoppy' Hopkins retired in 1970, the good old days looked like they might become a thing of the past. Around the same time, Luna Park survived an attempt to be turned into a multi-storey building, first in 1969, then again in the 1980s – both plans were knocked back by the council. But Luna's reputation shot up in flames following a fatal fire in the Ghost Train ride in 1979, in which one adult and six children died. The park closed.

A brief reopening in 1982 was lacklustre, mainly for its over-American feel, and, by 1988, the park was closed once again, left dilapidated and empty.

Then, after years of lobbying by the Friends of Luna Park, the site was deemed Crown land and its doors jubilantly reopened in 1995. But the noise of the Big Dipper was keeping residents in plush Kirribilli awake at night, and remarkably, the park was once again brought to a standstill.

But Luna Park is the queen of the comeback. On 4 April 2004 she rose for one final roll of the dice, showing off a brand-new spit and polish, with a contemporary-meets-nostalgic feel. The latest state of play? At last count, some 4.5 million visitors had crossed her path and the old gal's rides keep on trucking.

**Manly Beach**

# Manly

Getting to Manly is half of its appeal. Either jump on a trusty green and gold, double-ended **Manly ferry** from Circular Quay or take the slick JetCat. The trip takes you out through the harbour, past millionaires' mansions towards Manly Wharf in Manly Cove, where there's a small harbour beach and a netted swimming area. The real **Manly Beach** is on the ocean side of this gateway to the northern beaches. Head across the pedestrianised **Corso** with its colourful array of shops and restaurants and you'll reach the Norfolk pines that line the promenade behind Manly Beach. It's quite a sight and the walk around the next cove to **Shelly Beach** is a favourite with locals. Traditionally, Manly has been a mecca for migrant Brits and,

consequently, real Sydneysiders have mixed feelings about the beachside haven. Nevertheless there's a lot to like here. The living is relaxed, people are very friendly and it lacks the urban edge of the city on the other side of the water.

## Sights & museums

### Manly Art Gallery & Museum

*West Esplanade (9976 1420/ www.manlyaustralia.com.au/ManlyArt Gallery/). Ferry Manly.* **Open** 10am-5pm Tue-Sun. Closed public holidays. **Admission** free. **Map** p143 A2 ❶ Opened in 1930, this small museum has an 845-strong collection of paintings by Australian artists, alongside more than 2,000 historic photographs of the northern beaches and some impressive ceramics. It is also the setting for some edgy exhibitions by local students and

# Surfie speak

Thinking of hitting the surf? First get clued up on the Surfer's Code of Ethics. Surfing is all about respect – respect for the beach and ocean, and, of course, respect for safety

Surf Life Saving Australia has a member patrolling every surfing beach in the country. And they are especially on the lookout for the gremmies and grommets – young, mischievous surfers who are perhaps too brave for their own good. This bunch never get clucked (scared of a wave). Instead they just get amped (charged up) at the sight of a bump (a big set of waves).

Keeping up? Good. Because if you want to fit in, you've got to learn the lingo. You may be a kook (a bad surfer or learner) or even a wannabe (you've got the clobber but not the board). But even if you have no boards in your quiver (that's the sack that the serious guys carry their boards in), you can at least earn respect by getting the wording right. Another way to spot the pros is to look for the ones doing the 'cheater five, hanging the toes on the nose', meaning they're keeping their weight on the back of the board, squatting down and extending one foot, Beckham-style, in front.

These are the dudes who complain of having noodle arms (from paddling out to sea). Be sure to give them a wide berth if they've just been snaked – some kook has just stolen their wave by paddling inside them… let's just hope it wasn't you.

photographers. The museum recounts the history of Manly with the help of a marvellously kitsch collection of beach memorabilia, including some great vintage swimming costumes.

## Manly Visitor Information Centre

*Manly Wharf (9976 1430/www.manly tourism.com). Ferry Manly.* **Open** 9am-5pm Mon-Fri; 10am-4pm Sat, Sun (5pm in summer).* **Map** p143 A3 **②**
Situated at the front of the wharf, this is the place to find brochures, bus timetables, free maps and lots of other information about what's going on.

## North Fort

*North Fort Road, off North Head Scenic Drive (9976 6102/www.north fort.org.au). Ferry Manly then bus 135.* **Open** 9am-4pm Wed-Sun. **Admission** $11; $5-$8 reductions. **Map** p143 C3 **③**
The remote location of North Fort means its landscape has changed little since early colonial paintings of the spot. Wind-blown sand dunes cover the headland, with hillside 'hanging' swamps among the coastal shrub. Today it is home to the Royal Australian Artillery National Museum, once part of the School of Artillery constructed between 1935 and 1938 in the shadow of war and the need to defend Sydney Harbour from naval attack. You can still tour around the fortifications, underground tunnels and a memorial walkway – the last undergoes continual upgrades as more and more inscribed paving stones are added, honouring nationals who have served in the defence of Australia.

## North Head Quarantine Station

*North Head Scenic Drive (bookings 9976 6220/www.q-station.com.au). Ferry Manly then bus 135.* **Open** (pre-booked tours only) *Day tour* 3-5pm Sat; 10am-12pm & 3-5pm Sun. *Adults' ghost tour* 8-11pm Wed-Sun. *Family ghost tour* 6.30-8.30pm Sun, Thur. **Admission** *Day tour* $25; $19 reductions. *Adults' ghost tour* $34; $32 reductions. **Map** p143 C3 **④**

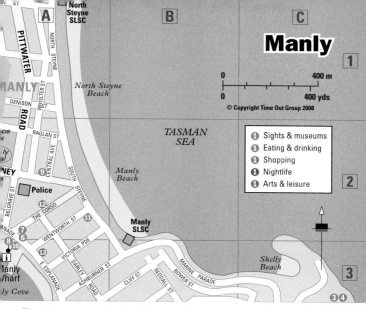

The ghost tours at the North Head Quarantine Station may just be the creepiest sightseeing excursion you'll ever come across. Several visitors claim to have seen the resident ghosts – a moustachioed man in a three-piece suit and a stern matron – and many more have reported feeling decidedly nauseous after getting a whiff of putrid and inexplicable smells. If you take the adults' night tour, bring a torch and wear flat shoes.

### Oceanworld Manly

*West Esplanade (8251 7877/ www.oceanworld.com.au). Ferry Manly.* **Open** 10am-5.30pm daily. **Admission** $17.95; $9.50-$12.95 reductions; discount after 3.30pm. **Map** p143 A2 ❺
This three-level attraction has a floor devoted to Australia's most dangerous creatures (among them poisonous snakes, funnel web spiders, giant monitor lizards and crocodiles) plus another floor dedicated to tropical fish, corals and venomous sea creatures.

The main attraction, however, is the oceanarium on the lower-ground floor, which holds the largest sharks in captivity in the whole of Australia, alongside several giant rays and sea turtles.

## Eating & drinking

### Alhambra Café & Tapas Bar

*54 West Esplanade, opposite Manly Wharf (9976 2975). Ferry Manly.* **Open** 6-10.30pm Tues; noon-3pm, 6-10.30pm Wed-Sun. **$$$**. Licensed/ BYO (wine only). **Moroccan/ Spanish. Map** p143 A2 ❻
Moorish by theme, moreish by nature, this loud, fun restaurant in Manly does a great line in tapas, as well as richly spiced tagines, fluffy jewelled couscous and luscious *pastillas* – shredded braised chicken in light, crisp pastry dusted with sugar. The sunny outdoor seating and wild flamenco on Saturday nights only serve to up the ante.

## Bacino

*Shop 1A, The Corso (9977 8889/ www.bacinobar.com). Ferry Manly.* **Open** 6am-6pm Mon-Thur; 6am-10pm Fri, Sat; 7am-10pm Sun. Licensed/BYO. No credit cards. **Café. Map** p143 A2 **7**

Manly folk happily queue up for their morning fix from this popular Italian corner café. The Little Italy coffee blend is rich and addictive and there are generously stuffed paninis on offer for lunch too.

## Bavarian Beer Café

*Shops 2-5, Manly Wharf (9977 8088/ www.bavarianbeercafe.com.au). Ferry Manly.* **Open** 10am-late Mon-Fri; 8.30am-late Sat, Sun. **$$**. Licensed. **German. Map** p143 A2 **8**

Despite the name, it's actually all about the meat at the Bavarian Beer Café. Try a whopping veal schnitzel with sauerkraut or Bavarian meat platter stacked with sausage and mashed potato. And, for a few more calories, there are giant pretzels served with a wad of butter.

## Ground Zero

*18 Sydney Road, at Central Avenue (9977 6996). Ferry Manly.* **Open** 8am-5pm daily. BYO. **Café. Map** p143 A2 **9**

Sun, surf and… short blacks? The folk at Ground Zero serve one of the best blends of coffee in Sydney. It's a loungey establishment just a hop and a skip from the sands of Manly Beach and perfect for whiling away a sunny afternoon. For lunch or dinner the fresh salmon is always succulent.

## Manly Wharf Hotel

*Manly Wharf, East Esplanade (9977 1266/www.manlywharfhotel.com.au). Ferry Manly.* **Open** noon-midnight Mon-Sat; noon-10pm Sun. **$$**. **Pub. Map** p143 A3 **10**

The slick Manly Wharf development is a divine (if loud) place to meet for a drink with a waterside view but it's also a really lovely spot to rendezvous for more solid sustenance. While the steaks, duck potsticker dumplings with pineapple relish and such like are pretty good, the seafood is, fittingly

enough for the wharf location, the main highlight. You can decide to dine à la carte and enjoy such piscatorial delights as open lobster ravioli with scallops and asparagus. Or, if there are a few of you, just opt for the enormous seafood platter ($130).

## Shore Club

*36-38 South Steyne (9977 6322). Ferry Manly.* **Open** *Sand bar* 11.30am-midnight Mon-Wed; 11.30am-2am Thur-Sat; noon-midnight Sun. *Sound bar* 8pm-2am Fri, Sat; 7pm-midnight Sun. *Sun deck* 4pm-midnight Mon-Wed; 4pm-2am Thur, Fri; noon-2am Sat; noon-midnight Sun. **Bar. Map** p143 A2 **11**

The list is designed by bar guru Alexx Swainston. The balcony is as breezy, laidback and cool a location as you'd wish to find yourself, drink in hand. Go for the Pimm's jug – a bargain at $26. There's also the Mexican Ponyride (tequila, tequila and more tequila) if you're feeling serious. Manly's looking up in bar land.

## Shopping

## Platypus Shoes

*47 The Corso (9977 1500/www.platypus shoes.com). Ferry Manly.* **Open** 9am-6pm Mon-Sat; 10am-5.30pm Sun. **Map** p143 A2 **12**

Platypus does hip brands such as Diesel, Onitsuka Tiger, Crocs, Vans and Birkenstock, at reasonable prices. There are loads of cool trainers, as well as hats and sunglasses for the beach.

## Arts & leisure

## Manly Cinemas

*25/43-45 East Esplanade, opposite Manly Wharf (9977 0644/www.manly cinemas.com.au). Ferry Manly.* Screens 2. **Admission** $14; $7-$12 reductions. **Map** p143 A3 **13**

This modest two-screener opposite Manly Wharf shows quality art-house flicks and cherry-picked mainstream hits to a culture-vulture crowd. There's a recently upgraded sound system, stadium-style seating and fresh juice on sale in the foyer.

Cremorne Point p149

# Neighbouring Sydney

While the CBD is compact, the rest of Sydney sprawls. Here are a few places that are worth the trip – some close by, some further away (no trip further than three hours from the city).

## Vaucluse & Watsons Bay

Vaucluse, on the harbour in the east, is one of Sydney's super-rich suburbs and always has been. Consequently, there's an air of ownership from its locals but don't let that put you off. A trip to **Nielsen Park** and **Shark Beach** is a Sydney highlight and the harbour swimming is some of the best in the city.

It is claimed that **Watsons Bay** was the country's first fishing village. Now largely the province of **Doyles on the Beach** seafood restaurant (11 Marine Parade, 9337 2007, www.doyles.com.au) and rowdy weekend pub the **Watsons Bay Hotel**, it has stunning views back across the harbour to the city, particularly at night, and retains vestiges of its old charm, including original weatherboard houses and terraces. These are best seen by walking north to the First Fleet landing spot at **Green Point Reserve** and on to Camp Cove and Lady Bay beaches, and the Hornby lighthouse on the tip of **South Head**. On the other (ocean) side of the peninsula from Watsons Bay beach is the bite in the sheer cliffs that gives the **Gap** its name – and from which many have jumped to their doom. Gap Park is the start of a spectacular cliff walk that runs south back into Vaucluse and also the best place to watch the annual **Sydney to Hobart Race** (p38).

## Sights & museums

### Nielsen Park

*Greycliffe Avenue, Vaucluse (9337 5511/www.nationalparks.nsw.gov.au). Bus 325.* **Open** 5am-10pm daily. **Admission** free.

Generations of Sydneysiders have been flocking to Nielsen Park since the early 1900s. They sit on Shark Beach, the grassy slopes behind it, or climb the headlands either side of the sands for a great view across the harbour. With its abundance of shady trees, gentle waters, panoramic views and excellent Nielsen Park Café and Restaurant (serving à la carte meals, plus snacks and ice-creams), it's the perfect picnic spot. It's also a favourite viewing point for the New Year's Eve fireworks over the harbour (p38). Nestled in the grounds to the rear of the grassy slopes lies Greycliffe House, a Gothic-style mansion built in 1862 as a wedding gift from the co-founder and first editor of the *Australian* newspaper, William Charles Wentworth, for his daughter Fanny and her husband John Reeve. In 1913, it became a baby hospital, then a home for new mothers. Nowadays it's a NSW National Parks & Wildlife Service office, providing info on parks throughout the state. Keep an eye out for the seaplanes that take off from neighbouring Rose Bay (p47) and begin their ascent over the waters of Shark Bay.

### Vaucluse House

*Vaucluse Park, Wentworth Road, Vaucluse (9388 7922/www.hht.net.au). Bus 325.* **Open** *House* 9.30am-4pm Fri-Sun. *Grounds* 10am-5pm Tue-Sun. **Admission** $8; $4 reductions.

The oldest 'house museum' in the country sits prettily in a moated 19th-century estate, surrounded by ten hectares (28 acres) of prime land, with its own sheltered beach on Vaucluse Bay. From 1827 to 1853 and 1861 to 1862 this was the opulent home of William Charles Wentworth. His house originally stood in a much larger estate, and 26 servants were required to look after the master's three sons and seven daughters, not to mention his vineyards, orchards and beloved racehorses. The Historic Homes Trust has endeavoured to keep the place as it was when the Wentworth family was in residence. In the kitchen a fire burns in the large grate and hefty copper pans line the walls. Look out for the tin bath, taken on trips to Europe, that still displays a sticker from London's Victoria Station, and the door in the sumptuously furnished drawing room that hides its own little secret piece of history (ask a guide to open it).

## Eating & drinking

### Watsons Bay Hotel

*1 Military Road, at Cliff Street, Watsons Bay (9337 5444/ www.watsonsbayhotel.com.au). Ferry Watson's Bay/bus 324, 325, 380.* **Open** 10am-midnight daily. **Pub**.

Let's be honest. The fish and chips are so-so. The drinks aren't that thrilling or cheap. But the Watto (as it's fondly known) is still on most Sydneysiders' list of the city's top pubs. The place is an eastern suburbs institution, and there really is something to be said for watching the sun sink over the harbour from the comfort of its capacious veranda, surrounded by other beer-swilling day-trippers.

## Mosman, Cremorne & Balmoral

On the north side of the harbour, the enclaves of **Mosman**, **Cremorne** and **Balmoral** are where Sydney's seriously moneyed

# Sydney's best beaches

There are more than 50 beaches along Sydney's coastline, from the surfers' wild Whale Beach in the north, to picnic spot Clovelly in the south. The harbour beaches are smaller and protected while the bigger ocean beaches attract surfers and serious swimmers.

From September to May, nearly all of Sydney's ocean beaches are patrolled by lifeguards (see also box p127). Rules are stringent: alcohol and fires are banned, and on many beaches, ball games and frisbees are also illegal.

Locals swim all year round in the warm waters of the sheltered harbour inlet at **Shark Beach** (Nielsen Park, Vaucluse). If you don't swim, you can watch the ferries, yachts and kayakers vie for space in the harbour, or just grab a bite to eat at the (licensed) café. Sun-seekers love the strip of bright yellow sand at **Camp Cove** (Victoria Street, Watsons Bay) but it's not good for surfing.

The Bathers' Pavilion at **Balmoral Beach** (p151), now one of Sydney's most popular eateries, was built in the late 1920s. Families flock to Balmoral for its sheltered waters and two large sandy beaches, separated by

Rocky Point, a picnicking island accessible by a footbridge.

**Chinamans Beach** (McLean Crescent, Mosman) is a hidden gem, stumbled upon via the dunes on the edge of the Rosherville bushland reserve.

Australia's most famous strip of sand, **Bondi Beach** (Campbell Parade, Bondi) can attract up to 40,000 people a day, but go at certain times of the week and you'll find it comparatively quiet. The central area near the Pavilion is safest for swimming; surfers favour the southern end, with its strong rips. Nearby at **Clovelly Beach** (Clovelly Road, Clovelly), the sand slopes into a long inlet of calm water, surrounded by a boardwalk and promenade.

Jumping aboard a Sydney ferry to **Manly Beach** (Manly) is a must. To reach the open sea, head across the busy pedestrianised street, the Corso. Manly has all the facilities of a big resort and on a hot day can attract up to 50,000 sun-seekers. Meanwhile, the 700-metre (2,230-foot) stretch of salmon-pink sand at **Whale Beach** (The Strand), approached via a set of mind-bendingly steep roads, offers seriously big surf.

Airline flights are one of the biggest producers of the global warming gas $CO_2$. But with **The CarbonNeutral Company** you can make your travel a little greener.

Go to **www.carbonneutral.com** to calculate your flight emissions then 'neutralise' them through international projects which save exactly the same amount of carbon dioxide.

Contact us at **shop@carbonneutral.com** or call into the office on **0870 199 99 88** for more details.

**CarbonNeutral**®flights

Taronga Zoo

live in conspicuous splendour. **Cremorne Point**, a sliver of a peninsula, offers one of the finest panoramas of Sydney Harbour and a great coastal walking path through the bush. Further back in Mosman, vast houses line winding roads and **Mosman Village** is packed with cafés, cake shops and delis for the ladies who lunch.

Further east lies **Taronga Zoo**, extremely popular with tourists and occupying a splendid vantage point overlooking Bradleys Head. On the other 'Middle Harbour' side of Mosman is Balmoral, one of Sydney's prettiest harbour suburbs. Boasting not one but two beaches, plenty of open green space and a Romanesque bandstand (the venue for many local events), Balmoral is also a scenic place to eat and boasts a few excellent restaurants, including the pioneering Bathers' Pavilion (p151).

## Sights & museums

### Taronga Zoo

*Bradleys Head Road, Mosman (9969 2777/www.zoo.nsw.gov.au). Ferry Taronga Zoo/bus 247.* **Open** 9am-5pm daily. **Admission** *Zoo only* $37; $18-$23 reductions. *Zoopass* $44; $30-$21.50 reductions.

Only 12 minutes by ferry from Circular Quay, the 'zoo with a view' covers 17.5 hectares (43 acres) on the western side of Bradleys Head. The zoo moved here from Moore Park in Sydney's eastern suburbs in 1916. The animals arrived by ferry – the story goes that Jessie the elephant actually walked from Moore Park to Circular Quay before gingerly climbing aboard ship. The zoo contains some 2,600 animals of more than 340 species: best of all, especially for tourists, are the native ones, including cute koalas, kangaroos, platypuses, Tasmanian devils and lots of colourful, screechy birds (follow the zoo's well trodden Wild Australia Walk to see them all). Visitors are no longer

**SYDNEY BY AREA**

allowed to actually cuddle koalas, but a 'koala encounter' (11am-2.45pm) lets you have a photo taken beside one of the sleepy critters.

Other highlights include the Free Flight Bird Show, the Seal Show, Giraffes in Focus – meet the giraffes face to face, listen to a keeper talk and grab a close-up photo – the huge Komodo dragon and the Gorilla Forest, where, at the time of writing, a very cute baby gorilla was born, drawing huge crowds. Backyard to Bush is a journey from an Aussie backyard through an adventure-packed farm-yard into a bush wilderness, and the new Asian Elephant Rainforest is quite a sight, with its deep swimming pool waterfall and mud wallows. The zoo's elephant exhibit is part of a large new area called Wild Asia, which includes a 2.3km (1.4-mile) stretch where the elephants walk past other species including gorillas and penguins.

The zoo is on a hill, so if you arrive by ferry, take the SkySafari cable car to the main zoo compound at the top and then walk back down to the wharf. You can buy a Zoopass at Circular Quay to cover the return ferry trip, cable car and zoo admission. It's a huge place and tricky to find your way around (the free map is pretty poor), so allow at least three to four hours for a visit. There are several cafés, but the food isn't great either, so it's a good idea to take your own picnic.

## Eating & drinking

### Alchemy 731

*731 Military Road, between Gouldsbury Street & Belmore Road, Mosman (9968 3731/www.alchemy731.com.au). Bus 169, 175, 178, 180, 247.* **Open** 6-9.30pm Tue-Thur, Sat; noon-2pm, 6-10pm Fri. **$$**. Licensed. **Modern European**.

European-style dining in all its glory can be found on the busy main drag of Mosman. Go for the traditional European lunch special with every-thing from gravadlax to saltimbocca on the menu.

Bathers' Pavilion

## Bathers' Pavilion

*4 The Esplanade, between Awaba Street & Mandolong Road, Balmoral Beach (9969 5050/www.bathers pavilion.com.au). Ferry Taronga Zoo then bus 238/ferry Mosman South then bus 233.* **Open** *Café* 7am-late daily. *Restaurant* noon-2.30pm, 6.30-9.30pm daily. *Café* **$$**. Set menu *Restaurant* **$$$$**. Licensed. **Mod Oz**.

Pioneering chef Serge Dansereau has one of the best located restaurants in the north of Sydney, looking straight out over Balmoral Beach. His chestnut soup is delicate, sweet and bold and while the steep prices are almost enough to cause a drop in appetite, the Pavilion is still an incredibly popular choice with locals and tourists alike. The paintings of Balmoral that adorn the covers of the restaurant's menus are by local artist Kerry Lester, who has been exhibited at the Archibald Prize (p37) 11 times.

## Mino

*521 Military Road, between Gurrigal & Harbour Streets, Mosman (9960 3351). Bus 169, 175, 178, 180, 247.* **Open** 6-10pm Tue-Sun. **$$**. Licensed/BYO (wine only). **Japanese**.

Mosman's Military Road is home to many Japanese eateries that range from several pretty ordinary mass-market sushi joints to the well hidden charms of this little restaurant. Not much to look at from the outside, Mino is quite nice once you're through the door – and though the à la carte options are wide-ranging, regulars all seem happy to put their faith in the chef's *kaiseki* menu.

## Ripples at Chowder Bay

NEW *Deck C, Chowder Bay Road, Mosman (9960 3000/www.aqua dining.com.au). Bus 244.* **Open** 9-11am, noon-3pm, 6-9.30pm Mon-Fri; 8-10.30am, noon-4pm, 6-9.30pm Sat, Sun. **$$**. Licensed/ BYO (wine only). **Italian**.

A rare restaurant in Sydney where the food actually stands up to the view. Try the skewers of pork, polenta and cabbage or perhaps the *fregolone*

(that's Italian for little balls of pasta). This 140-seater restaurant, with its beautiful views (and a welcome breeze to boot), is the perfect place to while away a Saturday afternoon.

## Vera Cruz

*314 Military Road, between Winnie Street & Langley Avenue, Cremorne (9904 5818). Bus 169, 175, 178, 180, 247.* **Open** 6-10pm Mon-Sat. **$$**. Licensed/BYO. **Mexican**.

You won't find traditional Mexican – that great gap in the Australian culinary landscape – at Vera Cruz. But then this very designer boîte isn't so much aiming for authenticity as a crowd-pleasing lightness and clarity of flavour – no bad thing, either. Try the kitchen's killer chicken *mole*, washed down with a couple of cervezas.

## Arts & leisure

## Hayden Orpheum Picture Palace

*380 Military Road, between Winnie & Macpherson Streets, Cremorne (9908 4344/www.orpheum.com.au). Bus 143, 144, 151, 228, 229, 230, 243, 246, 247, 257. Screens 6.* **Admission** $15.50; $8.50-$12 reductions. *Special* Tue $7.50-$10.50.

Without doubt the grandest cinema in Sydney, Cremorne's art deco picture palace is a stunning step back in time. The Hayden Orpheum was built in 1935 by George Kenworthy, the top theatrical architect of the period. Today's version is actually even more glitzy than the original, thanks to a $2.5-million restoration by owner and local TV celeb Mike Walsh. Each of the six auditoria has its own colour scheme and decor, but the 744-seat Orpheum is the true star of the show. It even boasts a genuine Wurlitzer cinema organ, which rises out of a stage pit on weekend evenings, complete with flashing lights and a grinning organist. Expect a mix of mainstream US, British and Australian fare, with some art house, special presentations and occasionally the odd cabaret show.

## Northern Beaches

Beyond the environs of the city lies Sydney's longest-kept secret – the seemingly endless stretch of sensational surf beaches that lines the north coast like a priceless string of pearls. This really is no exaggeration and locals know it, which is why they have fiercely protected the northern beaches from tourist overload.

The northern beaches start over the **Spit Bridge**, which crosses Middle Harbour connecting Mosman to Seaforth and Manly, but it's the more distant suburbs such as **Collaroy**, **Narrbeen**, **Newport**, **Avalon**, **Whale Beach** and **Palm Beach** that set the tone for the area, which is lush, laidback and totally devoted to beach, surf and the good life.

## Sights & museums

### Ku-ring-gai Chase National Park

*NPWS office 9472 8949/www. nationalparks.nsw.gov.au.* **Open** sunrise-sunset daily. **Admission** $3 arriving by boat/ferry; $2 reductions; $11 per vehicle.

Set where the Hawkesbury River meets the sea and occupying nearly 15,000 hectares (37,000 acres) of dense forest, hidden coves and sheltered beaches, Ku-ring-gai Chase was designated a national park in 1894. It is located within one of Sydney's wealthiest municipalities, stretching from the southern suburbs of St Ives North and Wahroonga, to Broken Bay in the north. Every visitor to Sydney should take in the West Head lookout if they can, with its views over the mouth of the Hawkesbury, the beginning of the Central Coast, Barrenjoey Lighthouse and Palm Beach. Walking tracks lead to significant examples of Aboriginal rock art. Guided walks and canoe and boat tours can also be arranged. There are various walking routes into the

park depending on where, and how far, you want to go – contact the park office for more information.

## Eating & drinking

### Chelsea Tea House

*48 Old Barrenjoey Road, Avalon (9918 6794). Bus 188, 190, E88, L88, L90.* **Open** 8.30am-4pm daily. Licensed/BYO. No credit cards. **Café**.

Lucienne Francisco's wagyu beef brisket sandwich doused in homemade barbecue sauce is so good, you won't care about the extra juice dripping down your chin and collecting on the table. And your lap. In fact, you'll want an extra piece of bread to mop it up.

### Cook's Larder

*Shop 1, 21-23 Old Barrenjoey Road, near Avalon Parade, Avalon (9973 4370/www.thecookslarder.com.au). Bus 188, 190, E88, L88, L90.* **Open** 8am-4pm Mon-Sat; 8am-3.30pm Sun; 6.30pm-late Fri. BYO. **Café**.

The cake at Cook's Larder is legendary. But that's not all – it also has a beaut breakfast menu stuffed with goodies such as homemade baked beans and (joy of joys) crumpets. You can BYO, as well as purchase a couple of kitchen utensils while you're at it and take some cake for the drive (or walk) home. And just to sweeten the deal, it's only a two-minute walk from the beach.

### Jonah's

*69 Bynya Road, between Norma & Surf Roads, Palm Beach (9974 5599/www.jonahs.com.au). Bus 190, L90.* **Open** 8am-11am, noon-3pm, 6.30-9.30pm Mon-Thur, Sun; 8am-11am, noon-3pm, 6.30pm-late Fri, Sat. **$$$**. Licensed. **Mod Oz**.

California-born George Francisco is maestro of Mod Oz cuisine, cooking up such savoury delights at Jonah's as roasted marrow bone with crunchy garlic croutons and Murray cod. Menu highlights include snow crab and Francisco's dessert of soufflé with mixed berries. For a complete blow-out, catch the seaplane over to the restaurant from Rose Bay (p47).

# Into the wild

Not all Aussie animals can hurt you – honest.

**Fruit bats**

While visitors may tremble at the sight of a plump huntsman spider, a swooping ibis, or a squeaking fruit bat, the locals fiercely guard their native species (which are protected by NSW law). Thankfully, once you get to know the wildlife, there's not so much to fear.

## Brush-tailed possum

Possums make a lot of noise as they thump across the city's rooftops, and just as much mess, eating fruit, leaves and flowers. But despite the carnage, they're harmless. The solitary marsupials with pointy snouts, pink noses, long whiskers and large ears can grow to the size of a large cat and only come out after dark.

## Kangaroos & wallabies

You won't find the nation's iconic marsupials hopping around down at the harbour, but you won't have to go far to spot them. They are most active at night, dusk and dawn, grazing in the Blue Mountains and country areas.

## Koalas

This shy bear only eats one type of eucalyptus leaf and is tricky to spot in the wild. Your best bet is to head to Taronga Zoo (p149) or Sydney Wildlife World (p87).

## Birds

Sydney boasts an astonishing amount of birdlife. Look out for the kookaburra (the world's largest kingfisher) with its white and brown plumage and distinctive laugh, the ibis with its long beak and spindly legs, sulphur-crested cockatoos, pink galahs and the plump pelicans which follow ships around the harbour. And if you're by the water around Manly, watch out for the fairy penguins.

## Fruit bats

At dusk, Sydney's central and eastern skies fill with these bats heading out in search of food.

## Snakes

The most dangerous snakes to be found in NSW are the tiger snake, brown snake, death adder, king brown snake and several species of sea snake. The good news is that most are more scared of you than you are of them.

## Spiders

There are two Sydney spiders with a potentially fatal bite – the funnel web (reddish-brown and hairy) and the redback (small and black with a red stripe on its body). Other (harmless) spiders you're more likely to encounter are the huntsman, which often hangs out indoors, catching mosquitoes, and the golden orb, found along the foreshore in Manly and Vaucluse.

**SYDNEY BY AREA**

## Newport Arms Hotel

*Corner of Beaconsfield & Kalinya Streets, Newport (9997 4900/ www.newportarms.com.au). Bus 188, 190, L88, L90.* **Open** 10am-midnight Mon-Sat; 10am-10pm Sun. **Pub**.

This Newport landmark (est. 1880) has a mammoth beer garden out the back boasting a spectacular view over Pittwater and the eucalyptus-clad hills of Ku-ring-gai Chase National Park (p152). It's the perfect spot for a post-beach beer as you contemplate your sunburn. Three restaurants, a giant outdoor screen and guest rooms are the Newport's added attractions.

## Swelter

*1112 Barrenjoey Road, Palm Beach (9974 3169). Bus 190, L90.* **Open** 8am-4pm Tue-Sun; 6-10pm Thur-Sat. Licensed & BYO. **Café**.

A lengthy chalked-up blackboard menu that runs the length of the room encapsulates the easy, no-nonsense Aussie/Italian vibe at this stylish new addition to Barrenjoey Road. Swelter's kitchen does a good line in panini, steak sangas and organic fizzies.

## Brighton-le-Sands, Cronulla & Bundeena

Traditionally, Sydney's south starts at **Brighton-le-Sands** in the district of Rockdale and then a very cliquey district known as the **Shire**. **Cronulla** is the stronghold of the Shire, championing a lifestyle of sun, surf, sea and anything (preferably motorised) that allows you to travel on water.

Brighton-le-Sands involves a different sense of community, having largely been claimed by generations of Greeks. Neither the noisy swoop of planes into Sydney Airport at next-door Mascot, nor the view of billowing smoke from the oil refinery at Kurnell across Botany Bay, can dim their enthusiasm for recreating the spirit of a Greek coastal town.

During the week the Shire remains a relatively insular peninsula with few interlopers. On Sundays, however, families from the outer southern and western suburbs catch Sydney's only train-to-beach service to Cronulla, where they come to picnic under the shady beachside trees.

A 20-minute ferry ride from Cronulla's Tonkin Street Wharf across Port Hacking delivers you to **Bundeena**, a small township (population 2,300) and former artists' colony, that spreads out along the top of the north-eastern section of the **Royal National Park**. Bundeena's charm is that it's quiet. Very quiet.

Established in 1879, the Royal was Australia's first national park – and only the second in the world, after Yellowstone in the US. Covering 150 square kilometres (58 square miles) on the southern boundary of Sydney's metropolitan area, it offers stunning coastline, rainforest, open wetlands, estuaries and heath. Visitors can spend days bushwalking, picnicking, swimming and birdwatching. The depths of the park are best explored by car, though Bundeena is a handy haven from the wilds, especially if you're fed up with camping. There are three main beaches here, two of which fall within the national park.

## Sights & museums

### Royal National Park

*9542 0648/www.national parks. nsw.gov.au.* **Open** *Park* 7am-8.30pm daily. *Visitor centre* 9.30am-4.30pm Mon-Fri; 8.30am-4.30pm Sat, Sun. **Admission** $11 per vehicle.

You can get to the Royal by following walking paths from various nearby CityRail stations – namely Engadine, Heathcote, Loftus, Otford, Waterfall – but once there, driving is by far the easiest way to explore its vast expanse.

The park's nerve centre is at Audley, on the Hacking River, once the heart of the park's Victorian 'pleasure gardens'. Here you'll find the main visitor centre (drop in for information on the park's walking trails), alongside spacious lawns, an old-fashioned dance hall and a causeway. If you've brought some provisions, you can hire a rowing boat or canoe from the Audley boathouse and head upstream to the charming picnic spots at Ironbark Flat or Wattle Forest. If you're a surfer, Garie Beach provides some suitably animated waves, while further south is Werrong Beach, set among littoral rainforest and the park's only authorised nude bathing spot. At secluded Wattamolla Beach you'll often be lucky enough to glimpse migrating whales out in the blue. The park's many walking trails include Lady Carrington Drive, an easy 10km (six-mile) track along the Hacking River, and the more arduous 26km (16-mile) Coast Track, which hugs the coastline from Bundeena to Otford, providing gorgeous views out to sea en route.

## Eating & drinking

### Blackwater

*Shop 1, 8 Water Street, Sans Souci (9529 4893/www.blackwaterrestaurant. com.au). CityRail Rockdale then bus 477/bus 303.* **Open** 6-9.30pm Tue; noon-2.30pm, 6-9.30pm Wed-Fri, Sun; 6-9.30pm Sat. **$$**. Licensed/ BYO. **Italian**.

Traditional Italian food hits Sans Souci with the help of chef Riccardo Roberti who dishes up the likes of gnocchi with housemade pesto, arancini with eggplant ragu and light-as-a-feather, pear sorbet in stylish surrounds.

### Nun's Pool

*103 Ewos Parade, Cronulla (9523 3395/www.thenunspool.com). CityRail Cronulla then bus 985.* **Open** 8am-4pm Tue-Sun. **$$**. Licensed. **European**.

The waitresses at Nun's Pool wear cut-off jeans, and walking into the homely room is like stepping in to a sunny lounge. Breakfast is a modern-day take on the fry-up, with balsamic tomatoes, mushrooms with prosciutto and thyme and poached eggs on asparagus.

**Parramatta JetCat**

## Parramatta & Olympic Park

Parramatta – the 'capital' of the west – boasts a historical importance to rival any area in Sydney, as well as housing the city's second business district. Historically, western Sydney belonged to the Dharug, Dharawal and Gandangara people before the white settlers moved in, and the word Parramatta is, like many Sydney place names, Aboriginal in origin. Parramatta also has a rich colonial heritage as Australia's second-oldest white settlement, making it an important tourist stop for heritage buildings. Closer to the city, the Olympic Park in **Homebush Bay** was where the Aussies proudly held the 2000 Olympic Games. The area has since been turned into a family-oriented sports and leisure complex.

## Sights & museums

### Elizabeth Farm

*70 Alice Street, between Arthur & Alfred Streets, Rosehill (9635 9488/ www.hht.net.au). CityRail Parramatta then 15min walk.* **Open** 9.30am-4pm Fri-Sun. **Admission** $8; $4 reductions. Elizabeth Farm is notable for being the birthplace of the Australian wool industry – John Macarthur imported merino sheep for breeding at the site – and for the farm's main building. With its deep, shady verandas and stone-flagged floors, it became the prototype for the Australian homestead. Parts of the original 1793 construction – the oldest surviving European building in Australia – remain. The interior has been restored to its 1830s condition, with a recreated Victorian garden to match. The museum's genteel Tearooms are open from 11am to 3pm. The farm is run by the Historic Houses Trust, which looks after various museums and historic sites in Sydney.

### Experiment Farm Cottage

*9 Ruse Street, Harris Park (9635 5655/ www.nsw.nationaltrust.org.au). CityRail Harris Park then 10min walk/RiverCat Parramatta then 20min walk.* **Open** 10.30am-3.30pm Tue-Fri; 11am-3.30pm Sat, Sun. **Admission** $6; $4 reductions. *Joint admission with Old Government House* $10; $7 reductions.

In 1789, Governor Phillip set up an experiment 'to know in what time a man might be able to support himself'. The guinea pig for Phillip's study was convict James Ruse, who became self-sufficient in two years and was given the colony's first land grant as a reward, thereby becoming Australia's first private farmer. He subsequently sold the land to a surgeon, John Harris, who built this modest cottage.

### Old Government House

*Parramatta Park, Parramatta (9635 8149/www.nsw.nationaltrust.org.au). CityRail/RiverCat Parramatta then 15min walk.* **Open** 10am-4pm Mon-Fri; 10.30am-4pm Sat, Sun. **Admission** $8; $5. *Joint admission with Experiment Farm Cottage* $10; $7 reductions.

Set in 105 hectares (260 acres) of park-land, Old Government House was built between 1799 and 1818 on the foundations of Governor Phillip's 1790 thatched cottage, which had fallen down, and is Australia's oldest public building. Previously a vice-regal residence and, at the turn of the 19th century, a boarding house for a local boys' school, it has been restored to its former glory via a multi-million-dollar revamp. The house also boasts the nation's most important collection of Australian colonial furniture, and, if you find yourself there on the right day, the ghost tours on the third Friday evening of each month are a real hoot.

### Parramatta Heritage & Visitor Information Centre

*346A Church Street, next to Lennox Bridge, Parramatta (8839 3311/ www.parracity.nsw.gov.au). CityRail/RiverCat Parramatta then 10min walk.* **Open** 9am-5pm daily.

Experiment Farm Cottage

# Hunter's top drop

Head to the Hunter Valley where the wines are corkers.

About two hours' drive north of Sydney is Australia's oldest wine-growing region, the Hunter Valley. About 3,500 hectares (8,650 acres), are under vine here, with an annual crushing in the vicinity of 35,000 tonnes. Famous for its sémillon and shiraz grapes, the Hunter is now making a name for itself with chardonnay, verdelho and chambourcin.

With 120 wineries in the region, it can be hard to know where to start. Pokolbin is as good a place as any, and boasts a number of fantastic wineries. Tyrell's Wines has been in the Hunter Valley since the 1850s. Its 2007 Lost Block Sémillon, $17, is a blend of citrus and melon flavours that you can drink now or cellar for five years (Tyrell's Wines, Broke Road, Pokolbin, 4993 7000). Although it's making a name for itself as a contract winemaker, First Creek Wines also owns the Chatto label. The Chatto Hunter Valley Shiraz 2004, $40, is an excellent medium-bodied, spicy wine (First Creek Wines, corner of McDonalds and Gillards Roads, Pokolbin, 4998 7293).

Chambourcin is a French/American hybrid that's found some favour in the Hunter. Tamburlaine Wines is an organic grower that produces a Member's Reserve Chambourcin, a medium-bodied dry red (Tamburlaine Wines, 358 McDonalds Rd, Pokolbin, 4998 7570). Excellent value is the McGuigan Bin 6000 Verdelho 2007. At about $10, it's a fresh wine full of fruit. Also have a crack at the sémillon (McGuigan Wines, corner of Broke and McDonalds Roads, Pokolbin, 4998 7402).

Worth a diversion from Pokolbin is Two Rivers Wines near Denham. Its award-winning Reserve Chardonnay 2006, $20, has spicy oak and stone fruit (Two Rivers Wines, 2 Yarrawa Road, Denham, 6547 2556). Other cellar doors of interest include Hungerford Hill – the Terroir restaurant is excellent as are its sémillon and shiraz (Hungerford Hill, 1 Broke Road, Pokolbin, 4998 7666) and Poole's Rock (Poole's Rock, DeBeyers Road, Pokolbin, 4998 7356), where you'll find its eponymous label, as well as Cockfighter's Ghost and Firestick.

## Eating & drinking

### Temasek

*71 George Street, between Church &*
*Smith Street, Parramatta (9633 9926).*
*CityRail Parramatta.* **Open** 11.30am-
2.30pm, 5.30-10pm Tue-Sun. **$$**.
BYO. **Malaysian**

Long held to be the purveyor of
Sydney's finest laksa, this plastic table-
clothed place also takes top honours
in the beef rendang and Hainan
chicken stakes. House specialities at
Temasek also include fishhead curry
(a whole lot tastier than it sounds) and
fiery chilli crab.

## Arts & leisure

### Acer Arena

*Olympic Boulevard, at Edwin Flack*
*Avenue, Sydney Olympic Park,*
*Homebush Bay (8765 4321/*
*www.acerarena.com.au). CityRail*
*Olympic Park/RiverCat Homebush Bay*
*then bus 401.* **Admission** prices vary.
Built for the 2000 Olympics, the Acer
Arena (formerly known as the Sydney
SuperDome) has a whopping 21,000-
seat capacity and multiple layouts
for anything from rock and pop to rap.
Elton John, Justin Timberlake and
Gwen Stefani have all played here and
the joint also hosts big-scale dance par-
ties, monster truck shows and various
equestrian events.

### Parramatta Riverside Theatres

*Corner of Church & Market Streets,*
*Parramatta (8839 3399/www.riverside*
*parramatta.com.au, CityRail/RiverCat*
*Parramatta.* **Admission** $25-$55; $15-
$35 reductions.
This costly Bicentennial project is a
council-mandated and multi-theatre
complex, perched beside the pleasant,
if a little brownish, Parramatta River.
It hosts shows touring from central
Sydney venues and across Australia,
as well as the annual (and very good)
Big Laugh Comedy Festival, which
takes place in late March/early April.
Visit the website for more details.

### Sydney International Aquatic Centre

*Olympic Boulevard, Sydney Olympic*
*Park, Homebush Bay (9752 3666/*
*www.sydneyaquaticcentre.com.au,*
*CityRail Olympic Park/RiverCat Sydney*
*Olympic Park then bus 401.* **Open** 5am-
9pm Mon-Fri; 6am-8pm Sat, Sun. Tours
on request only. **Admission** *Swim*
*& spa* $6.40; $4.40-$5 reductions. *Swim*
*& gym* $13; $9.30 reductions. *Tours* $3,
call for group guided tours.
Having hosted the pool events during
the Olympics, this place is still home to
high-quality international meets and a
handful of somewhat less illustrious
inter-school competitions. The centre is
a really excellent venue for serious,
lane-pounding swimmers, but also
impressive enough to visit as a land-
mark in its own right.

### Sydney International Athletics Centre

*Edwin Flack Avenue, Sydney Olympic*
*Park, Homebush Bay (9752 3444/*
*www.sydneyathleticcentre.com.au).*
*CityRail Olympic Park/RiverCat Sydney*
*Olympic Park then bus 401.* **Open**
*Visits* 3-8pm Mon-Fri; 8am-1pm Sat;
9am-1pm Sun.

### Sydney Olympic Park Sports Centre

*Olympic Boulevard, Sydney Olympic*
*Park, Homebush Bay (9763 0111/*
*www.sports-centre.com.au). CityRail*
*Olympic Park/RiverCat Sydney Olympic*
*Park then bus 401.* **Open** *Visits*
7.30am-10.30pm daily.
It hosted tae kwon do and table tennis
in the Olympics and now this sports
centre is home to various spectator
sports, including gymnastics, soccer,
badminton, volleyball, hockey and
martial arts.

### ANZ Stadium – Australia's Home Ground

*Olympic Boulevard, Sydney Olympic*
*Park, Homebush Bay (8765 2000/*
*guided tours 8765 2300/*
*www.anzstadium.com.au). CityRail*
*Olympic Park/RiverCat Sydney Olympic*
*Park then bus 401.*

In 2008, the former Telstra Stadium was renamed by its new sponsor ANZ bank. Crowds fill almost half of its 83,500 capacity at regular rugby league games, while it tends to be nearly full for exhibition events. You'll struggle to get a ticket for rugby union tests or State of Origin rugby league games.

## Blue Mountains

Two hours west of the CBD and well worth a day, overnight or weekend trip are the World Heritage-listed Blue Mountains, boasting breathtaking views across deep valleys, waterfalls and bush.

### Sights & museums

#### Scenic World

*Corner of Cliff & Violet Streets, Katoomba (4782 2699/www.scenic world.com.au).* **Open** 9am-5pm daily. **Admission** *Skyway return trip* $16; $8 reductions. *Cableway & Railway return trip* $19; $10 reductions.

This collection of tourist transports is all about views and vertigo. The Scenic Skyway – a cable-car system over the Jamison Valley – was renovated a few years ago. The new cars have glass floors, so now visitors can see exactly how far the drop is – 270m (890ft), in fact. The Scenic Railway features an old coal train reinvented as the world's steepest rail incline, which takes you down into the rainforested valley – as does the Scenic Cableway, another cable-car ride. There's a 2km (1.25-mile) boardwalk between the Railway and Cableway stations, so you can go down on one and back on the other.

## Hunter Valley

The second most visited region in New South Wales after the Blue Mountains is the state's main wine-growing region, which is precisely what makes it so popular. The area surrounding the town of **Pokolbin**, two to three hours north of Sydney,

boasts more than 75 wineries, offering tastings and cellar-door sales of wine ranging from semillon and shiraz to chardonnay. Nestled among the vineyards are award-winning restaurants and luxury hotels, but there are plenty of cheaper options for those on a budget as well.

## Arts & leisure

### Activity Tours Australia

*9904 5730/www.activitytours.com.au.* **Admission** (with lunch) $100; $94 reductions.

Organises day trips from Sydney to the Hunter Valley, taking in five wineries, a tour to see how wine is made and a cheese factory. Maximum 19 people.

### Balloon Aloft

*1800 028 568/4938 195/www.balloon aloft.com.*

Offers hot-air balloon rides for people staying overnight; you meet an hour before dawn so it's probably best not to sample too much of the local drop the night before. The relaxing balloon trip takes in the spectacular landscape of vineyards, rivers, forests and the rolling hills of the valley, followed by a Champagne reception back on land.

### Hunter Vineyard Tours

*4991 1659/www.huntervineyardtours. com.au.* **Admission** from $55; *with lunch* $80.

Offers full daytrips in 12- or 22-seat buses, taking in five wineries (lunch optional) in the Cessnock area. Pick-up from local hotels.

### Trekabout Tours

*4990 8277/www.hunterweb.com.au/ trekabout.* **Admission** *half day (Mon-Fri only)* $45; *full day* $55.

Arranges half- or full-day winery tours for up to six people. The shorter tour visits four to five wineries; the full-day option gets to six or seven. You'll need to get yourself to the Hunter Valley – pick-up is from hotels in the Cessnock/Pokolbin area.

# Essentials

**Medusa p175**

# Hotels

After an initial post-Olympics slump at the start of the Noughties, which saw many hotels converted into apartment blocks, Sydney's hotel industry is growing, and predominantly at the upper end. This growth is underpinned by business visitors, as well as by the visiting celebrities and dignitaries who flood the city to attend the increasing number of glitzy events being held these days in the Emerald City.

For the common tourist, the sheer variety and numbers of hotels, serviced apartment blocks, backpacker hangouts and boutique offerings available can be quite dazzling – the bad news is that you'll have to devote a bit of time to researching where you want to stay, the good news is that there really is something suitable for

everyone. Prices at the top end can be pretty dazzling too, matching those you'll find in any of the world's top cities. The secret to nabbing the best rooms is to peek behind the glass palaces, look outside the city centre and seek out the many unusual, individually-run places. On prices, the key is to work the internet. Booking online can save you hundreds of dollars with prices often as much as half the rack rate. Standards are pretty high across the board.

In the centre, you'll by and large find the five- and six-star joints in prime positions around the city, many affording the visitor fantastic harbour views. The four-star-plus hotels are strung around the central sightseeing areas: the Rocks, Circular Quay, George Street, Hyde Park and Darling Harbour.

Meanwhile, a swag of backpacker joints congregate around Kings Cross and in nearby Potts Point, Darlinghurst and Elizabeth Bay. Staying in these areas means you'll have access to a good assortment of restaurants and bars, although if you want to see the main tourist sights, you'll need to catch a CityRail train back into town.

The inner-west suburbs of Balmain, Newtown and Glebe are likewise a short train or bus ride from the city centre, but have the advantages of good pubs and a student atmosphere, if that's your scene. Newtown's bustling King Street can be noisy and traffic-polluted, but many consider that part of its charm.

If you fancy staying near the beach, you can't go wrong with Bondi, Coogee or Manly. The bus journey from Bondi and Coogee into the city can be a pain, but the beach atmosphere is fabulous. If you stay in Manly (a popular option

**ESSENTIALS**

www.yhotel.com.au

# Y hotels
## SYDNEY
...designed for your enjoyment

## City South

Y Hotel City South is a funky boutique hotel in Sydney's hip inner city. The rooms, while compact have been designed for comfort and feature the latest interiors. There is also a large 2 bedroom apartment ideal for families or small groups. Facilities include a gymnasium, roof top garden, café and terrace, secure parking, internet kiosk, guest kitchen and laundry. All rooms include breakfast.

179 Cleveland Street, Chippendale 2008
t: 61 2 8303 1303
f: 61 2 8303 1300
e: citysouth@yhotel.com.au

## Hyde Park

Y Hotel Hyde Park is a great value CBD hotel ideally located opposite Hyde Park and Oxford Street. There are studio, deluxe and traditional style rooms to choose from. City attractions are on your doorstep. Facilities include a café and guest lounge, internet kiosk, guest kitchen, laundry and fully equipped Conference Centre. All rooms include breakfast.

5 -11 Wentworth Avenue, Sydney 2000
t: 61 2 9264 2451
f: 61 2 9285 6288
e: res@yhotel.com.au

The Hotels that work for the community
(YWCA NSW)

with British visitors), you're limited by the ferry service from the city, which stops around midnight. For the full seaside experience, head for the northern beaches, such as Newport, Collaroy or the stunning but pricey Palm Beach.

There are two new hotels opening in late 2008. The first is the Accor-run Pullman Sydney Olympic Park (www.pullman hotels.com) – a 212-room tower, perfectly placed for concerts at Homebush. The second is the Barclay (www.thebarclay.com.au) in Kings Cross – a 41-room renovation of an existing hotel that promises to bring more jet-set glamour to the already sparkling Bayswater Road in the heart of Sydney's red light district.

Serviced apartments are listed at the end of this chapter and can be a very good option for long stays, when visitors can often negotiate lower rates as well as benefitting from the use of home comforts such as a kitchen and washing machine.

## Timings and rates

Where you stay may well depend on when you come. The busiest tourist times in the city are between November and May. The beach areas are packed from mid-December to late January, when the school holidays are in full swing. If you want a room during Gay and Lesbian Mardi Gras (February/March, p34) or a harbour view at New Year, you'll have to book well in advance.

The hotels listed in this chapter have been sorted into categories, according to the price for one night in a double room with bathroom: deluxe ($$$$) from around $350; expensive ($$$) from around $250; moderate ($$) from around $100; or budget ($) from around $80, with much cheaper options available if you stay in shared dorms.

Blacket

## CBD, Circular Quay & the Rocks

### Blacket

*70 King Street, CBD, NSW 2000 (9279 3030/www.theblacket.com). CityRail Martin Place or Wynyard.* **$$$**.
A stylish boutique hotel, with a typical boutique aesthetic: all muted colours, clean lines and minimalist furniture. Opened in 2001, the Blacket is set in a 19th-century bank built by architect Edmund Blacket, so there are a few period flourishes here and there.

### Central Park Hotel

*185 Castlereagh Street, CBD, NSW 2000 (9283 5000/www.centralpark. com.au). CityRail Town Hall/Monorail Galeries Victoria.* **$$**.
A compact urban hotel, the Central Park offers en suite rooms and studios (with double sofa beds and spa baths), plus seven light and airy, split-level loft apartments that can sleep up to four.

ESSENTIALS

## Establishment

*5 Bridge Lane, CBD, NSW 2000 (9240 3100 www.establishmenthotel.com). CityRail Circular Quay or Wynyard/ ferry Circular Quay.* **$$$$**.

Though it has only 33 rooms and two split-level penthouse suites, the Establishment's cool clout more than outweighs its capacity. Exceedingly stylish, this place would be perfectly at home in the smarter districts of London or New York. As for the guest rooms, half are all sharp angles, minimalist Japanese elements and flashes of bright colour, while the others are a lot more subdued – choose whichever suits your mood. Expect luxurious touches at every turn (think Philippe Starck taps, Bulgari toiletries, Bose stereos).

## Four Points by Sheraton Darling Harbour

*161 Sussex Street, at Market Street, CBD, NSW 2000 (1800 074 545/9290 4000/www.fourpoints.com). CityRail Town Hall/ferry Darling Harbour/ Monorail Darling Park.* **$$$**.

With 630 rooms including 45 suites, this vast hotel caters to tour groups, business types and the international conference crowd – the Convention and Exhibition Centre is a stone's throw away, and the hotel is within walking distance of several museums, as well as Chinatown, the CBD and the central shopping district. Rooms have all the mod cons and some also have balconies overlooking Darling Harbour.

## Four Seasons Hotel Sydney

*199 George Street, at Essex Street, CBD, NSW 2000 (1800 142 163/ 9238 0000/www.fourseasons.com). CityRail/ferry Circular Quay.* **$$$$**.

All the rooms at the Four Seasons are spacious and have marble bathrooms; some overlook Walsh Bay, the Harbour Bridge and the Opera House, the rest have city views. The executive floor caters to business types, with its own check-in, concierge, meetings facilities and complimentary refreshments.

## Grace Hotel

*77 York Street, at King Street, CBD, NSW 2000 (9272 6888/www.grace hotel.com.au). CityRail Martin Place or Wynyard.* **$$$**.

This charming hotel is housed in an 11-storey corner block (a loose copy of the Tribune Tower in Chicago) that

Palisade Hotel

began life in 1930 as the headquarters of department store giant Grace Brothers. During World War II the building was to become the site from which General MacArthur directed South Pacific operations. A complete refurbishment was finished in 2005, but many of the building's attractive original features, such as the marble floors, lifts, stairwells and ornate ironwork, have been retained and restored to great effect. Rooms, however, are modern, large and comfortable, and all have bathtubs. The indoor heated lap pool is small, but there's a sauna and steam room, plus a sun-filled fitness centre and rooftop terrace.

### Hilton Sydney

*488 George Street, between Park & Market Streets, CBD, NSW 2000 (9266 2000/reservations 9265 6045/www.hiltonsydney.com.au). CityRail Town Hall.* **$$$$**.
Since its refurb three years ago, the Hilton has reinstated itself as one of the city's premier five-star hotels – quite a feat considering it has no harbour view. From the light-filled, four-storey high lobby with its striking spiralling aluminium sculpture (by Australian artist Bronwyn Oliver) to the hotel's 31 'relaxation' rooms and suites, it is an undeniably classy establishment.

### InterContinental Sydney

*Corner of Bridge & Phillip Streets, at Bridge Street, CBD, NSW 2000 (1800 221 335/9253 9000/www.sydney. intercontinental.com). CityRail/ferry Circular Quay.* **$$$$**.
Built in 1851, the InterContinental now features such high-tech extras as high-speed internet access and digital TV in all rooms, plus two TV broadcast and video conferencing studios. Rooms have a classic-contemporary feel and come with either harbour or city views.

### Lord Nelson Brewery Hotel

*19 Kent Street, at Argyle Street, Millers Point, NSW 2000 (9251 4044/ www.lordnelson.com.au). CityRail/ferry Circular Quay.* **$$**.

Time marches on, but you wouldn't know it at the Lord Nelson where the motto is 'You've been praying, the Lord has delivered'. The clean and pretty spacious Victorian-style rooms with plantation shutters are air conditioned, but the look and feel of the place is pure 19th-century colonial – the pub opened in 1841 and claims to be the oldest in the city. There are nine guest rooms, all with original bare sandstone walls, and most en suite.

### Observatory Hotel

*89-113 Kent Street, between Argyle & High Streets, Millers Point, NSW 2000 (9256 2222/www.observatoryhotel. com.au). CityRail/ferry Circular Quay.* **$$$$**.
A consistent favourite among Sydney's most well-heeled visitors, the service-oriented Observatory has the feel of a very grand European hotel. Tones are hushed as the army of impeccably trained staff attend to their guests' every need and furniture is mainly of polished mahogany with a mass of antiques and lush drapes. Rooms boast original artworks, plus sparkling, crisp marble bathrooms, TVs, CD players and high-speed internet. Most rooms have killer views of either Walsh Bay or Observatory Hill. But the jewel in the crown is the hotel's renowned day spa. Its indoor pool, with its twinkling night-sky ceiling, is quite something and in late 2006 the spa added La Prairie's signature treatments to its menu, including the much-written-about Caviar Firming Facial.

### Palisade Hotel

*35 Bettington Street, at Argyle Street, Millers Point, NSW 2000 (9247 2272/ www.palisadehotel.com). CityRail/ferry Circular Quay.* **$$**.
Things are pretty basic at the Palisade – there's no air conditioning, no private bathrooms in the guest rooms and the building doesn't have a lift either. But if you're looking for views and old-time charm at very affordable prices, then this is a good choice. Another historic Rocks property, the Palisade was built

in 1916, and behind its imposing brown brick façade are a popular pub, with crackling log fires in winter, and very good restaurant (p73) that attracts the pre-theatre crowd. Hot tip: when booking, request one of the rooms on an upper floor, as these provide the best harbour views.

**Park Hyatt Sydney**

### Park Hyatt Sydney

*7 Hickson Road, The Rocks, NSW 2000 (9241 1234/ www.sydney.park. hyatt.com). CityRail/ferry Circular Quay.* **$$$$**.
Since opening in 1990 the plush Park Hyatt has played host to a steady stream of celebrities, heads of state and international jet-setters, all with money to burn. The jaw-dropping, close-up vista of both the Opera House and the Harbour Bridge is a major selling point, but you get what you pay (a lot) for – cheaper rooms offer just glimpses. Extras include a rooftop swimming pool, deluxe spa and much-vaunted 24-hour butler service.

### Russell

*143A George Street, at Globe Street, The Rocks, NSW 2000 (9241 3543/ www.therussell.com.au). CityRail/ferry Circular Quay.* **$$**.
With a great location in the middle of the Rocks, just a stroll away from the hustle and bustle of Circular Quay, the Russell feels like a cosy country B&B. Housed in a turreted 1887 building, rooms feature such period flourishes as ornate fireplaces, antique brass beds, marble washbasins, pine dressers and floral bedspreads and wallpapers.

### Rydges World Square

*389 Pitt Street, at Liverpool Street, CBD, NSW 2000 (1800 838 830/8268 1888/www.rydges.com). CityRail Central or Town Hall/Monorail World Square/LightRail Central.* **$$$**.
Set in the shopping and entertainment precinct of World Square, Rydges was converted from the previous Avillion hotel, and, at the time of writing, work is still in progress. Rooms are comfy and functional, bathrooms are good, furnishings are bland.

# Apartment hotels

Somewhere in between a hotel suite and a rented apartment, apartment hotels used to be strictly the domain of the business traveller – no more. These days, holidaymakers can't get enough of their space, flexibility, in-built kitchens, washing machines and other home comforts.

**Apartment One** (297 Liverpool Street, Darlinghurst, 9331 2881/ www.contemporaryhotels.com.au). A hip split-level apartment with no less than three outdoor terraces. Long-stay rates available.

**Medina Executive Sydney Central** (2 Lee Street, at George Street, Haymarket, 8396 9800/ www.medinaapartments.com.au). Most of these one- and two-bed flats and studios have kitchens. There's a laundry, café and bar, plus a grocery delivery service.

**Regents Court Hotel** (18 Springfield Avenue, off Victoria Street, Potts Point, 9358 1533/ www.regentscourt.com.au).

These swish boutique-style studio suites are favoured by arty types. The rooftop terrace has great views of the city skyline and there are free refreshments in reception.

**Meriton World Tower** (91-95 Liverpool Street, at George Street, CBD, 8263 7500/www.meriton apartments.com.au). World Tower, part of World Square, is the tallest residential building in Sydney. One-beds and studios are on levels 18-36, while the two- and three-beds are on levels 62-74. The higher you go, the better the view.

**Quay Grand Suites Sydney** (61 Macquarie Street, East Circular Quay, (9256 4000/ www.mirvachotels.com.au). Close to the Opera House, these five-star one- and two-bed apartments deliver on all fronts. They're very spacious (double the standard apartment hotel size), and offer balconies, harbour views, en suite bathrooms, two TVs per flat, well equipped kitchens and more.

## Sebel Pier One

*11 Hickson Road, on Dawes Point, Walsh Bay, NSW 2000 (1800 780 485/8298 9999/www.sebelpierone. com.au). CityRail/ferry Circular Quay then 15min walk.* **$$$**.

A very successful marriage of historic architecture and contemporary design, this sleek, chic boutique hotel has water views in the most unexpected places, including beneath your feet – the glass floor in the lobby is quite the showpiece. Located in a converted warehouse at the quiet end of the Rocks, the Sebel's rooms feature much of the original timber and iron work which was once part of the working Pier One wharf. Some rooms even have telescopes for star-gazing.

## Shangri-La Hotel

*176 Cumberland Street, between Essex & Argyle Streets, The Rocks, NSW 2000 (9250 6000/www.shangri-la.com). CityRail/ferry Circular Quay.* **$$$$**.

Ideally located between the Opera House and the Harbour Bridge, the Shangri-La Hotel is another five-star spot with undeniably breathtaking views – from every room – which is one reason for its popularity. Its rooms are among some of the largest in the city and service is a major priority with lots of extra touches designed to maintain a loyal base of regulars. Decor is a mix of modern Eastern and classic hotel chic – but then, you probably won't be looking at the furniture with views like these. There's also a fitness centre and an indoor swimming pool.

## Sheraton on the Park

*161 Elizabeth Street, between Market & Park Streets, CBD, NSW 2000 (1800 073 535/9286 6000/ www.sheraton.com). CityRail St James.* **$$$$**.

Overlooking bucolic Hyde Park, this award-winning hotel is huge, with 557 rooms and suites, and a prime location within the central business and city shopping districts. The Sheraton's grand lobby screams luxury with its massive black marble pillars and curved staircase. The rooms have a refined, modern and quasi-nautical theme (think stripes and circles) and all feature more black marble in the bathrooms. There's a spacious pool and gym on level 22, the Conservatory Bar on level one and a lounge off the lobby.

## Westin Sydney

*1 Martin Place, between Pitt & George Streets, CBD, NSW 2000 (1800 656 535/8223 1111/www.westin.com). CityRail Martin Place.* **$$$$**.

At the Westin Sydney you get the best of both worlds – a real sense of local history married to some very modern design and deluxe service. Located in pedestrianised Martin Place, smack-dab in the middle of the CBD, the Westin is partly housed in what used to be the General Post Office, built in 1887. Rooms in the heritage-listed building feature high ceilings and lots of period detail, while tower rooms have floor-to-ceiling city views and a more modern look.

## Y Hotel Hyde Park

*5-11 Wentworth Avenue, at Liverpool Street, CBD, NSW 2010 (1800 994 994/9264 2451/www.yhotel.com.au). CityRail Museum.* **$**.

Run by the venerable old YWCA, this spot attracts all kinds of traveller (and both sexes), from budget-conscious business visitors to families and young singles. The Y Hotel's deluxe, studio and corporate rooms are all en suite while high-speed internet, TVs and fridges are all standard.

## Darling Harbour, Pyrmont & Chinatown

## Hotel Ibis Darling Harbour

*70 Murray Street, at Allen Street, Darling Harbour, NSW 2000 (1300 656 565/9563 0888/www.accorhotels. com.au). CityRail Town Hall/Monorail/ LightRail Convention.* **$$**.

The Hotel Ibis is a no-frills, get-what-you-pay-for option in a very convenient location. The rooms may be on the small side, but they were refurbished in late 2007 and now have a pretty cool

**ESSENTIALS**

new look. For location alone, it's still pretty good value for money, all the more so if you can bag yourself a last-minute value deal – check the website before you book for the best offers.

## Novotel Sydney on Darling Harbour

*100 Murray Street,Darling Harbour, NSW 2000 (1300 656 565/9934 0000/www.noveldarlingharbour.com. au). CityRail Town Hall/Monorail/ LightRail Convention.* **$$$**.

Another good option next door to the Sydney Convention and Exhibition Centre, the Novotel Sydney is aimed mainly at business travellers. All the rooms have LCD TVs, a bath and shower with huge bath towels, plus broadband and wireless internet access, and mobile phone and laptop charging stations.

## Railway Square YHA

*8-10 Lee Street, at Railway Square, Haymarket, NSW 2000 (9281 9666/ www.yha.com.au). CityRail/LightRail Central.* **$**.

This YHA hostel, built in a former parcels shed incorporates an old and disused railway platform into its design. Some dorms are even housed inside replicas of train carriages (very Harry Potter), while the bathrooms are in the adjacent main building. Most of the dorms have four to eight beds with lockers, and there are also a couple of en suite double rooms.

## Star City Hotel & Serviced Apartments

*80 Pyrmont Street, between Jones Bay Road & Union Street, Pyrmont, NSW 2000 (1800 700 700/9657 8393/ www.starcity.com.au). LightRail Star City/Monorail Harbourside/bus 443, 449.* **$$$$**.

Gambling's big business in Australia (see also box p89). And nowhere is it bigger than at this little slice of Las Vegas, Sydney-style. The numbers are dizzying: 306 standard rooms, 43 suites with 24-hour butler service, 131 fully serviced apartments, two penthouses, 11 restaurants and bars, two theatres

and – of course – a casino that's open 24 hours a day. Facilities include a spa and health club and an indoor-outdoor pool with panoramic views of the city.

## Wake Up!

*509 Pitt Street, at George Street, Haymarket, NSW 2000 (1800 800 945/9288 7888/www.wakeup. com.au).CityRail/ LightRail Central.* **$**.

This brilliant, award-winning hostel is part of a new and fully comprehensive generation – big, clean, efficiently run and offering very proactive security, despite the party atmosphere. The common areas are like a twentysome-thing's dream with circular lounge-around sofas, a funky TV lounge, an endless bank of computers for logging on to the internet, a street café, kitchen, ATMs, even a travel agent to help organise your trip and help you find local work. The air-conditioned dorms sleep four, six, eight or ten, and some are women-only. There are also double and twin rooms, some with private showers. Bedlinen is provided and check-in is 24-hours.

## Kings Cross to Potts Point

## Blue, Woolloomooloo Bay

*Woolloomooloo Wharf, 6 Cowper Wharf Road, opposite Forbes Street, Woolloomooloo, NSW 2011 (9331 9000/www.tajhotels.com). CityRail Kings Cross then 10min walk/bus 311.* **$$$$**.

The former W hotel in the historic Woolloomooloo Wharf is now owned by India's luxury hotel and resort chain Taj Hotels. And, while Blue's cutting edge may have been blunted a little, it's still a funky, alternative hotel with plenty to offer those visitors who like something a little bit different from their five-star hangout. The very plush rooms feature original elements from the old wharf building and there's a gy and indoor pool. The attached Water Bar (p97) is deservedly popular.

Sebel Pier One p171

### Diamant Hotel

*14 Kings Cross Road, at Penny's Lane, Potts Point, NSW 2011 (1800 816 168/9295 8888/ 8899/www.diamant. com.au). CityRail Kings Cross.* **$$$**.

This newly opened boutique hotel is perfectly placed near the Coca-Cola sign in Kings Cross and features the best accommodation in the area. It's part of the Eight Hotels Group, which also owns, among others, the Kirketon in neighbouring Darlinghurst (p175) – but the Diamant is undoubtedly the swishest hotel in the set. A big plus is that all rooms have opening windows – it may not sound revolutionary but in a city of air-conditioned high-rise towers, this is quite a boast. Other bells and whistles include 42-inch plasma screen TVs, iPod docks and DVD and CD players.

### Eva's Backpackers

*6-8 Orwell Street, at Victoria Street, Kings Cross, NSW 2011 (1800 802 517/9358 2185/www.evasbackpackers. com.au). CityRail Kings Cross.* **$**.

With its laidback atmosphere and its reputation for being very clean and quiet (pretty rare for a backpackers' hostel in this neighbourhood), Eva's

has rightfully gained a following. There are twin, double and dorm rooms, some en suite, some with air conditioning. Added extras include free breakfast, broadband internet access, luggage storage facilities, wake-up calls, a laundry room with free washing powder and a great rooftop terrace and barbecue area with fabulous views over Sydney.

### Hotel Formule 1 Kings Cross

*191-201 William Street, Kings Cross, NSW 2011 (93260300/www.formule1. com.au). CityRail Kings Cross.* **$**.

The Accor Group budget hotel with a chequered flag logo – the idea is you're having a pitstop, get it? – is basic, but clean and very functional, offering bunk, twin or double beds, en suite bathrooms and in-room TVs. Set on the busy part of William Street, it can feel a bit like you're on a race track at times and don't expect any special comforts, but everything you need is here.

### O'Malley's Hotel

*228 William Street, Kings Cross, NSW 2011 (9357 2211/fwww.omalleyshotel. com.au). CityRail Kings Cross.* **$**.

ESSENTIALS

It may be attached to a popular Irish pub and live music venue, and, yes, it's dangerously close to everything that's wrong with Kings Cross, but don't write off O'Malley's. Its 1907 building houses 15 en-suite and non-smoking rooms with lovely period touches and old-fashioned charm, and the location is actually quite convenient.

### Original Backpackers Lodge

*160-162 Victoria Street, between Darlinghurst Road & Orwell Street, Kings Cross, NSW 2011 (9356 3232/ www.originalbackpackers.com.au). CityRail Kings Cross.* $.

Established in 1980, this sprawling hostel in a Victorian mansion may look a little lived-in, but it's got plenty of character and lots of extras such as a lovely and spacious courtyard, free bedlinen and towels, 24-hour check-in and free airport pick-up. The Original has single, double and family rooms, as well as 10-bed dorms, some of which are women-only.

### Simpsons of Potts Point

*8 Challis Avenue, at Victoria Street, Potts Point, NSW 2011 (9356 2199/www.simpsonshotel.com). CityRail Kings Cross.* $$.

A very elegant and charming place, combining the style and comfort of a boutique hotel with the informality and sociability of a B&B. At the quieter end of a tree-lined street in Potts Point, this lovingly restored mansion was built in 1892 and still retains a host of of its original arts and crafts details, such as its mouldings and fireplaces. The 12 high-ceilinged guest rooms (all en suite, air-conditioned and featuring originals by Australian artist Ellis Rowan) are old-fashioned, but elegantly so, and by no means dowdy.

### Victoria Court Hotel

*122 Victoria Street, Potts Point, NSW 2011 (1800 630 505/9357 3200/ www.victoriacourt.com.au). CityRail Kings Cross.* $$.

This small hotel, formed from two 1881 terraced houses, is a celebration of Victorian extravagance, from the four-poster beds to the floral-print designs on everything else (wallpaper, curtains, carpeting). All its rooms have air-con and private bathrooms; some also have marble fireplaces and nice wrought-iron balconies.

## Darlinghurst & Surry Hills

### Kirketon

*229 Darlinghurst Road, between Farrell & Tewkesbury Avenues, Darlinghurst (1800 332 920/9332 2011/www.kirketon.com.au). CityRail Kings Cross.* $$.

Alongside the Diamant Hotel in Kings Cross (p174), the Kirketon is one of the Eight Hotels group, owner of various budget boutique operations in Sydney. The Kirketon got a refurbishment in 2007, its rooms, dining room and bar benefitting from a major spit and polish. Rooms are all en suite and have Kevin Murphy toiletries and chocs. The overall design is contemporary minimalist with rich colours and slick bathrooms with showers.

### Medusa

*267 Darlinghurst Road, between Liverpool & William Streets, Darlinghurst, NSW 2010 (9331 1000/ www.medusa.com.au). CityRail Kings Cross.* $$$.

What's not to love about this heritage-listed Victorian mansion, decked out in bright pink paint? Embodying a very Darlinghurst sense of urban chic, the Medusa is an ode to colour and quirky design, all interesting angles and bright flourishes of imagination. The lobby is (bubblegum) pink too, with bulging floral mouldings and an over-sized paper chandelier. The expansive Grand Rooms feature period fireplaces, groovy chaises longues and sitting areas. All rooms are en suite, with kitchenette, CD player and minibar. There's a diminutive courtyard at the back, which has a water feature and seating area.

**ESSENTIALS**

## Paddington to Woollahra

### Hughenden Hotel

*14 Queen Street, at Oxford Street, Woollahra, NSW 2025 (9363 4863/1800 642 432/www.hughenden hotel.com.au). Bus 333, 352, 378, 380.* **$$.**

This four-star boutique hotel was something of a lost cause when sisters Elizabeth and Susanne Gervay bought it back in 1992. But together they set about transforming the crumbling, grand 1870s mansion into an award-winning hotel which today combines old-school charm with modern-day comfort. All rooms are en suite, and there's also an attached four-bedroom terraced home that can be rented in its entirety. Elizabeth is an artist and Susanne an author, so literary events and art exhibitions also take place here regularly, if that's your bag.

### Sullivans Hotel

*21 Oxford Street, between Greens Road & Verona Street, Paddington, NSW 2021 (9361 0211/www.sullivans. com.au). Bus 352, 378, 380, L82.* **$$.**

Sullivans is a Paddington stalwart. All rooms have private bathrooms, with some interconnecting family rooms also available. The hotel has wireless internet, a solar heated pool, fitness room, complimentary evening chocs, a grand courtyard, free secure parking and free bicycles.

## Bondi to Coogee

### Coogee Bay Hotel

*Corner of Arden Street & Coogee Bay Road, Coogee Beach, NSW 2034 (9665 0000/www.coogeebayhotel.com.au). Bus 372, 373, 374* **$$.**

Not exactly a quiet beachside retreat, this complex is very big and very busy. The brasserie serves hearty fare for breakfast (included in the room price), plus lunch and dinner seven days a week, and there are seven different bars (p126). The Boutique wing has

spacious and modern rooms with marble bathrooms, balconies and, in some, kitchenettes. The Heritage wing in the main part of the pub is more basic.

### Dive Hotel

*234 Arden Street, opposite the beach, Coogee Beach, NSW 2034 (9665 5538/ www.divehotel.com.au). Bus 372, 373, 374.* **$$.**

A smart and elegant guesthouse with a contemporary design that's all bold colours, polished wood and crisp bed-linen. The cosy, sun-filled breakfast room (serving complimentary brekkie from 7am to 1pm) and kitchen give way on to a bamboo-bordered garden. All rooms are en suite, with a microwave, fridge, TV and VCR, and the spacious front rooms – nos. 1, 2 and 19 – have ocean views.

### Ravesi's

*118 Campbell Parade, at Hall Street, Bondi Beach, NSW 2026 (9365 4422/www.ravesis.com.au). CityRail Bondi Junction then bus 333, 380, 381, 382/bus 333, 380.* **$$.**

Ravesi's is known primarily for its noisy street-level bar and second-floor Drift bar (p126), but upstairs there's also a chic boutique hotel. All rooms have en suites and are impeccably furnished, designed by renowned abstract artist Dane van Bree, using a palette of earthy Aboriginal colours – mainly copper, black and bronze. The split-level suites have terraces and superb sea views.

### Surfside Backpackers

*35A Hall Street, between Gould & O'Brien Streets, Bondi Beach, NSW 2026 (9365 4900/www.surfside backpackers.com.au). CityRail Bondi Junction then bus 333, 380, 381, 382/bus 333, 380.* **$.**

You might feel out of place if you're over 25 at the Surfside. It caters to young, fun-loving backpackers from around the world who are willing to overlook the questionable artwork in the hallways (cartoonish drawings of topless beach babes). Dorms come with six, eight or 12 beds.

Railway Square YHA p173

ESSENTIALS

### Swiss-Grand Resort & Spa

*180-186 Campbell Parade, Bondi Beach, NSW 2026 (1800 655 252/9365 5666/www.swissgrand.com.au). CityRail Bondi Junction then bus 333, 380, 381, 382/bus 333, 380.* **$$$**.

The Swiss-Grand looks oddly like a wedding cake, with its gleaming white columns and tiered levels, but it's still the classiest hotel in Bondi (which may say something about the state of the latter's accommodation, especially given that the Grand is looking a little tired). Rooms are spacious, with two TVs, bath and shower and a minibar. There are rooftop and indoor pools, a good gym, plus the renowned Samsara Day Spa, offering Balinese treatments.

## Glebe, Newtown & Balmain

### Alishan International Guesthouse

*100 Glebe Point Road, Glebe, NSW 2037 (9566 4048/www.alishan.com.au). LightRail Glebe/bus 370, 431, 432, 433, 434.* **$**.

This converted century-old mansion is a good inner-west budget choice. The spacious dining room has a black stone floor and rattan furnishings, and the very large commercial-grade kitchen is for guest use (no meals are provided). There are dorms, simple single, double and family rooms, plus a Japanese-style twin room with low beds and tatami mats. Some rooms have private bathrooms, but there's no air-con.

### Australian Sunrise Lodge

*485 King Street, Newtown, NSW 2042 (9550 4999/www.australiansunrise lodge.com). CityRail Newtown.* **$**.

Rooms have a TV, fridge, microwave and tea, coffee making facilities. Some have balconies overlooking a courtyard and are en suite, but none has air-con – although there are ceiling fans, and electric fans on request. The lodge is recommended by Sydney University for off-campus accommodation, so expect a studenty clientele.

### Billabong Gardens

*5-11 Egan Street, at King Street, Newtown, NSW 2042 (9550 3236/www.billabonggardens.com.au). CityRail Newtown.* **$**.

Bohemian and arty, the decor at this Newtown hostel-motel is a patchwork of bright colours, exposed brick and

Wake Up! p173

crazy patterns. Set just off bustling King Street, the Billabong Gardens attracts artists and musos – part of its appeal is that it offers special deals for touring bands, including space to store their equipment. The place is clean and all rooms have ceiling fans and wireless internet. Some rooms have TVs and fridges, but there's no air-conditioning.

### Tricketts Luxury B&B

*270 Glebe Point Road, Glebe, NSW 2037 (9552 1141/www.tricketts. com.au). LightRail Jubilee Park/bus 431, 434.* **$$**.
You might not expect it in a bed and breakfast, but Tricketts is something of a haven for antiques-lovers. The owners have gone to a lot of trouble and spared no detail, and, from the ornate moulded ceilings and imposing original cedar staircase to the cut-crystal glassware in the bedrooms and Persian rugs, practically everything is a collectible. The seven guest rooms (one kingsize, five queensize and one twin-bedded room) are decorated in different styles, but all are en suite, and two,with their four-poster beds, are aimed at honeymooners.

## Kirribilli & Milsons Point

### Glenferrie Lodge

*12A Carabella Street, between Peel Street & Kirribilli Avenue, Kirribilli, NSW 2061 (9955 1685/www.glenferrie lodge.com). Ferry Kirribilli.* **$**.
A pretty, rambling guesthouse, Glenferrie lacks air-con, but bedrooms do have ceiling fans and there's always a lovely harbour breeze. The shared facilities are spotless and bathrooms are ample and spacious. The lounge offers cable TV (rooms have TVs with standard broadcast plus DVD players) plus there's wireless internet. Dinner is served five nights a week.

## Manly

### Manly Pacific Sydney

*55 North Steyne, between Raglan & Denison Streets, Manly, NSW 2095 (9977 7666/www.accorhotels.com.au). Ferry Manly.* **$$$**.
The Manly Pacific is a so-so fourish-star seaside hotel. There's a restaurant, Zali's, which serves an upmarket café menu at night and a Mediterranean buffet on Saturday evenings and Sunday lunch, plus two bars, a heated outdoor pool, rooftop gym, sauna and spa. All rooms have balconies and the Corso, Manly's pedestrian shopping and cafe strip, is just a short stroll – as is Manly Beach.

### Periwinkle Guest House

*18-19 East Esplanade, at Ashburner Street, Manly, NSW 2095 (9977 4668/www.periwinkle.citysearch.com.au). Ferry Manly.* **$$**.
Perched above tranquil Manly Cove, within walking distance of the ferry wharf, this 1895 Federation building has iron-lace verandas and plenty of period charm without feeling stuffy. The 18 colourful rooms have ceiling fans and fireplaces, and 12 of them are en suite. Heaters and electric blankets are provided in winter.

**ESSENTIALS**

# Getting Around

## Arriving & leaving

### By air

#### Sydney Airport

*(9667 9111/www.sydneyairport.com.au)*

Sydney Airport is on the northern shoreline of Botany Bay, about nine kilometres (six miles) south-east of the city centre. There are three terminals: T1 is for all international flights on all airlines and for QF (Qantas) flights 001-399; T2 is a domestic terminal for Virgin Blue, Regional Express, Jetstar, OzJet, Aeropelican, Air Link, Big Sky Express and QF flights 1600 and above; T3 is the Qantas terminal for QF domestic flights 400-1599.

The best way to and from the airport is the efficient Airport Link rail service (131 500, www.airportlink.com.au) which runs between Sydney Airport and Central Station every ten minutes from both international and domestic terminals. The line is a spur of the green CityRail line, so it serves all the main inner-city interchanges. It takes ten minutes to reach Central Station from the domestic terminals and 13 minutes from the international one. Trains run from 5.19am to 11.45pm Monday to Friday and from 5.06am to 11.43pm Saturday and Sunday. A one-way ticket from the domestic terminal to Central Station costs $13.40; $9.20 reductions. It's $13.80; $9.40 reductions from the international terminal.

Bus-wise, the excellent KST Sydney Airporter (9666 9988, www.kst.com.au) shuttle runs a door-to-door service to all hotels, major apartment blocks and backpacker joints in the city, Darling Harbour and Kings Cross. A single costs $12-$13. Look for the white buses with a blue and red logo outside 'The Meeting Point' outside T1 and at 'The Horseshoe' outside both T2 and T3. Book three hours in advance for hotel pick-ups and give yourself plenty of time to get to the airport, as the shuttle will take twice as long as a taxi.

Each terminal has its own sheltered taxi rank, with supervisors in peak hours to ensure a smooth and hassle-free flow of taxis. You never have to wait for very long, even in the vast sheep pen-style queuing system of the international terminal, where some 190 vehicles are on call. If you have any special needs – wheelchair access, child seats or an extra-large vehicle – go to the front of the queue and tell the supervisor, who will call you to a taxi fitted out for your needs. It takes about 25 minutes to reach the city, depending on the traffic and time of day, and costs around $35-$40. The main car rental companies all have desks at the airport.

### By bus

Lots of bus companies operate throughout Australia. Handily, they all use the Sydney Coach Terminal in Central Station as their main pick-up and drop-off point. National carrier Greyhound (1300 473 946, or from abroad +61 2 9212 1500/www.greyhound.com.au), transports more than a million passengers a year.

### By rail

The country's State Rail Authority's CountryLink operates out of Central Station with extensive user-friendly services to all main NSW and interstate destinations (central reservations 13 2232/www.countrylink.info).

## By sea

International cruise liners, including the QE2, dock at the Overseas International Passenger Terminal, located on the west side of Circular Quay, or around the corner in Darling Harbour.

## Public transport

To get around Sydney you'll probably use a combination of trains, ferries, buses and maybe the 'airborne' Monorail or the LightRail streetcars. As well as the Sydney Buses network (run by the State Transit Authority, STA), there are CityRail trains and Sydney Ferries. The other transport services are privately run and therefore generally more expensive. The centre of Sydney is so small that if you're in a large group, it's often cheaper to pool together for a taxi. A great, consumer-friendly phone line and website that offers comprehensive timetable, ticket and fare information is the **Transport Infoline** (13 1500/ www.131500.info). Phone daily, 6am-10pm, for details on STA buses, Sydney Ferries and CityRail, plus timetabling for cross-city private bus services.

## Fares & tickets

There are several combination passes covering the government-run transit system, and they're worth buying if you plan extensive use of public transport.

The TravelPass offers unlimited seven-day, quarterly or yearly travel throughout the zones for which it has been issued, on all buses, trains and ferries. These TravelPass tickets are aimed at commuters, but can be useful if you're in Sydney for any length of time. To find the right TravelPass

for you, check the STA website or ask at any train station or bus information kiosk (where you can also buy them). Newsagents displaying a Sydney Buses Ticket Stop sign, and ticket offices or vending machines at Circular Quay and Manly also sell passes. Passes are also available for different combinations of buses and ferries, or for travel solely by bus, ferry or train. TravelPasses cannot be used on the STA premium Sydney Explorer and Bondi Explorer bus services, Sydney Ferry harbour cruises, JetCats or on private buses.

The SydneyPass ticket is aimed specifically at tourists, offering unlimited travel on selected CityRail trains, buses (including premium services such as the Explorer buses) and ferries (including premium services such as JetCats and cruises). Valid for any three, five or seven days within an eight-day period. A three-day pass is $110 ($55 reductions, $275 family); for five days it's $145 ($70 reductions, $360 family) or $165 ($80 reductions, $410 family) for a seven-day pass.

DayTripper tickets offer unlimited one-day travel on buses, ferries and CityRail trains until 4am – but not on the Explorer buses or JetCats. It costs $16 ($8 concessions) and is available on board buses, from STA offices and at Sydney Ferries ticket offices.

BusTripper passes offer unlimited all-day travel on buses only – except for the premium Explorer bus services. It costs $12.10 ($6 under-16s).

## Buses

Buses are slow but fairly frequent, and offer a better way of seeing the city than the CityRail trains, which operate underground within the centre. Buses are the only option for

**ESSENTIALS**

transport to popular areas such as Bondi Beach, Coogee and the northern beaches (beyond Manly), which aren't served by either train or ferry. Sydney is divided into eight zones; the city centre is zone 1. The minimum adult fare is $1.80 (90c reductions), which covers two zones.

The bus driver will not stop unless you hold out your arm to request a ride. Pay the driver (avoid big notes) or validate your travel pass in the machine at the door.

The bus route numbers give you an idea of where they go. Buses 131-193 go to Manly and the northern beaches; 200-296 the lower north shore, Taronga Zoo and the northern suburbs; 300-400 the eastern suburbs (including Bondi, Paddington, Darlinghurst and Sydney Airport); 401-500 the inner-south and inner-west, Balmain, Newtown, Leichhardt and Homebush; and 501-629 the north-west including Parramatta and Chatswood. The 100s and 200s generally start near Wynyard Station and the 300s-600s can be found around Circular Quay. Bus numbers starting with an 'X' are express services, which travel between the suburbs on the way into the city. Stops are marked 'Express'. Limited-stop or 'L' services operate on some of the longer routes to provide faster trips to and from the city.

Bus services in the central and inner suburbs run pretty much all night, but those from the centre to the northern beaches tend to stop around midnight. Nightrider buses run hourly services until 5am to all outer suburban train stations after the normal train services have stopped running. STA also runs the tourist-oriented Sydney Explorer and Bondi Explorer bus services. For full details of both these, go to www.sydneybuses.info.

## CityRail

CityRail (www.cityrail.info) is the city's main passenger rail service covering the greater Sydney region (it's the sister company to CountryLink which covers all country and long-distance routes within NSW). The sleek, double-decker silver trains run underground on the central City Circle loop – Central, Town Hall, Wynyard, Circular Quay, St James and Museum stations – and overground to the suburbs (both Central and Town Hall stations run connecting trains to all suburban lines). Although certainly quicker than the bus, Sydney's trains are not as frequent as many would wish them to be and a wait of 15 minutes, even during peak commuting hours, is not uncommon. For one of Sydney's best train rides, take the trip from the city to the north shore – the line passes over the Harbour Bridge and the views are spectacular.

You can buy CityRail tickets at ticket offices or vending machines at all rail stations. Expect huge queues in rush hour. A single ticket to anywhere on the City Circle costs $2.60 ($1.30 reductions); an off-peak return costs $3.60 ($2.60 under-16s).

For more details of CityRail services, call the Transport Infoline (p181) or visit www.cityrail.info. The website includes a detailed map of the CityRail city network.

## Ferries

No trip to Sydney would be complete without clambering aboard one of the picture-postcard ferries that ply the harbour and are used daily by hundreds of commuters. All ferries depart from Circular Quay. These stately vessels are a great way to explore the harbour: there's plenty of room to take pictures from the outdoor decks or just to sit in the sun and enjoy the ride. JetCats – fast catamarans – operate a service to Manly, taking 15 minutes, half the time of the ordinary ferry.

Ticket prices vary, but a single from Circular Quay to destinations within the Inner Harbour costs $5.20 ($2.60 concessions). A JetCat fare is $8.20. If you plan to use the ferries a lot, the FerryTen pass covers ten rides within the Inner Harbour and costs $33.50 ($16.70 reductions); and $48.10 ($24 reductions) to Manly (by ferry only, not JetCat). A JetCatTen is $67.80.

Tickets are sold at Circular Quay and Manly. Tickets for Inner Harbour services can also be purchased from on-board cashiers.

### Sydney Ferries Information Centre

*Opposite Wharf 4, Circular Quay (13 1500/www.sydneyferries.info). CityRail/ ferry Circular Quay.* **Open** 6.45am-6.15pm Mon-Sat; 7.15am-6.15pm Sun

## Metro LightRail

The Metro LightRail provides Sydney with a 14-station service from Central Station via Darling Harbour, Pyrmont and Star City to the inner-west. It's useful for visiting Darling Harbour, Paddy's Market, Sydney Fish Market, Glebe and the Powerhouse Museum.

Trams operate 24 hours a day, seven days a week, between Central and Star City stations, and from 6am to 11pm Monday to Thursday and Sunday, 6am to midnight Friday and Saturday, from Central all the way out to Lilyfield in the west. Trams run about every ten to 15 minutes from 6am to 11pm, and every 30 minutes at other times. The line is divided into two zones. Tickets for both zones cost $4.20 ($3.20 reductions). A Day Pass

offers unlimited trips for $9 ($6.50 reductions). Buy tickets from Central Station or on board the train. For more, call 8584 5288 or visit www.metrolightrail.com.au.

## Metro Monorail

The monorail around central Sydney runs every three to five minutes, 7am to 10pm Monday to Thursday, 7am to midnight Friday and Saturday, 8am to 10pm Sunday. The seven-station loop costs $4.80 (free under-fives) whether you go one stop or all the way. A Supervoucher Day Pass ($9.50) offers a day of unlimited travel, plus discounts on museum admissions. Buy tickets at station ticket offices or vending machines. For details, call 8584 5288 or visit www.metromonorail.com.au.

## Taxis

It's easy to flag down a taxi in Sydney and there are many taxi ranks in the centre. A yellow light indicates the cab is free. Tipping is not expected, but passengers sometimes round up the bill. The standard fare is $1.79 per kilometre from 6am to 10pm (add an extra $1.20 per km from 10pm to 6am), plus a $3 hiring fee and, if relevant, a $1.60 telephone booking fee. If a cabby takes you across the Bridge, the $3 toll will be added to the fare, even if you travelled via the toll-free northbound route.

### Taxi companies

**Legion Cabs**
13 1451/www.legioncabs.com.au
**Silver Service Taxis**
3 3100/www.silverservice.com.au
**Taxis Combined Services**
13 3300/www.taxiscombined.com.au
**Zero200**
Wheelchair Accessible Taxis Service
8332 0200/www.zero200.com.au

## Water taxis

Water taxis are fun, but expensive. The cost depends on the time of day and the number of passengers, but the fare for two from Circular Quay to Doyles fish restaurant at Watsons Bay, which takes ten to 12 minutes, is around $60.

**Water Taxis Combined**
9555 8888/www.watertaxis.com.au

## Driving

Under Australian law, most visitors can drive for as long as they like on their domestic driving licence without the need for any further authorisation. Residents must apply for an Australian driving licence after three months, which involves a written test. You must carry your licence and passport when in charge of a vehicle; if the licence isn't in English, take an English translation as well as the original.

Driving is on the left. The speed limit in cities is 60kph (38mph), but many suburban roads have a 50kph (30mph) limit. The maximum speed on highways is 100kph (60mph), and 110kph (70mph) on motorways and freeways. Speed cameras are numerous and there are heavy penalties for speeding. The legal blood alcohol limit is 0.05 per cent for experienced drivers and zero for provisional or learner drivers. Seat belts are mandatory and baby capsules or child seats must be used for children.

## Parking

In central Sydney parking is a pain and not recommended. In some suburbs, such as tree-lined Paddington, the quality of the road surfaces is poor, and narrow one-way streets with parking on both sides only compound the problem. Note that you must park in the same direction as the traffic on your side of the road. Rates at city-centre car parks range from $16 to $23 for one hour, with $20 to $62 the day rate. 'Early Bird' special rates often apply if you park before 9am and leave after 3.30pm.

## Tolls

The toll for the Harbour Bridge and Tunnel is currently $3 for cars heading south (free for northbound cars). There are also tolls for the 'eastern distributor' and the Cross-City Tunnel. Visit www.crosscity.com.au for further information.

## Vehicle hire

All the major car rental firms are situated near one another on William Street in Kings Cross, with additional outlets at Sydney Airport. Rates vary almost hourly and all offer deals. You will need to show a current driver's licence and probably your passport. Credit cards are the preferred method of payment and are nearly always asked for to cover insurance costs, even if you do eventually pay by cash or travellers' cheque. A few firms will rent to 18-year-olds, but in most cases you have to be 21 and hold a full driving licence. If you're under 25, you'll probably have to pay an extra daily surcharge, and insurance excesses will be higher.

**Avis**
9357 2000/www.avis.com.au

**Budget**
8255 9600/www.budget.com.au

**Hertz**
9360 6621/www.hertz.com.au

**Red Spot**
9356 8333/www.redspotrentals.com.au

**Thrifty**
8374 6177/www.thrifty.com.au

# Resources A-Z

## Accident & emergency

Call 000 for police, fire or ambulance. The hospitals below have 24-hour A&E departments.

### Royal North Shore Hospital

*Pacific Highway, St Leonards (9926 7111). CityRail St Leonards.*

### Royal Prince Alfred Hospital

*Missenden Road, Camperdown (9515 6111). Bus 412.*

### St Vincent's Public Hospital

*Corner of Burton & Victoria Streets, Darlinghurst (8382 1111). CityRail Kings Cross/bus 378, 380, 333.*

## Credit card loss

To report lost or stolen cards, call the (free) 24-hour numbers below.

### American Express

*1300 132 639/ www.americanexpress.com.*

### Diners Club

*1300 360 060/ www.dinersclub.co.uk.*

### MasterCard

*1800 120 113/ www.mastercard.com.*

### Visa

*1300 651 089/ www.visa.com*

## Customs

Before landing on Australian soil you will be given an immigration form to fill out, as well as several customs and agriculture declaration forms. You will pass through either the Green channel (nothing to declare) or the Red channel (something to declare). Your baggage may well be examined by Customs, regardless of which channel you use.

Anyone aged 18 years or over can bring in $900 worth of duty-free goods ($450 for under-18s), 2.25 litres of alcohol and 250 cigarettes or 250g of other tobacco products. You must declare amounts of $10,000 or more. Visitors can bring items such as computers into Australia duty-free, provided that Customs is satisfied that these items are intended to be taken away again on departure. UK Customs & Excise (www.hmce. gov.uk) allows travellers aged 18 and over returning from outside the EU to bring home £145 worth of goods, 200 cigarettes or 250g of tobacco, one litre of spirits or two litres of fortified wine, 60ml perfume and 250ml toilet water. US Customs (www.customs.ustreas.gov) allows Americans to return from trips to Australia with gifts and goods valued up to US$800.

## Quarantine

You must declare all food, seeds, plant cuttings, nuts or anything made from plant or animal material that you bring into Australia. This includes many souvenirs and airline food. If you don't, you could face an on-the-spot fine of $220, or prosecution and fines of $60,000. Sniffer dogs will hunt out the tiniest morsel as they roam the airport with their handlers.

Quarantine officers use high-tech X-ray machines to check your luggage. Bins are provided at the airport for you to ditch any food and plants you may have in your possesion before reaching immigration. Visit the website of the Australian Quarantine & Inspection Service (www.daffa.gov.au) for details.

Australia also has strict laws prohibiting the export of native animals and plants, and items deemed 'moveable cultural heritage'. These include birds and their eggs, fish, reptiles, insects, plants, seeds, fossils and rock art. Products made from protected wildlife, such as hard corals and giant clam shells, are not allowed to be taken out of the country. If in doubt, check with the Department of the Environment & Heritage (6274 1111, www.deh.gov.au).

If you need to carry medicines in or out of the country, transport them with a prescription or doctor's letter. Penalties for carrying illicit drugs (including prescription drugs in suspiciously large quantities) in Australia are severe and could result in a jail term. If in doubt, phone the Customs National Information Line (1300 363 263, www.customs.gov.au).

## Dental emergency

Dental treatment is expensive and not covered by Medicare, or any reciprocal health agreement. If you need to see a dentist, check the Yellow Pages or ask locals to recommend a dentist they trust.

## Disabled

For information on disabled resources, visit the website of the Disability Information Resource (www.accessibility.com.au). It offers details on wheelchair access across the city, from bars and restaurants to museums and public toilets. You can also contact the following:

### Information on Disability & Education Awareness Services (IDEAS)

*Suite 208, 35 Buckingham Street, Surry Hills (1800 029 904/ 9657 1796/www.ideas.org.au).*
Provides information and referral on all disabilities for the whole of NSW and also has a database on services in the eastern suburbs.

### Spinal Cord Injuries Australia

*9661 8855/www.scia.org.au.*
Provides consumer-based support and rehabilitation services to help those with physical disabilities to participate fully in society.

### State Library of NSW Disability Information

*State Library of NSW, corner of Macquarie Street & Cahill Expressway, CBD (9273 1583/ www.sl.nsw.gov.au/access).*
Helpful information line and a good starting point for disabled visitors.

## Electricity

The Australian domestic electricity supply is 230-240V, 50Hz AC. UK appliances work with a basic plug adaptor, but US 110V appliances will need a more elaborate form of transformer as well.

## Embassies & consulates

### Canada

*Level 5, Quay West Building, 111 Harrington Street, CBD (9364 3000/ www.canada.org.au). CityRail/ferry Circular Quay.*

### Ireland

*Level 26, 1 Market Street, CBD (9264 963 /www.dfa.ie). CityRail Town Hall.*

### New Zealand

*Level 10, 55 Hunter Street, at Castlereagh Street, CBD (8256 2000/). CityRail Martin Place or Wynyard.*

## South Africa

*Rhodes Place, State Circle,
Yarralumla, Canberra (6272 7300/
www.sahc.org.au).*

## United Kingdom

*Level 16, The Gateway, 1 Macquarie
Place, at Bridge Street, CBD (9247
7521/www.britaus.net). CityRail/ferry
Circular Quay.*

## USA

*Level 59, MLC Centre 19-29
Martin Place, CBD (9373 9200/
http://sydney.usconsulate.gov/sydney).
CityRail Martin Place.*

## Internet

Cybercafés are everywhere in
Sydney. Most backpacker hotels
have internet links and most
libraries will provide access.

## Opening hours

Shops are usually open from 9am
to 5pm or 6pm Monday to
Saturday, and from 11am to 4pm
or 5pm Sunday. Thursday is late-
night opening (which is usually
until 9pm). Some shops also close
at noon on Saturdays. Banks are
normally open from 9.30am to 4pm
Monday to Thursday, until 5pm on
Friday, and closed at the weekend.

## Police

To report an emergency, dial 000.
If it is not an emergency, call the
police at 13 1444. The City Central
Police Station is at 192 Day Street,
CBD (9265 6499). Visit www.police.
nsw.gov.au for more information.

## Postal services

Australia Post (www.auspost.
com.au) promises that about 90 per
cent of all letters mailed within the
metropolitan area arrive the next
business day. Post is delivered once

a day Monday to Friday, with no
delivery on Saturdays or Sundays.
Post to Europe takes four to ten
days. Stamps for postcards to
Europe and the USA cost $1.10; for
letters it's $1.85 (for mail up to 50g).
International aerogrammes cost
95¢. Letters within Australia cost
from 50¢ to $2.45.

Most post office branches
open from 9am to 5pm Monday to
Friday, but the GPO Martin Place
branch is also open on Saturdays.
Stamps can be bought at some
newsagents and general stores.
Suburban post offices will receive
post for you; otherwise have it sent
Poste Restante (general delivery)
to GPO Sydney, NSW 2000 – and
collect it from the address below.
Most post offices rent out PO
boxes, but only on an annual basis.

## General Post Office

*1 Martin Place, CBD (9244 3713).
CityRail Martin Place or Wynyard.*

## Poste Restante

*Level 2, Hunter Connection Building,
310 George Street, CBD (13 13 18).
CityRail Martin Place or Wynyard.*

## Smoking

Sydney is heavily anti-smoking.
Smoking is banned on public
transport and in cafés, restaurants,
pubs, clubs and a range of enclosed
spaces, including shopping malls
and theatres. There are hefty fines
for tossing cigarette butts out of car
windows as many life-threatening
bushfires have started this way.

## Telephones

The country code for Australia
is 61; the area code for NSW,
including Sydney, is 02. You don't
need to dial the 02 from within the
state. Numbers starting with 1800
are free when dialled within

**ESSENTIALS**

Australia; numbers beginning 13 or 1300 are charged at a 25¢ flat rate.

To make an international call, you dial an international access code – either 0011 or 0018 (the cheaper rate for longer calls) – followed by the country code, area code (omitting the initial 0 if there is one), and then the number.

Standard local calls are untimed flat-rate calls between fixed telephone services within a local service area. To check if local call charges apply, call 13 22 00. STD calls (national long-distance calls) are charged according to their distance, time and day, plus a fee. Each call starts with five pip tones.

There are public phones dotted around the city, as well as in bars, cafés, railway stations and post offices. You can also make long-distance and international calls at many internet cafés. Most public phones accept coins ($1, 50¢, 20¢, 10¢) and some accept major credit cards. You can buy cheap-rate international phonecards at most good newsagents. For directory enquiries, dial 1223 to find a number within Australia, and 1225 for international enquiries. For operator-assisted national or international calls, phone 1234.

Australia's mobile phone network operates on dual-band 900/1800 MHz (megahertz). This means that if you're coming from the UK you should be able to use your own mobile phone – although it's not as simple as it sounds.

If you keep your UK SIM card in the phone, when you arrive your phone will register itself with a local network with which your UK service provider has an agreement. If you want to use this facility, check with your service provider before you go, as you may need to set your phone up to work abroad. This is the easiest method, but potentially very expensive: calling

numbers in Australia will cost the same as calling back to the UK – ie a lot – and you'll have to pay to receive calls as well as make them.

Another simple option is to buy or rent a phone. Many Sydney companies offer competitive mobile phone rentals with local networks, for a minimum of three days, billed to your credit card. Or you could just buy or rent a SIM card for an Australian network and slot it into your UK phone (and top up as required). However, your phone may have been 'locked' so that it works only with your UK service provider's SIM card. You're entitled to get the phone unlocked, and the service provider has to give you an unlocking code – for free – if you ask for it. Once you've unlocked your phone you can put any SIM card in it. In practice, Australian service providers tend not to make this especially easy, and the process can be fraught with difficulties. Alternatively, any mobile phone repair shop will do it, for about $40.

## Time

New South Wales operates on Eastern Standard Time (GMT plus ten hours). Between October and March, Daylight Saving Time comes into operation, and the clocks go forward one hour. Australia has three time zones – the others are Western Standard Time (GMT plus eight hours) and Central Standard Time (GMT plus 9.5 hours). Note that Queensland doesn't recognise Daylight Saving.

## Tipping

Tipping is appreciated but not expected in restaurants and cafés, where ten per cent is the norm. Locals never tip in taxis.

## Tourist information

As well as the visitor centres below, the City of Sydney's website – www.cityofsydney.nsw.gov.au – and Tourism NSW's site – www. visitnsw.com.au – offer lots of information. If you plan to travel around Australia, then the official website – www.australia.com – is packed with ideas.

### Sydney Visitor Centre
*Level 2, corner of Argyle & Playfair Roads, The Rocks (9240 8788/1800 067 676/www.sydneyvisitorcentre.com). CityRail/ferry Circular Quay.*
This is the main official information resource, with two city-centre locations in the Rocks and in Darling Harbour.

### Cadman's Cottage/ Sydney Harbour National Park Information Centre
*110 George Street, between Argyle Street & Mill Lane, The Rocks (9247 5033/www.nationalparks.nsw.gov.au). CityRail/ferry Circular Quay.*

## Visas & immigration

All travellers, including children – except for Australian and New Zealand citizens – must have a visa or an ETA (Electronic Travel Authority) to enter Australia. An ETA is sufficient for tourists from EC countries – including the UK and Ireland, except in the case of holders of GBN (British National Overseas) passports – the USA, Canada and Japan (but not South Africa) – who are intending to stay for up to three months.

ETAs, for straightforward tourist and business trips, are the simplest to arrange: your travel agent or airline or a commercial visa service can arrange one on the spot if you give them details or a copy/fax of your passport (no photo or ticket is required). You don't need a stamp in your passport:

ETAs are confirmed electronically at your port of entry. Alternatively, you can apply for an ETA online at www.eta.immi.gov.au. This service costs $20, and you can be approved for entry in under 30 seconds.

If your entry requirements are more complex or you want to stay longer than three months, you will need a non-ETA visa, which you apply for by post or in person at the relevant office. Do this well in advance of your trip. For up-to-date details of overseas office where visa applications can be made, visit the official government website, www.immi.gov.au.

## When to go

Sydney has a moderate climate, with warm to hot summers, cool winters and rainfall all year round. Spring brings blossoming flowers and clear blue skies, with temperatures warm enough to shed the woollies, especially when the sun shines. In summer, Sydneysiders live in shorts. In January the sun bakes the city, and temperatures can top 30°C (90°F) – and even go over 40°C (104°F). In autumn, the city is swept by strong winds, while winter mornings and nights mean low temperatures that can – but rarely do – dip down to 6°C (43°F). Winter daily maximums tend to hover between 14°C (57°F) and 18°C (64°F), and on occasion snow falls in the Blue Mountains.

### NSW public holidays
**New Year's Day** (1 January); **Australia Day** (26 January); **Good Friday**; **Easter Monday**; **Anzac Day** (25 April); **Queen's Birthday** (2nd Monday in June); **August Bank Holiday**(1st Monday in August); **Labour Day** (1st Monday in October); **Christmas Day** (25 December); and **Boxing Day** (26 December).

ESSENTIALS

# Index

**ESSENTIALS**

# Treat yourself to the ultimate shopping experience

While you're in Sydney make sure you visit the premium fashion destination of choice, Westfield Bondi Junction. With world-class retailers including Paul & Joe, Chanel Beauté, Pepe Jeans London, Zimmermann, Leona Edmiston and many more, get ready to walk into a shopping haven.

Our award winning customer service ensures that all customers can shop with ease whilst using one of our Black Label services including valet parking, world-first Hands Free Shopping ™ and Personal Styling; providing our customers with the ultimate shopping experience.

You'll find the locals are very friendly (and stylish) at Westfield Bondi Junction.

For more info. visit Westfield.com/bondijunction